NEW ORLEANS

NEW ORLEANS

A CULTURAL HISTORY

Louise McKinney

OXFORD
UNIVERSITY PRESS

2006

OXFORD
UNIVERSITY PRESS

Oxford University Press, Inc., publishes works that further
Oxford University's objective of excellence
in research, scholarship, and education.

Oxford   New York
Auckland   Cape Town   Dar es Salaam   Hong Kong   Karachi
Kuala Lumpur   Madrid   Melbourne   Mexico City   Nairobi
New Delhi   Shanghai   Taipei   Toronto

With offices in
Argentina   Austria   Brazil   Chile   Czech Republic   France   Greece
Guatemala   Hungary   Italy   Japan   Poland   Portugal   Singapore
South Korea   Switzerland   Thailand   Turkey   Ukraine   Vietnam

Published by Oxford University Press, Inc.
198 Madison Avenue, New York, New York 10016

www.oup.com

Oxford is a registered trademark of Oxford University Press

Co-published in Great Britain by Signal Books

Library of Congress Cataloging-in-Publication Data
McKinney, Louise, 1958–
New Orleans : a cultural history / Louise McKinney.
p. cm. — (Cityscapes)
Includes bibliographical references and indexes.
ISBN-13 978-0-19-530135-9 ; 978-0-19-530136-6 (pbk.)
ISBN 0-19-530135-8; 0-19-530136-6 (pbk.)
1. New Orleans (La.)—Civilization. 2. New Orleans (La.)—Social life and customs.
3. New Orleans Region (La.)—Description and travel. 4. New Orleans Region (La.)—
History, Local. I. Title. II. Series.
F379.N55M39 2005
976.3'35—dc22   2005049878

9 8 7 6 5 4 3 2 1

Printed in the United States of America
on acid-free paper

Foreword

"New Orleans is, among cities, the most feminine of women, always using the old standard of feminine distinction. . . Has she not been called frivolous?. . . It is true, New Orleans laughs a great deal."
—Grace King, *New Orleans: The Place and the People*, c. 1895

By Grace King's reckoning, or that of anyone else who is inclined to think fanciful thoughts as they walk these old streets, our city is utterly, palpably and indisputably female. Not that she is simply *like* a woman, but that she *is* a woman who may speak to those inclined to listen.

Regardless of the conclusions one draws from this assertion, anyone who has spent more than a moment in New Orleans knows what it means to be enveloped by a distinctly voluptuous presence.

Consider her geographical location, tucked into a turn of the Mississippi River, which for a brief spate actually sends the water flowing *north* instead of south, thus defying all customary logic of rivers and geography. This not only gives New Orleans her beautiful curvaceous shape, but also renders her incapable of being mapped in a linear masculine grid pattern. In order to fit her curvy crescent, streets often have to converge into unexpected pie-shaped pieces or they disappear altogether for no reason. So forget about making rational decisions about how to get where you are going. Here you navigate with an intuitive compass because the shortest distance between two points is not necessarily the straight line you thought it was.

New Orleans' geographical address, putting her as it does at the bottom of the Mississippi's muddy outflow, also contributes to her female identity by making her rich with a dense, fertile soil, a chthonic womb that births the near obscene beauty of her foliage, the gorgeous flowers practically turning themselves inside out in a frenzy to be seen. This heaviness of her mud, this bottoming out, end-of-the-line location also places her in a deep psychic realm. It is the subconscious, the basement of the soul, where dark inexplicable alchemy occurs, often considered the root of creativity and expressly feminine.

And of course there is the weather. Much has been made of her steamy, watery character, her soft air after the rain, hung with the fragrances of jasmine and gardenia. This is all true. However, the climate can turn murderous at any moment. We frail humans, with our frail levees against the river, live with the constant threat of death by drowning. To understand New Orleans fully as a woman, you have to accept that despite all the sweet gifts she bestows she can also take away with a vengeance. Call her fickle if you like, but those are the terms of this feminine engagement.

The true character of the city may lie in the mysterious indeterminate space between the real, geographical New Orleans and what we bring *to her*, what we imagine or desire her to be. With all her dangers and delights, the essence of New Orleans is the ability to suggest an invitation into your own dark, creative feminine nature with the added condition that you must be brave enough to follow it without a guarantee of fulfillment. In this book, Louise McKinney seeks out the essence.

"But why bother? Isn't it time for gin and tonics?" New Orleans herself might ask, looking at her wrist, as if there might be a wristwatch there, but of course there isn't because she has never cared for punctuality, save for her attendance to the cocktail hour. "Go sit on the porch and smell the sweet olive trees," she would advise. "Write a poem instead."

Constance Adler,
New Orleans, 2005

Preface and Acknowledgments

For those who haven't been to New Orleans, perhaps only the smallest shard of recognition resides lodged in the memory. It may be a detail of a photograph or a bit of television documentary—say, an aerial glimpse of the city's streets at Mardi Gras, a blur of humanity in bright colors, grimacing (or is it smiling?) harlequin faces, the tight corridors of the French Quarter, topped by crumbling rooftops and chimneypots. Perhaps a refrain, just a few bars, of a song about New Orleans. "Do You Know What It Means to Miss New Orleans?" A quick search on ASCAP (the American Society of Composers, Authors, and Publishers) website yields nearly 200 song titles with the place name New Orleans: from Duke Ellington's "New Orleans Suite" to Hoagie Carmichael's "New Orleans Medley," from "New Orleans Bounce" to "New Orleans Remembered."

These images—visual, oral, aural—are a palimpsest upon the colorful passages, both travel and travelogue, created by countless writers, artists, historians, ethnographers, and scholars who have either lived in, or visited, this mythic American—yet Euro-Caribbean—city. Lying as it does at the nexus of three Americas (North, Central, and South), located at the same latitude as Cairo, this port at the mouth of the mighty Mississippi River, where it meets the Gulf of Mexico, has attracted many visitors, in times of prosperity and poverty.

Now picture an image of a naked "odalisque" reclining beneath the subtropical sun in an attitude of lassitude, seeking relief in cool shadows. Both Lafcadio Hearn, the author and ethnographer who stayed in New Orleans from 1877 to 1888 before moving on to international fame as a chronicler of Japan, and Nobel Prize–winning William Faulkner, who wrote his first novel *Soldier's Pay* in the French Quarter of the early 1920s, pictured New Orleans thus. Hearn daubs his literary canvas, a portrait of a "dead bride" recumbent in the state of Louisiana. She is rendered in warm hues:

The wealth of the world is here—unworked gold in the ore . . .
The paradise of the South is here, deserted and half in ruins.
I never beheld anything so beautiful and so sad. When I saw
it first—sunrise over Louisiana—the tears sprang to my eyes.
It was like a young death—a dead bride crowned with orange
flowers—a dead face that asked for a kiss. I cannot say how fair
and rich and beautiful this dead South is. It has fascinated me.

Faulkner unveils his silk-swathed mistress. She is:

this courtesan, not old and yet no longer young. . . . who shuns
the sunlight that the illusion of her former glory be preserved.

How peculiar that two very different writers, separated by three
decades, should seize upon the same female image to portray one of
America's oldest and most exceptional cities. In both cameos she is a sad
beauty, neither dead nor alive. In both she is illumined by sunlight; there
is no need to wonder why. The unrelenting laser sun, refracted from the
surface of the Mississippi, miles of swampy wetlands, lakes, and the gulf,
shines upon her face.

But why refer to chiaroscuro shadings of death in the depiction of
a reclining female form as appropriate for New Orleans? Certainly, the
city's planter era of slavery and sprawling antebellum mansions is dead
and gone forever. There is also New Orleanians' own preoccupation with
death, viz. its famous second-line funerals. And there are the "deadening" clichés of tourism's *ad reductio* promotion of New Orleans and its
fascinating cultures. But the more interesting question, and the one I
have sought to answer here is this: "What is *alive* about New Orleans?"
The answer has to be its people, the way so many different cultures have
come here, come together, to create something new. This interchange is
physically reflected in the interracial history of New Orleans, the actual
mixing of bloodlines and blurring of cultural demarcation. The miscegenation of Euro/African/Native American cultures, and successive
waves of immigrants, have resulted in what one researcher has called
"creolized energy"—adding life to urban development through cultural
borrowings.

As is seen in the history of the birth of jazz—America's first indigenous music, blending classical structures with African-American syncopation—in New Orleans at the turn of the nineteenth and twentieth
centuries, the mingling of people and their traditions allows for com-

radeship, so that the very coexistence of people from various racial and ethic backgrounds actually eclipses their differences. The result makes for expressive urban folk art. This is also true in the transmutation of Roman Catholicism into practices of Haitian *vodou* and in the cultural veneration of Native Americans by the blending of native folkways and Afro-Caribbean traditions in rituals of New Orleans' vividly colorful Mardi Gras Indians.

Says cultural commentator Ivor Miller, "Unlike post-modernist strategies, which emphasize the dismantling and breaking up of traditions, creolization tends to synthesize existing fragments together into a seamless whole." He goes to the source, quoting early jazz innovators "Jelly Roll" Morton and Sidney Bechet in an interview with musicologist and ethnographer Alan Lomax: "'We had all nations in New Orleans,' said Jelly Roll; 'But with the music we could creep in close to other people,' adds Dr. Bechet." Miller concludes: "Jazz was the hybrid of hybrids and so it appealed to a nation of lonely immigrants. In a divided world struggling blindly toward unity, it became a cosmopolitan musical argot."

In a city like New Orleans, which for its very economic survival strives always to reinvent itself, cultural invention is valued. What is more, it is "hip." In *Hip: The History*, John Leland suggests that coinage of the word "hip" is from the African Wolof verb *hepi*, to see, or *hipi*, to open one's eyes, and its first use in the context of "enlightenment" dates to America in the 1700s. Leland writes:

> From these origins, hip tells a story of black and white America, and the dance of conflict and curiosity that binds it. In a history often defined by racial clash, hip offers an alternative account of centuries of contact and emulation, of back-and-forth. This line of mutual influence, which we seldom talk about, is not a decorative fillip on the national identity but one of the central, life-giving arteries.

As my narrative moves out from the urban center, which is the people themselves, it moves to the influence of the Mississippi River on the "Crescent City," then spirals both historically and geographically outward as the city developed. First it is the old city, the French Quarter, the Creole heart of New Orleans; then to America's first suburbs, the *faubourgs* Tremé and Marigny; then Uptown, where the influx of

"Americans" in the mid-nineteenth century turned the city into a bilingual, divided place (French Catholic vs. Anglo Protestant, southerner vs. northerner); out into the contemporary enclaves of Mid-City, the urban revitalization of Downtown; to the exurbs across Lake Pontchartrain and its 24-mile causeway; and finally to Cajun country, Acadiana, where one culture in exile still thrives today. The thread holding ten chapters—and almost four centuries—together is the resilience of the people who carry their cultural legacies forward, or, the way they would say it in New Orleans, who "keep on keepin' on."

• • •

I am grateful to everyone who, wittingly or unwittingly, has contributed to this account of the New Orleans experience, albeit from my own perspective: Constance Adler, Neil Alexander, Kevin Allman and all my WHERE friends, Wilbur "Junkyard Dog" Arnold, Darilyn Barousse, Linda Bays Powers, Jason Berry, Rev. Marie Bickham, Jerry Brock, Karen Celestan (New Orleans Jazz & Heritage Festival), Sandra Russell Clark, Davell Crawford, Jo "Cool" Davis, Marq de Villiers, Carlo Ditta, Andrea duPlessis, Eddie Edwards, Martha Eller, Susan Erickson, David and Michelle Fine, Dennis Formento, Elizabeth Fane Goliwas, Jenny Hamilton (New Orleans Ballet Association), Don Hoffman, Lou Hoffman, David Jansen, Ellen Johnson, Pat Jolly, "Louisiana" Jones, Mary and James Jumonville, Jerry Jumonville, Merline Kimble, Earl Lindsay, Keenan Lupton, Lisa LeBlanc-Berry, Don Marquis, Lionel Milton, Leo Palamara, Barbara Pann, Arthur Perley, Stephen "Spike" Perkins, Warren Perrin (CODOFIL), Arthur Pfister, Mischa Philippoff, Bruce Raeburn (William Ransom Hogan Jazz Archive, Tulane University), Eddie Richard, David Richmond, Georgia Ross, Michael Sartisky (*Cultural Vistas*), Elsa Schneider (Historic New Orleans Collection), Jamil Sharif, John Sinclair, Ava Sommé, Dan Swanson, Anne Williams (New Orleans Museum of Art), and Steve Winn.

Many thanks, also, to the kind people of The Hambidge Center, in Rabun Gap, Georgia, where the first chapters of this book were written, and to Sandra Rouse who suggested the retreat. Thanks, also, to Sheila Bauer for her attention to the manuscript. And, while New Orleans does not really need any more myth-makers (there are hundreds of books by experts on just about every aspect of New Orleans—particularly its music and cuisine, Creole cookbooks alone could fill a number of library shelves), I hope this volume will provoke explorers to discover the city's all-embracing, all-accepting spirit.

Hearn in his essay "The Glamor of New Orleans" attempted to define the indefinable (what is "mysterious" about New Orleans). Hearn called it charm, but is it charm—or a spell? He wrote:

> There are few who can visit her for the first time without delight; and few who can ever leave her without regret; and none who can forget her strange charm when they have once felt its influence. And assuredly those who wander from her may never cease to behold her in their dreams—quaint, beautiful, and sunny as of old—and to feel at long intervals the return of the first charm—the first delicious fascination of the fairest city of the South.

But Lillian Hellman says it more simply: "New Orleans does odd things to people. It did odd things to me."

This book is dedicated to my parents Harold and Stephanie McKinney, my husband Avery Lamar Miller, and to Len Gasparini, "the Driver."

Louise McKinney
Atlanta, June 2005

• • •

POSTSCRIPT

At time of publication, hurricanes Katrina and Rita had drastically altered the landscape of Gulf states Louisiana, Mississippi, and Alabama. Due to storm damage and resulting restoration efforts, services at many airports, hotels, restaurants, museums and other travel-related destinations may have been affected.

Contents

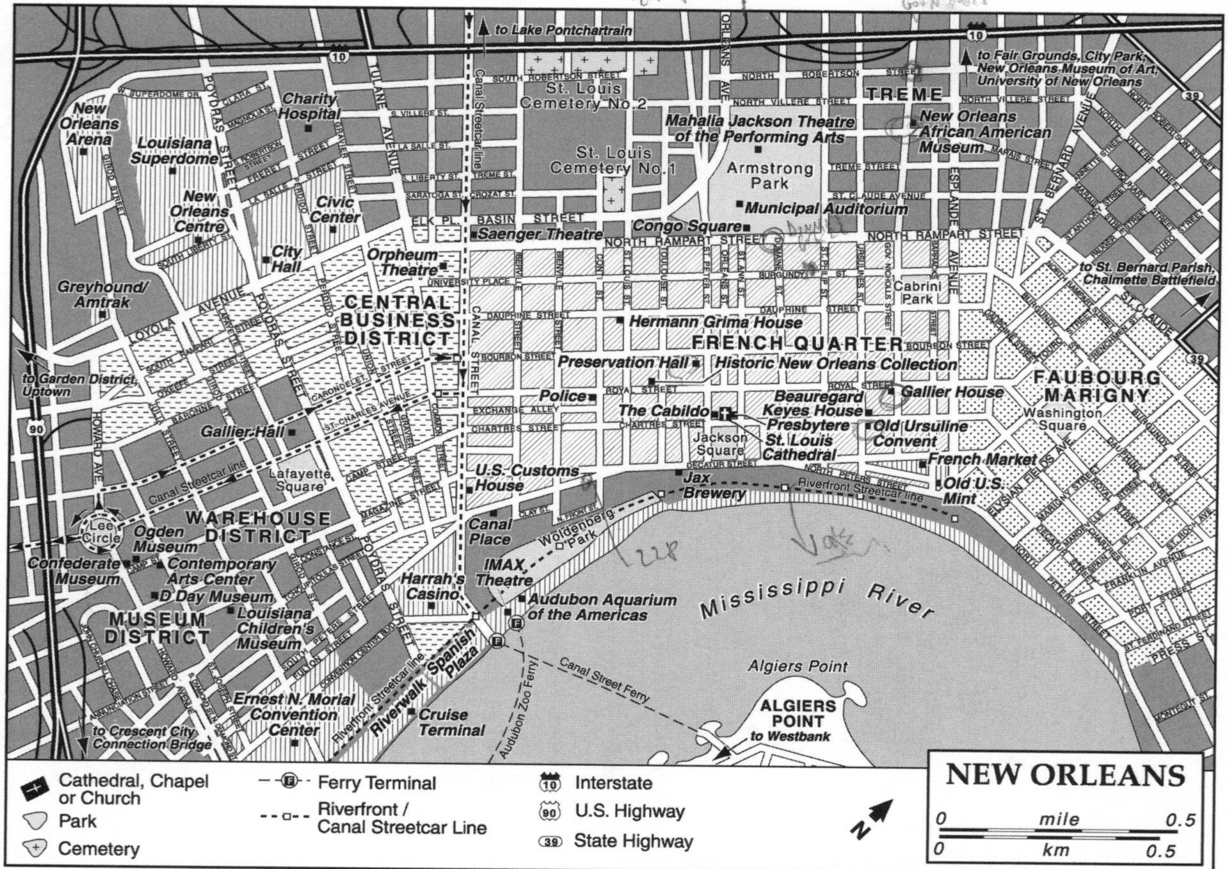

NEW ORLEANS

Scale:
0 — 0.5 mile
0 — 0.5 km

Map legend:
- Cathedral, Chapel or Church
- Park
- Cemetery
- Ferry Terminal
- Riverfront / Canal Streetcar Line
- Interstate
- U.S. Highway
- State Highway

Handwritten notes (top of map):
Wellesley Crole light cars 1125 north Rober about
Ho spelling
Vote

Map labels:

to Lake Pontchartrain

to Fair Grounds, City Park, New Orleans Museum of Arts, University of New Orleans

to St. Bernard Parish; Chalmette Battlefield

TREME
New Orleans African American Museum
St. Louis Cemetery No. 2
St. Louis Cemetery No. 1
Mahalia Jackson Theatre of the Performing Arts
Congo Square Theatre
Saenger Theatre
Armstrong Park
Municipal Auditorium
Cabrini Park

ESPLANADE AVENUE
ORLEANS AVE
BASIN STREET
NORTH RAMPART STREET
ST. PHILIP ST.
DUMAINE ST.
ST. ANN ST.
ST. PETER ST.
TOULOUSE ST.
ST. LOUIS ST.
CONTI ST.
BIENVILLE STREET
URSULINES ST.
GOV. NICHOLLS STREET
BARRACKS STREET

FRENCH QUARTER
Hermann Grima House
Historic New Orleans Collection
Preservation Hall
The Cabildo
Beauregard Keyes House
Presbytere
St. Louis Cathedral
Old Ursuline Convent
Galier House
French Market
Old U.S. Mint
Jackson Square
Jax Brewery
Police

FAUBOURG MARIGNY
Washington Square
Riverfront Streetcar line

CANAL STREET
CENTRAL BUSINESS DISTRICT
Orpheum Theatre
Charity Hospital
Civic Center
City Hall
Louisiana Superdome
New Orleans Centre
New Orleans Arena
Greyhound / Amtrak

TULANE AVENUE
POYDRAS STREET
HOWARD AVE.

WAREHOUSE DISTRICT
MUSEUM DISTRICT
Confederate Museum
Ogden Museum
Contemporary Arts Center
D-Day Museum
Louisiana Children's Museum
Ernest N. Morial Convention Center
Gallier Hall
Lafayette Square
Lee Circle

to Garden District, Uptown
to Crescent City Connection/Bridge

U.S. Customs House
Canal Place
Harrah's Casino
IMAX Theatre
Woldenberg Park
Spanish Plaza
Riverwalk
Cruise Terminal
Audubon Aquarium of the Americas
Canal Street Ferry
Audubon Zoo Ferry

Mississippi River

ALGIERS POINT
to Westbank
Algiers Point

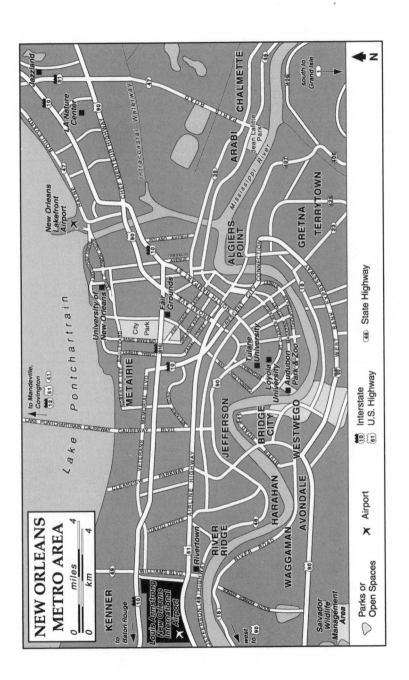

NEW ORLEANS

Introduction

"The Good Lord willin', and if the flood wall don't float away. . ."
—Radio Station WWOZ disk jockey

People always say, "I'm going down to New Orleans," even if they live south, east, or west of it. It always seems to be *down* to New Orleans. Yet that is really how it happens. The adventure begins driving towards the Crescent City, maybe via Highway 61, penetrating mythic "De-e-e-e-p South" countryside, past Memphis, Tennessee, Vicksburg and Natchez, Mississippi. Elvis intones "Love Me Tender" on the car radio and kudzu vine breaks the sun into pieces on the road. The traveler stops at a greasy spoon on the way, whose menu reads, "If'n you don't find what you want, just holler." Then fed "tight as a tick," it's time to take the road again, down through the Mississippi River Valley, into the L-shaped state of Louisiana, sitting snugly between Texas, Arkansas and Mississippi.

Or it might be flying high above the Gulf of Mexico, peering over a bourbon and Coke (the South's *vin ordinaire*), looking out of the plane's tiny window. Far below, about a hundred miles inland, floats the "island" of New Orleans (proper), barely twenty square miles, buoyed on a raft of natural and man-made levees, languorously settled into two silvery loops of the Mississippi, which has flowed nearly 4,000 miles, cleaving the US to meet the Gulf.

Coming in on the more utilitarian Interstate Highway 10 via capital city Baton Rouge to the north and west, the traveler descends to lower and lower sea levels. Outside suburban Slidell to the east, a billboard for the psychiatric hospital across Lake Pontchartrain queries solicitously, "Overwhelmed? Depressed?" Then, it's over the Industrial Canal. Suspended on I-10's concrete bands, you may first see the city spread out as in a fog. Its peculiar air is "pearl gray, luminous", Simone de Beauvoir once remarked; there is an omnipresent "fine haze… soft and subtle, with opalescent hints", suggested historian Oliver Evans. It envelops the tops of office buildings, and the convex roof of Louisiana Superdome is like a moon-like mushroom growing up out of nowhere;

the river, the Vieux Carré (or "Old Square"), noted on I-10's green-and-white highway signs, are invisible from this vantage point—they are down there somewhere, even lower. It seems mysterious.

Down into the city streets. Climb out of the frigidity of the car's air conditioning and it hits you—the solid wall of heat that averages 92° during August (and abates only during the brief seasonal modulation called "winter"). Eyeglasses fog up. This is, as de Beauvoir worried, something that could make you insane. Not just the foggy eyeglasses, but sweat pouring down the back; brow, upper lip constantly covered with a moist dew. Walk just one city block, say along Poydras in the CBD (Central Business District), or not even that far. Clothes become saturated and cling to the body like a cheap suit. The most innocuous of activities works up a sweat: flossing one's teeth. But some like it hot, it should be said. Some carry umbrellas around at midday because the sun "pours down," while others on the bus count on their "do rags" (bandanas)—flapped on head, stuffed in pocket, tied like an Indian headband—or cool, clean facecloths to keep off what some locals call "the humility [sic]." "New Orleans, The City That Air Forgot," reads one T-shirt, improvising on the old slogan about a city care forgot.

Sherwood Anderson (1876-1941) a writer perhaps more closely associated with the Midwest, began spending time in New Orleans in 1922 and wrote *Many Marriages* and *Dark Laughter* while living in the city. He claimed that he thrived on the humidity, and that, "like an old horse [he] went better in it"; he also loved the "soft, smoky" New Orleans nights. Humidity is at its highest after sunset, and the voluptuous nighttime is sometimes interwoven with the smell of hickory wood burning, lemony trumpet flower or too-sweet jasmine, sweet olive, with the chirping of cicadas and tiny tree frogs, with the presence of the river and its river sounds (tugboats signaling to one another around treacherous curves), and with the occasional nocturnal call of a mockingbird.

They all come together, as one heavy sense impression: the heat, the jumble of Caribbean-style dwellings, their raggedy louvers sequestering something, dark streets with names like Abundance, Music, Mystery, Desire, the ghostly fronds of palmettos and swags of Spanish moss. There is even a ubiquitous New Orleans scent, something profoundly sensual and redolent of dampness, decay. The must is everywhere, exuding from the very cells of vegetation growing in the lush abandon of a hothouse climate—for this is the sixth-greenest city in the nation, according to the Metro Green Index, home (in City Park) to the largest collection of live oaks anywhere in the world.

City Afloat

This Euro-Caribbean port city, whose population within city limits now hovers somewhere around 500,000, looks on the map like a saucer of land, floating below 641-square-mile Lake Pontchartrain to the north, Lake Borgne and the Gulf of Mexico to the south and east, smaller Lake Salvador to the west, threaded throughout by the Mississippi which snakes through wetlands to reach Venice, Louisiana (at the tip of the "L's" boot), and finally out to the Gulf at Pass-a-Loutre. Nowhere is the ground in New Orleans more than 17 feet above sea level, and much of it is at least five feet below. And New Orleans is the rainiest major city in the US with an average annual rainfall of 60 inches, the drenching months being March, July and September. "Water is the city's natural element," noted one historian, remarking that even the early French colonists at the beginning of the eighteenth century called it *Île d'Orléans*. As Ari Kelman notes in his environmental history, *A River and Its City*, it is essentially an "amphibious city".

If Pacific Northwesterners have their mountain mists (just harmless droplets of water, really), this city offers up regular terror-inspiring afternoon thunderstorms of epic proportion. At 11 a.m. or 3 p.m.(people can set their watches, it seems), the sky becomes bruised and begins to glower; the crepe myrtle trees, especially the mature ones all along Napoleon Avenue, turn incandescent, even neon pink, and there follows a raging, ferocious lashing of trees. But just as quickly the weather changes again, and it is a benign sunny day once more. ("The Devil be beatin' his wife and marryin' his daughter," goes the politically incorrect Creole saying when, rarely, it rains and the sun shines at the same time.) Read the journal of A. Oakley Hall, a former mayor of New York City who resided in La Nouvelle Orléans from 1845 to 1848. One gets the idea of the extremes in climate from his memoirs and a chapter aptly entitled "Rain and Mosquitoes":

I never realized the capacity of the clouds for water until "going through a course" of the wet season in New Orleans... the rain was now dogged, obstinate and persevering; and now the rapidly succeeding showers charged the earth like reserve after reserve of cavalry in a battle.

Storms are one thing, but hurricanes are yet another and nothing to fool with. Present-day residents are still able to recall floods born by Hurricane Betsy in 1965 and recount childhood memories of standing with their families on rooftops to escape the rising tide. In 2004 four severe hurricanes and one tropical storm battered the entire Gulf Coast region in one hurricane season, resulting in $4.27 billion of damage. But the harrowing event that everyone feared took place 29 August, 2005, when Category 4 Hurricane Katrina, with sustained winds of up to 145 mph, came barreling toward the Crescent City. At first, residents thought they had been spared the worst when the hurricane veered at the last minute to the east. But the worst was yet to come. Engineers studying the failures at the floodwalls had always warned of storm surge "overtopping" the levee as a specter that could mean New Orleans' ruin. (Overtopping occurs when rising waters spill over the top of a floodwall.)

But what happened was this: in the early hours of 30 August, when a 500-foot breach of the floodwalls occurred in the 17th Street Canal on the border of Metairie and New Orleans proper, eighty percent of the city took on water, the hardest-hit areas being outlying Jefferson, St. Bernard, Plaquemines, and St. Tammany parishes. This along with other possible breaches allowed the water of Lake Pontchartrain, whose level during the storm was some six feet above sea level, to flow downward into northern New Orleans proper, which lies between two and ten feet below sea level.

As the water level in homes and businesses rose dramatically, what followed was sheer pandemonium as the New Orleans' metro area of some 1.4 million people was forced to carry out the mandatory evacuation announced by Mayor Ray Nagin two days earlier. Local officials also seemed to have grossly underestimated the needs of those who did not own cars, as well as sick and elderly citizens. Meanwhile, the Federal Emergency Management Agency was taking too long to mobilize supplies (water, ice, packaged meals), claiming it was difficult passage into the city, while the media was seen to be far more successful than FEMA at reaching hard-hit areas. The politicians began battling over jurisdictions and finger-pointing. For her part, Louisiana Governor Kathleen Blanco defended the state's actions, saying it had requisitioned many school buses to evacuate those without cars. Residents, however, complained that they were left stranded, unaware of any such service. The slow process of helicopter evacuation began as thousands made their way to the "shelters of last resort", the Louisiana Superdome and Morial Convention Center. When conditions in those buildings descended into squalor and lawlessness, with more and more people arriving each day, evacuation of thousands to distant shelters such as the Houston, Texas, Astrodome became necessary. President George W. Bush finally came to see the devastation wrought in New Orleans and throughout the Gulf Coast region.

Failing proper preparation—or should all the supplies vanish from the shelves—citizens have simply learnt to help one another during the deluge. It would not be unusual, for instance, for one stranger in a car to pick up another human being caught in the rain—accompanied, of course, by a lot of "hollering'"—and take him to a counter for a cup of coffee to while away the time. Random acts of kindness can still occur in New Orleans, which might quite properly be called a Small Town Masquerading as a Big City. This is what prompted Covington, LA, author and 1961 National Book Award winner Walker Percy to write, "In New York if you trip and fall down, people will curse and grumble about having to step over you; in New Orleans, on the other hand, there's still a chance that someone will pick you up, take you to the nearest barkeep, and pay for a shot of Early Times."

Splendid Decay

"In the balconies and on the mouldering window-ledges flowers bloomed, and in the decaying courts climbing-roses mingled their perfume with the orange; the shops were open; ladies tripped along from early mass or to early market; there was a twittering in the square and in the sweet old gardens; caged birds sang and sang the songs of South America and the tropics; the language heard on all sides was French...Nothing could be more shabby than the streets, ill-paved, with undulating sidewalks, and open gutters, little canals in

> *which the cat became the companion of the crawfish, and the*
> *vegetable in decay sought in vain a current to oblivion."*
>
> —New England novelist Charles Dudley Warner,
> on a Sunday morning Downtown in 1887

Rain, heat, humidity, the profusion of plant life, the wear and tear of human life: New Orleans continues to absorb, and attempts to repel, the effects of its own history. But as anyone with an eye for the passage of time can see, this city in the older sectors—the French Quarter, Tremé, Bywater, the Faubourg Marigny—sports its sagging rooftops, crumbling chimney pots, and heaving sidewalks like a tarnished badge of honor.

Architecture is a metaphor for time, mystery and decay. There is a feeling that grows up from the streets, out of the cracked sidewalks Uptown, and *banquettes* (sidewalks) of the French Quarter—and emanates from the buildings themselves, many of which have managed to survive the past 250 years sheltered from blazing sun rays by the generous outstretched limbs of live oaks and magnolias. Architects such as Benjamin Latrobe have tried to at least impose order on New Orleans' subtropical wildness and its below-sea-level terrain. But a constant battle wages as structures yield to their patinas of acid- and bottle-green moss, gnarled root systems creep under peaceful yards just floating above the water table, and as dampness and insects (the voracious Formosan termite, for example, which is quickly eating up both trees and buildings) conduct their assaults. Author George Scheer III wrote in 1991 about visiting a friend in New Orleans who was renovating her house (an interminable activity):

> *More than the faded paint, more than the dark windows, something*
> *made that house a forbidding presence. There is about much of New*
> *Orleans an air of decay... Lizards and cockroaches are the living*
> *things best adapted to the climate. It's a climate that breeds mosqui-*
> *toes. And it breeds indolence and madness.*

American photographer Clarence John Laughlin spent weekends away from his job with the US Corps of Engineers during the 1930s and documented New Orleans' historic buildings and cemeteries. Laughlin's perspective sensitively reveals architecture as a key to understanding New Orleans, and in his book *Lost Louisiana: An Essay in the Poetry of Remembrance*, he observes: "I approached the buildings as psychological and poetic manifestations… [the French Quarter] has the overall feelings of buildings completely involved in the mysterious process of time… It had the psychic taste and *frisson* of another age, and that is what captured my heart and moved me so deeply."

Historian Oliver Evans, too, appreciates the worn beauty of the city's houses, but points out an important architectural caveat: the truth is that everything looks much older than it really is (the Ursuline Convent in the French Quarter, designed in 1827, is, for instance, the only survivor of the colonial French period). "These houses look indescribably ancient," he writes. "Actually, the oldest of them are no earlier than the latter part of the eighteenth century, but they look as old as the houses of Pompeii."

Long before the conservationist movement of the 1960s and 1970s, and as early as the 1930s, such associations as the Vieux Carré Commission, the Historic Landmarks Commission and the Preservation Resource Center sprang up to save the city from the decay and other various forms of blight: abandonment, deterioration, ill-conceived makeovers and the onslaught of souvenir and T-shirt shops. For New Orleans today, as most people know, is considered one of North America's ultimate meeting spots for conventioneers and partiers, and it hosts as many as 8.5 million visitors (the polite word for "tourist") every year. That statistic is imperative enough to keep the city looking good. A study conducted in the mid-1990s by the Mayor's Office of New Orleans even found that it is the desired destination for as many as three million visiting friends and family of the city's residents, who stay on average three to five days. To keep its tourism-based economy vital (that is, $4.5 billion annually for the city; $9 billion for Louisiana), the Crescent City strives always to reinvent itself, and to improve in the name of, not only progress, but also survival.

But does the average New Orleanian worry about his/her hometown's stagnation and decay? Of course, it *is* aggravating to wake up and find mould in one's shoes, and the book pages curled overnight. But the city's inhabitants tend not to get worked up over much (unless it is another defeat for the local Saints football franchise, the team with one of the worst records throughout the 1990s). New Orleanians could not care less about how their city is received by strangers. Small wonder: many locals have never been farther away from home than the sweet olive tree in the backyard and, therefore, have little or nothing with which to compare it. Driving somewhere for more than ten minutes—say, over to the West Bank—is wholly unnecessary and tantamount to an excursion to Macchu Pichu. Some of New Orleans' enduring charm is the very insularity that keeps the city what it is, and that is usually what New Orleans "mythmakers" (and there are a lot of them) want it to be. According to the literary historian Kenneth Holditch:

> New Orleans is, of course, a city in love with its myths, mysteries, and fantasies…Possessed of boundless unwillingness to acknowledge any serious faults in their hometown or to do anything other than praise it, [citizens] are fond of boasting certain records of questionable virtue and veracity: that New Orleanians drink more coffee and liquor and eat more bread per capita than people anywhere else in the country; that the city has more churches and bars than any American city; and other distinctions, which, they seem to believe, not only make the place distinct but also glorious.

As regards dealing with dampness and decay—that sounds too much like work to many New Orleanians. As the New England novelist Charles Dudley Warner noted, do not ask too much from "this thriftless, battered, stained and lazy old place". Certainly, as one journalist remarked recently, "New Orleans is a place that doesn't ask for too much back."

The *laissez-faire* aura of "the Big Easy" is perhaps comparable to such far-flung places as the Caribbean islands or an Italian hill town such as Siena. One might liken New Orleans' customs to the Mediterranean; "midday languor, the appreciation of the good things in life: food, drink are taken seriously, ease is valued, hustle is absent," observes Richard Kennedy in *Literary New Orleans in the Modern World*. Considering New Orleans' European heritage as both a French and Spanish protectorate, and its later waves of African, Caribbean and Italian peoples, Kennedy further suggests, "One can expect here inhabitants who savor the possibilities of relaxation and pleasure and [who] have created… warmth and tolerance."

"Red Beans and Ricely Yours"

> *"How do you say New Orleans? Ya ready? 'New Orlunz!'"*
> —Trumpet master Al Hirt
> *"I don't know… sometime I say New Orlunz, sometime I say New Orleenz. Like that song, 'This time I'm walkin' to New Orlunz'.… If someone ask where I live at, I say, 'New Ahleens.' It all depends. I jus' say it the way I feel it."*
> —"Fats" Domino
> *"It's something special. We can call it the Big Easy, we can call it whatever the hell we want. It's 'New Ah-wins.'"*
> —Dr. John

The truth is, people say the place name in whatever way will rhyme best with the song lyrics preceding or following it. That is appropriate. New Orleans has not come by its nickname "the Big Easy" for nothing. By now, locals, not to mention the tourist trade, have cultivated this distinction of an easygoing place—tolerant of individuality—both consciously and unconsciously. If it happens that you are not a wealthy scion of an "old French family", it is certainly easier to get by here on little or nothing than in other North American cities where the work ethic reigns supreme.

In many neighborhoods, there is still a chance to take a *passeggiata,* a European-style leisurely evening stroll or, especially when it is really hot, the subtropical equivalent: stoop-sitting. Free red beans 'n' rice is often ladled out in bar-rooms (the traditional budget-conscious Monday meal created in some distant year so that the dish's slow cooking would allow housewives time to do their laundry). An old-fashioned little girl's ditty goes: "*Quartée* red beans, *quartée* rice/Little piece of salt meat to make it taste nice/Lend me the paper, and tell me the time/When papa passes, he'll pay you the dime."

And, as in any good Catholic city, there is fish fry Friday to look forward to, advertised in church newsletters and local publications. At private yard parties or local church functions (at the Tremé's St. Augustine Catholic Church, for example) the proverbial "plate" (at a nominal cost of maybe $3) is piled high with starchy southern/Creole/soul staples such as potato salad or macaroni and cheese, snap beans, tangy mustard or collard greens, and piping-hot catfish fried in the crust of spicy cornmeal coating called, of all things, "fish fry" (local brand Zatarain's is a favorite). There are still some hole-in-the-wall bars that serve $1 drinks that actually have liquor in them, although these establishments are off the beaten track in some rough and tumble neighborhoods. Even the venerable Pontchartrain Hotel's Bayou Bar, on St. Charles Avenue, Uptown, usually puts out an elaborate spread of hot and cold hors d'oeuvres for anyone who comes in for a cocktail—*gratis*.

This is the part about New Orleans that John Kennedy Toole's protagonist Ignatius Reilly extols in the Pulitzer-winning satirical novel *Confederacy of Dunces* (1980). Says Toole's oafish yet lovable Crescent City Quixote, it is "a comfortable metropolis which has a certain apathy and stagnation which I find inoffensive... I am assured of having a roof over my head and a Dr. Nut [now-extinct local soft drink] in my stomach." It is the part that every writer, artist and eccentric who has ever made it to New Orleans has liked. Lafcadio Hearn, ethnographer, translator, essayist and journalist, depended on the nickel plate lunches and wrote to a friend shortly after he arrived in the city in 1877, insisting that "it's better to live here in sackcloth and ashes... than to own the whole state of Ohio."

Chapter One
NEW ORLEANS PEOPLE: GUMBO IN A MELTING-POT

It is New Orleans' long-held customs and tradition, drawn from an exotically diverse mix of cultures, that continue to define it; these are not the ones held dear either by traditionally Protestant north Louisiana, or even by those living in the general direction north. The journalist A. J. Liebling wrote perceptively on the difference between the Big Easy and, say, the Big Apple (in a piece about Louisiana and former governor Earl Long for *The New Yorker* in 1961):

> *New Orleans resembles Genoa or Marseilles, or Beirut or the Egyptian Alexandria more than it does New York, although all seaports resemble one another more than they can resemble any place in the interior. Like Havana and Port-au-Prince, New Orleans is within the orbit of a Hellenistic world that never touched the North Atlantic. The Mediterranean, Caribbean and Gulf of Mexico form a homogenous, though interrupted, sea.*

Historian Oliver Evans, one of the literati who formed a charmed intellectual circle around such notables as Sherwood Anderson, Hamilton Basso and William Faulkner during the 1920s heyday of the literary journal *The Double Dealer*, goes so far as to say, with an effective, caffeine-inspired simile, "New Orleans is unlike any other city anywhere else; like the local coffee, a dark roast flavored more or less discreetly with chicory, it has its special flavor, and the visitor is aware of it immediately."

When writers, ethnographers, cultural historians or journalist cast around for a metaphor to describe the racial/cultural/spiritual hodge-podge that makes up New Orleans, the most common one they seize upon is the indigenous stew "gumbo". Creole cuisine offers up particularly apt figures of speech because form fits content: Creole cuisine, with its blending of French, Spanish, African, Native American, Caribbean and Acadian elements, expresses the very make-up of New Orleans' present-day population. Not only that, the city's fare customarily ranks New Orleans in Condé Nast *Traveller* magazine's "Top 10" of culinary destinations.

What is gumbo, after all, other than an Old World potage? Only this *pot au feu* features some different New World ingredients: a vegetable, okra (*kingumbo*), brought to America through the Middle Passage from Africa by slaves, who, it is said, secreted its seeds in their hair. The Creole version of this highly seasoned thick soup is served with rice and includes lots of seafood (shrimp, crab legs, along with the pot liquor), while the darker-brown Cajun gumbo (this traditionally peasant cuisine relies on one-pot dishes too) favors a combination of chicken and boldly spiced *andouille* sausage, perhaps even some seasonal game, and ground sassafras leaves, known as *filé* (an ingredient contributed by neighboring native Indian tribes) for thickening.

Well-loved chef and television personality Justin Wilson fills his cooking programs with traditional humorous Cajun folk tales and jokes, promising excellent results every time, enjoining his audiences to try his delicious wares: "I guar-*on*-tee!" (An important note: one has to be careful not to fall for the marketing of ersatz Cajun culture [see Chapter Nine], the subject of a book by Shane Bernard, *The Cajuns: Americanization of a People*.) Cajun culture is, more accurately, to be located in the 22 parishes of Acadiana, a good hour-to-two-hours' drive west of the city.

Still, when in New Orleans, there is nothing like sampling steaming bowls of gumbo cooked by Louisiana "natives" (whatever their background, white or African-American, Cajun or not, New Orleanian or not) in their own homes, usually at the beginning of the "cooler" weather. One finds that each chef usually has his or her own secret recipe, special ingredient, or jazzy innovation. Gumbo, the truly multicultural dish, is also more than competently prepared at such establishments as The Gumbo Shop on St. Peter Street in "the Quarter" (which used to supply it to former president Bill Clinton on Air Force One), Mr. B's Bistro on Royal Street, stewarded by one branch of the famous Brennan restaurant dynasty, and at Zachary's, an African-American-owned restaurant bordering Oak and Cambronne streets Uptown.

The First "Creoles"

"The air is broken by every language—English, French, Italian and German, veried [sic] by gombo [sic] languages of every shade; languages whose whole vocabulary embraces but a few dozen words, the major part of which are expressive, emphatic and terrific oaths."
—A turn-of-the-century traveler describing the French Market

Who makes up the New Orleans family, then? If language and idioms are any indication, then the Crescent City is a marvelous hybrid mix chock-a-block with influences of every kind: "America's first melting pot". But visitors are advised not to pronounce the street names with a French or Spanish accent; it will reveal them as non-native. Rather, "Chartres" is "CHAR-ders." "Dumaine" is "DEW-main." The diarist who penned the epigram above observed of the French Market:

Here the abuse is more flagrant, for not "king's English" alone is subjected to pretty rough handling, but every language spoken on the globe is slanged, docked, or insulted by uncivilized innovations on its original purity. This commingling of languages is swelled to an absolute uproar by sunrise, when the market-goers begin to arrive.

The study of New Orleans' settlement is one of drama and diversity and shows how the market scene could present such a "Babel". New Orleanians, as one discovers (and even as some families aware of their mixed heritage are at great pains to disguise), can tell a fascinating story of their forebears, who brought ethnic, racial and religious diversity to a place that began as a struggling, swamp-bound settlement. It would ultimately become "Paris on the Mississippi", the most affluent, fashionable nineteenth-century conurbation of the South. "No city perhaps on the globe, in an equal number of human beings, presents a greater contrast of national manners, language, and complexion than does New Orleans," wrote William Darby (1775-1854), a frontier geographer who had arrived in the Crescent City to draw land surveys for a number of planters.

Taken together, in the multicultural mix you can even count the original French-Canadian founders themselves: the brothers Pierre LeMoyne, Sieur de Bienville, who established the first capital of

Louisiana Territory, Biloxi (in present-day Mississippi), twenty years before New Orleans' founding in 1718; and Jean-Baptiste LeMoyne, Sieur d'Iberville, who had also claimed Mobile (in present-day Alabama) in 1702 for the French King Louis XIV. From the very lowest rungs of the social classes came the first settlers, an "ill-assorted collection", according to Oliver Evans, of beggars, former prison inmates, salt bootleggers, and brothel denizens—"rogues and paupers" all, summarized d'Iberville.

The settlement persevered despite the terrible living conditions heaped upon the small first village and its inhabitants—heat, mosquitoes, yellow fever, malaria, floods, attacks by neighboring Chickasaws, and famine. Survival was difficult in a place that was frequently threatened by hurricanes, says historian John Churchill Chase: "Just a year after its beginning hurricane winds and flooding brown waters of the Mississippi, each in turn, sought to blow [the settlement] away and wash it away." It was the first human outpost dug into the Mississippi Valley, marking the end of an ancient portage on a low wetland plain where, as research shows, even the native people refused to settle.

A vivid description by Englishwoman Frances Trollop, who journeyed to America in 1827 to join an experimental settlement run by a friend in Tennessee, is included in the beginning of her book of adventures. It gives a notion of the bleak aspect of the land in the early years of settlement:

> *The first indication of our approach to land was the appearance of this mighty river pouring forth its muddy mass of waters, and mingling with the deep blue of the Mexican Gulf. The shores of this river are so utterly flat, that no object upon them is perceptible at sea, and we gazed with pleasure on the muddy ocean that met us, for it told us we were arrived, and seven weeks of sailing had wearied us; yet it was not without a feeling like regret that we passed from the bright blue waves, whose varying aspect had so long furnished our chief amusement, into the murky stream which now received us.*
>
> *Large flights of pelicans were seen standing upon the long masses of mud which rose above the surface of the waters, and a pilot came to guide us over the bar, long before any other indication of land was visible.*

*I never beheld such a scene so utterly desolate as this entrance of
the Mississippi. Had Dante seen it, he might have drawn images of
another Bolgia from its horrors.*

New Orleans' cultural beginnings took a significant turn with the
introduction of African slaves, taken as human import to serve as field
hands in the colony, whose miserable toils in the heat and humidity
made future construction and agriculture in Louisiana Territory
possible. It was mostly the Senegalese who were taken into the
Louisiana-bound slave trade, by virtue of the fact that that country's
climate was similar to the southern regions. By 1721, just three years
after the founding of the city, there were almost half as many more
black men than there were white men.

Next came the German settlers from the Upper Rhine area, who
traveled up the Mississippi about thirty miles to establish what is called
the "German Coast"—they readily intermarried with the French,
sometimes turning their own German names, for example "Troxler",
into French: "Trosclair". They, too, are the forebears of present-day
New Orleanians.

Louisiana finally became a French Crown colony in 1731, and the
crops that were grown on burgeoning plantations were indigo, rice,
tobacco, and eventually sugar cane; trade was primarily by water and
the few roads that had been built ran along levees on the river's edge. A
problem for the French was the continued presence of English agents in
the area where Natchez Indians were settled. England and France were
at war in Europe and the two countries competed for Native American
allies in the Mississippi River Valley. The Natchez tribe had been pulled
apart into pro-French and pro-English factions. When Natchez Chief
Great Sun died in 1728, the French colony lost its most influential ally.
The pro-English faction of the tribe gained control and led the Natchez
Indians in a revolt against the French in November 1729. In the war
that followed the French massacred many Natchez or forced them to
leave their homeland. By the mid-1730s, members of the tribe that
escaped capture by the French were adopted by other tribes, including
the Chickasaw, Cherokee, and Creek.

In 1762, as a result of the fractious French and Indian War, and
because Louis XV's ambitions did not really include empire-building,
Louisiana was ceded to Louis' cousin, Carlos III, of Spain, his ally in the

war against Britain. At about this time, Acadian immigrants from the area that is today New Brunswick and Nova Scotia, who were dispersed in the 1755 *Grand Dérangement,* cast from their homes by the British because they had refused to take up arms against their French brethren, began arriving in the area from St. Domingue (Haiti) and other distant places to which they had been "scattered by the wind." Between 1 January and 13 May 1765, as many as 650 émigrés had traveled west across the river to settle the dry prairie region of the Attakapas and Opelousas, and later along the bayous of the Lower Mississippi and Bayou Lafourche.

It is simple but true to say that the French did not enjoy being "tenants" of the Spanish, nor neighbors with Spanish immigrants, who soon began arriving. The first Spanish governor, Don Antonio de Ulloa, was particularly reviled, and, as a result, the citizenry and French administration in combination revolted against his leadership with the purpose of driving him out. On 1 November 1768, de Ulloa sailed to Havana, whereupon he wrote a detailed report to the home government. In order to put down the uprising, the Spanish in 1769 sent 3,000 soldiers aboard ships with an Irish soldier of fortune, Don Alexander O'Reilly (perhaps the first "New Orleans eccentric"), in the service of Spain as commander. A fight was fought, the battle won, and in a ceremony in Place d'Armes (present-day Jackson Square) O'Reilly took formal possession of the colony for His Catholic Majesty, Carlos of Spain.

Twelve leaders of the revolution were arrested and tried—five of them sentenced to death. When it happened that no white man could be found to be hangman (it was forbidden for a black man to perform this duty), a firing squad was gathered that carried out the sentence at the corner of Barracks and Decatur streets, thereby stamping out one of the first revolts of a European colony in North America. O'Reilly reorganized New Orleans, instituting Spanish law (the French "Superior Council" became the Spanish "Cabildo"), but keeping Bienville's *Code Noir* (of 1724), whose terms enforced how the slave population should be treated, and which also forbade intermarriage between whites and blacks, between *les gens de couleur libres* and slaves, or even the taking of a "colored" concubine.

Nearly four decades of Spanish rule ensued, and it is the Spaniards' exuberant architectural structures of stucco-covered brick built around a patio, with open balconies and iron grilles, that remain today in the so-called "French" Quarter. The Spanish population never really offset the French, and New Orleans maintained its French character as a result. In 1800, through the Treaty of San Ildefonso, Louisiana was ceded back to France for certain concessions. Napoleon I then sold the Territory in 1803 to the newly formed United States and then-president Thomas Jefferson for $15 million. It was the 18th state to join the union and was known as the Territory of Orleans (the rest of the land became Missouri Territory). The entire 831,000-square-mile sale, then, represented a mere four cents per acre for land stretching west of the Mississippi River all the way to the Rocky Mountains! The transaction was done in high secrecy, because Napoleon's chief aim was to prevent the British from ever taking this land in ongoing conflicts with France. When Spanish rule had ended, New Orleans' population had tripled to just over 22,200 from 7,500 in 1731, and half of the city's citizens comprised "colored people".

Even the troops entrusted with the security of the new American colony would turn out to be especially "multicultural", one might say. During the War of 1812, between Britain and the United States, British ships moved up the Mississippi River to New Orleans and camped out on the north shore of Lake Borgne with as many as 14,000 soldiers. After fighting a brief engagement there, the British stalled, thinking New Orleans better defended than she was. In fact, American General Andrew Jackson's troops included his army of just 4,000 men, as well as an unusual assortment of "reinforcements": these were Jean Lafitte and his band of Barataria Bay pirates (by their involvement seeking grand-jury pardon for indictments of piracy); an outfit of free men of color; a band of Choctaw Indians; volunteer dragoons from Mississippi Territory; and some 2,250 Kentucky militiamen. Aware of the antipathy that many Creoles bore against Americans, the British printed circulars in French and Spanish and distributed them, exhorting residents: "Louisianans! Remain quiet in your houses; your slaves shall be preserved to you, and your property respected. We make war only against Americans." But the action was futile.

On 8 January 1815, the "Battle of New Orleans" on the Chalmette Battlefield bordering the river ended in victory for Jackson's ragtag army, due in large part to the excellent aim of the American gunmen. "It was an application of the formal methods of European warfare on a

terrain where these were an absurdity, and against men whose forte was a deadly marksmanship," explains historian W. Adolphe Roberts. Victory in the Battle of New Orleans was commemorated with much rejoicing in the Vieux Carré's Place d'Armes, the square that would eventually bear Jackson's name.

Neutral Ground

It was really the Louisiana Purchase that precipitated the greatest influx of cultures to the city of New Orleans. Among them were slaves and landowners who had escaped the 1793 uprising in St. Domingue that culminated in its independence in 1804; 8,000 refugees from Cuba (originally French-speakers from St. Domingue, one-third white, the rest *gens de couleur libres* or "free people of color"); wealthy American planters; and white adventurers called the Kaintucks, who arrived mostly from Kentucky on rafts down the Mississippi. Since it was predominantly French and Spanish citizens who inhabited the original walled French Quarter (the Vieux Carré, "Downtown", 66 square blocks set out along the river by architects Blondel de la Tour and Adrien de Pauger), the Americans took their cue and built their own conspicuous dwellings in the "American" quarter, which became known as the Garden District, located "Uptown". Canal Street represented a real dividing line between two cultures—French and Spanish Creole culture in the Vieux Carré, anchored by the St. Louis Cathedral, and the English-speaking culture that stayed on the other side of Canal's wide "neutral ground", as it is still called today. Creoles were resentful of the American newcomers, who were seen as usurpers, and intermarriage with *les Américains*, as they were called, was frowned on right up to the early twentieth century.

New Orleans' "Creolized" culture always fascinated travelers. Indeed, even today visitors are eager to understand, and are puzzled by, the complex racial and ethnic mix that is New Orleans. The following lengthy definition of the word Creole once noted on "Encyclopedia of Cajun Culture" www.cajunculture.com) is worth quoting at length in order to comprehend just how complex the term's etymology and usage is:

> *Always a controversial and confusing term, the word Creole, to put it simply, means many things to many people. It derives from the Latin* creare, *meaning, "to beget" or "create." After the New World's discovery, Portuguese colonists used the word* crioulo *to denote a New World slave of African descent. Eventually, the word was applied to all New World colonists regardless of ethnic origin, living along the Gulf Coast, especially in Louisiana. There the Spanish introduced the word as* criollo, *and during Louisiana's colonial period (1699-1803) the evolving word Creole generally referred to persons of African or European heritage born in the New World. By the nineteenth century, black, white, and mixed-race Louisianans used the term to distinguish themselves from foreign-born and Anglo-American settlers. It was during that century that the mixed-race Creoles of Color (or* gens de couleur libres, *"free persons of color") came into their own as an ethnic group enjoying many of the legal rights and privileges of whites. They occupied a middle ground between whites and enslaved blacks, and as such often possessed property and received formal educations. After the Civil War, most Creoles of Color lost their privileged status and joined the ranks of impoverished former black slaves. All the while, however, the word Creole persisted as a term also referring to white Louisianans, usually of upper-class, non-Cajun origin... It is generally understood among these Creoles of Color that Creole of Color still refers to Creoles of mixed-race heritage, while the term black Creole refers to Creoles of more or less pure African descent. Increasingly, both African-derived groups are putting aside old animosities (based largely on skin color and social standing) to work for mutual preservation, and as such often merely describe themselves as Creole... Ultimately, however, the word Creole remains murky, with some individuals (black, white and mixed-race) futilely claiming the right of exclusive use. As the* Encyclopedia of Southern Culture *states, perhaps the "safest" course is to say that a Creole is "anyone who says he is one."*

In any case, one can easily see, noting some of the family names in New Orleans, that its Franco-Spanish ancestry is still predominant— names, for citizens black, white and in between, such as Babineaux, Giarratano, Andry, Avegno, Paletou, Catalano, Ferro, Rodi, LaCaze, Taso, Tusson, Francher, Perrin, Pappalardo, Pavon, Blanq, Guillot, Charlot, Donato, Dumas, St. Etienne, Compagno, Dupuy, Rotolo, Hernandez and Cannizzaro, to name but a few.

Lafcadio Hearn, who as an ethnographer began living in New Orleans, drawing and documenting its strange customs for local as well as foreign consumption in such books as *Gombo Zhebes* (1885), wrote of the multicultural mix:

> *A man might here study the world. Every race that the world boasts is here, and a good many races that are nowhere else. The strangest and most complicated mixture of Negro and Caucasian blood, with Negroes washed white, and white men mulattoes would scorn to claim as of their own particular hybrid.*

The ethnic and racial diversity historically gave New Orleans a feeling of "foreignness" and "exoticism", as expressed by one visitor, William Kingsford, who wrote in the 1850s that "even the American part of the city [is] full of interest [and]… in the narrow French streets of the Creole population… with the varied appearance of the people… you are made to feel that you are a traveler." The above-quoted French Market visitor noted in his diary:

> *Aristocratic old gentlemen with their broadcloth, polished manners and boots puffed in and out; fat females with fat baskets hanging on their fat arms waddle to and fro; footmen, waiters, maids and small boys come and go away. Nearly all trades, professions, colors and castes are represented with baskets on their arms.*

The diarists are keen observers. And even the same modulations in human appearance can be seen today. For instance, much is made in songs and local legend about the beauty of New Orleans women. One finds dark-eyed, raven-haired beauties with skin as white and smooth as the sky, and lovely African-American woman with near-gleaming ebony skin, generously dusted with white baby powder to keep cool. Under a wide-brimmed Panama hat, you may find the most attractive male face you've ever seen—with café-au-lait-colored skin and amber-green or gray eyes. It is the legacy of cultural legacy that over the centuries has been, at turns, brutally forced (bastardization of a race through slavery), artfully arranged (see Chapter Four), forbidden, kept secret, stolen, just tolerated, and perhaps now commonplace.

Rich and Poor

Before the Civil War, New Orleans became the most prosperous city in the history of the South. Lloyd's of London predicted the boom: in 1835, New Orleans' commerce was valued at approximately $54 million. Louisiana had, in effect, become three states: urban, sophisticated, polyglot, multicultural Catholic New Orleans; Catholic rural Acadiana; and rural Protestant central/northern Louisiana. The state had been divided in two: the District of Louisiana (which included New Orleans and surrounding area) and the Territory of Orleans (which included most of the present state). Sixty years after the Louisiana Purchase, the population of New Orleans had grown to approximately 168,000. Tension between the regions provoked the state legislature to move the capital of the state to Baton Rouge, where it remains today.

After the Civil War and throughout the period of Reconstruction, New Orleans' fortunes changed dramatically as it became one of the poorest cities in the South. New waves of immigrants came: among them were the poor Irish escaping Ireland's Potato Famine of 1845-8, who settled the "Irish Channel" Uptown, and upon whose backs the building of the city's drainage systems was accomplished (many came as indentured servants). Italians arrived (95 per cent of them Sicilians, the highest percentage of Sicilians anywhere in the nation), sharing many traditions with the Spanish and French Creoles, including Roman Catholic faith, strong family ties, a love of opera, dancing and gambling (today they represent the largest white ethnic group in the city). On the heels of the 1990s North American Free Trade Agreement, Latinos were to come from countries such as Cuba, Venezuela, and Honduras. Long before their arrival had come the *Isleños,* a few thousand Spaniards from the Canary Islands who settled land near Bayou Manchac and the Amite River in 1778. They maintained an independent culture, and spoke their own archaic Spanish in settlements called Valenzuela (on Bayou Lafourche) and Galveztown (on the banks of Bayou Manchac). The Isleños Cultural Center and Museum is located on West Judge Perez Drive in St. Bernard Parish.

These were the times of greatest population growth in New Orleans. While in 1800 New Orleanians numbered fewer than 10,000, by 1900 the population was recorded at 287,104. The zenith of the *fin-de-siècle* era was the 1884-5 World's Industrial and Cotton Centennial Exposition held in Audubon Park & Zoological Gardens (today the zoo contains more than 2,000 species of animal life in a park that covers 55 acres along the riverfront, stretching between St. Charles Avenue and Magazine Street, between Exposition Boulevard and Walnut). The great exposition was celebrated in the spirit of stimulating Southern industry and in order to advertise the newly expanded port. In addition, the event marked a century of growth in the cotton trade (four million bales had been produced and packaged for foreign use). The exposition's main building covered 33 acres, bigger by 250,000 square feet than London's famous Crystal Palace, and its fairgrounds were illuminated by the biggest show of electricity in New Orleans' history: 4,000 incandescent and 1,100 arc lamps.

Passing into the twentieth century, New Orleans witnessed economic growth and stabilization as well as industrial and commercial expansion in the wake of the great Victorian age. The city received much-needed civic improvements in the form of a new water purification system that replaced old family cisterns. In 1904, sewers were replaced by underground water mains. And, thankfully, the last of the killing yellow fever outbreaks was in 1905.

There were educational advancements, too. When Reconstruction encouraged the admittance of African-Americans to the public schools, white parents had withdrawn their children. While some of them entered private schools, a great number of them received no education at all. In the late 1879s, the New Orleans public school system was restored, and in 1884 philanthropist Sophie B. Wright, who five years later also opened a private school for girls on Camp Street called the Home Institute, started a free night school. John McDonogh built John McDonogh High School, and Warren Easton, the boys' school on Canal Street, was constructed in 1913. In 1911, the Jesuits established Loyola University. Right next door, Tulane University, on St. Charles

Avenue directly facing Audubon Park, ceased being a facility of the old Louisiana University, and became a private institution by means of a donation of more than $1 million from Paul Tulane. Today, Tulane is recognized as a leader in the disciplines of law and medicine. The world-famous Amistad Research Center, which contains the largest collection in the US of historical materials pertaining to African-Americans and race relations, as well as the William Ransom Hogan Jazz Archive, are part of the important holdings at Tulane University.

During the Second Word War, New Orleans became a base for a group of military camps and during this time, in 1917, the Navy finally had to close Storyville, New Orleans' notorious bordello district (see Chapter Four, Early Jazzers) because troops were contracting sexually transmitted diseases. Because of the "War to End All Wars" Mardi Gras was actually suspended in 1918-9, and in 1927 a terrible flood caused $236 million in damages throughout the Mississippi River Delta. New Orleans barely escaped inundation, as the levee saved countless lives by holding back the floodwaters with only a few inches to spare. This was the era, during the late 1920s and early 1930s, that Louisiana politics was dominated by Huey P. Long, who served as governor from 1928 to 1932 and as US senator from 1932 to 1935. He was a controversial—some say megalomaniacal—figure, whose administration was "productive of benefits and evils in almost equal proportion", notes Oliver Evans. In his time he was compared by some to a dictator—railroading bills through passage, and commanding respect through nepotism, political patronage, and abuses of office:

> *The meetings of the legislature became an elaborate farce, and, on the frequent occasions that Huey came down from Washington to preside over them, presented a kind of comic opera which people flocked from miles around to witness: bills were adopted unread, and if a member hesitated Long would go to his desk and press the 'Aye' button himself.*

A Legacy in Progress

New Orleans' historic multiculturalism continues today in its welcoming of more and more immigrants into its midst. The most recent newcomers to date are the Vietnamese, many of whom have made New Orleans East their home. This is also where many locals in the know go to shop at weekends, at the Vietnamese Farmers' Market or at the Crescent City Farmers' Market at 700 Magazine St., set up in the Warehouse District for the sale of fresh local produce and other indigenous wares.

Every year, nearly every culture is celebrated in the Crescent City, and increasingly it seems that for each group of peoples there springs up a separate festival. They are many—the Cajun Music Festival, Chinese New Year, Dr. Martin Luther King, Jr. Commemorations, and Vietnamese Tet in January; Black Heritage Festival, St. Patrick's Day, the Irish Channel Parade, the Irish-Italian Parade, the Los Isleños Festival, the New Orleans Spring Fiesta and St. Joseph's Day in March; the Mensaje Spanish Festival and one great gigantic cultural celebration that is the New Orleans Jazz & Heritage Festival that begins in April; the Greek Festival and *Fête d'Amérique Française* in May; Juneteenth and Reggae Riddums Festival in June (African-American roots celebrations); Bastille Day in July; Deutsches Haus and Weindorf New Orleans in September; Celtic Nations Festival, the Italian Festival, the Oktoberfest Parade in October; Creole Christmas and Kwanzaa celebrations in December. And these are just the festivals held in New Orleans and closely surrounding areas, not inclusive of those ranging across the whole state of Louisiana.

Celebration comes with any number of faces in "The City That Care Forgot", a nickname first used in the *New Orleans City Guide* produced by the government make-work Federal Works Project of 1938. These "many voices speaking at once" are the inspiration for Lyle Saxon's seminal book that compiles the folk life of Louisiana, *Gumbo Ya-Ya*—and that is exactly what the book's title means. *Gumbo ya-ya*, literally and with alliteration, suggests many voices speaking at once. It makes fascinating reading for any student of New Orleans' multicultural legacy, as does *Cultural Vistas*, the Louisiana Endowment for the Humanities' magazine. But for those who would rather meet and greet in person, the streets are the best place to see the face, or faces, of this city

The citizens are quick to welcome strangers, and, as one local journalist remarked, many sojourners to New Orleans wind up having the time of their lives, finding themselves at short notice dancing in the streets (a peculiar notion to some), compelled to during some feast day or festival. Then, ultimately, the visitor must figure out how to make him- or herself leave such an inclusive and freeing place.

There is another, obvious reason one can reach out and touch New Orleans, and that is because the people return the intimacy. They are family-oriented to begin with, and each culture seems intent on sharing the customs that have brought meaning to their collective lives, many of which may have been brought a long way from a distant land, to be passed on to future generations and, ergo, transplanted into New Orleans' soil. Sometimes the folkways are merged and shared with those of others, only to create something brand-new and completely original out of that contact.

This is true of New Orleans' spectacular Mardi Gras Indians (see Chapter Six, Indian Red), whose complex combination of African-American and Native American music, design and dance is expressed in rituals to the delight and enrichment of native New Orleanians and those who are lucky enough to catch sight of them "suited" and "on the warpath" only a couple of times a year. A costume weighs as much as 100 to 150 pounds and costs each "Black Indian" thousands of dollars for brilliant-hued beads, feathers and sequins; it is carefully constructed over the months preceding Mardi Gras and Super Sunday (usually held on the Bayou St. John, following St. Joseph's Day in March). Then, after the days of celebration, each suit is de-constructed and the leftover beads handed down to the children and used as practice beads.

Family Business
This act of bringing children along in the way they should go spiritually and culturally is the very same impetus that gave, and gives, jazz such a firm roothold in New Orleans, its acknowledged birthplace. This is why it continues to grow and find new audiences today. For anyone who has stayed in the city long enough, it becomes apparent that there are certain family names and family members, who have been instrumental (pardon the pun) in assuring the continued life of New Orleans jazz, continued improvisation upon its form, and continued variations that result in creating new and exciting music genres (here one might mention the way the traditional jazz funeral brass bands have incorporated R&B and even hip-hop licks into the standard repertoire).

Mention the names Andrews (James and brother Troy), Barbarin (father Isidore, sons Paul, Louis and Lucien), Connick (father Harry Sr., and Harry Jr.), Crawford (grandfather "Sugar Boy" and grandson Davell), Jordan (Edward "Kidd" father, sons Kent and Marlon, daughter Stephanie), LaRocca (father Nick and son Jimmy), Lastie (father Deacon Frank, sons Melvin, David and Walter), Marsalis (father Ellis and sons Wynton, Brandford, Delfeayo, Jason), Neville (brothers Aaron, Art, Cyril, and daughter of Charles, Charmaine) Payton (father Walter and son Nicholas), and Turbinton (brothers Willy, Earl) among many others, and you conjure generations of musicians whose heritage not only reaches back, but continues to move forward with the new children of the family, grandsons and granddaughters, nephews, nieces, uncles, aunts and cousins. They, in turn, pass on the appreciation of music nurtured in the city of New Orleans. Jazz raconteur and mentor of a whole new generation of New Orleans musicians, Danny Barker, explained:

> *In New Orleans it was never a problem to have music for some social event because many of the musicians were related to one another. A party for some social event was planned and the musicians came and played. There your elders would explain to you, at length, how and why different musicians were related to you—when you greeted each other after that, it was "Hello, Cuz."*

Barker, who lived a musician's life extraordinaire, documented in his autobiographical *A Life in Jazz* (1986), was a wonderful model for future generations of musicians—a true "New Orleans Personality" and an example of an artist who passed the torch before passing on to a better place. He is credited with being largely responsible for the renaissance of New Orleans brass band music.

Barker was born on 13 January 1909, into a music-loving Creole family. His maternal grandfather, Isidore Barbarin, played alto horn in one of the most important brass bands of the early jazz era, the Onward Brass Band (1889-1930), which trained many an aspiring musician, such as Manuel Perez, Joe Oliver and Louis Armstrong. Isidore, whose "day job" was as driver of the horse-drawn hearse for a Creole undertaker, had nine children, and four of them became musicians. Barker's uncle, Paul Barbarin, who would become a noted jazz drummer in New York City, acted as mentor to Danny, who "came up" living at his paternal grandparents' house (now marked at 1027 Chartres St. in the lower end of the Quarter). There he lived out childhood years playing in the streets of the Creole neighborhood.

Later, after his mother remarried, he lived in the Faubourg Marigny, Seventh Ward, a more middle-class Creole enclave supporting cigar makers, brick masons, carpenters, music teachers, and other tradesmen. Barker was able to begin clarinet lessons with Barney Bigard, who then went on to Chicago and a career playing with "King" Oliver and Duke Ellington. Barker also experimented with the ukulele, banjo, and, later, guitar.

After marrying his young sweetheart, Louise (a.k.a. jazz vocalist "Blue Lu" Barker), in the early years of the Depression, Danny left the Crescent City, like many jazz musicians had before him, including "Jelly Roll" Morton and Sidney Bechet. It opened his eyes, gave him a breadth of experience he would not otherwise have received in New Orleans (meeting members of the Harlem Renaissance, for example), and allowed him to play with Morton, twice Danny's age, Cab Calloway's big band (which starred "Dizzie" Gillespie on trumpet), and Lionel Hampton. Meanwhile, "Blue Lu" was recording with Decca records.

Following a brief return home, upon which Barker recorded with the great father of jazz Sidney Bechet and trumpeter Bunk Johnson, the Barkers traveled to California, where "Blue Lu" was recording with Capitol and scored a hit on the *Billboard* charts. In ensuing years, Barker would record with Louis Armstrong, Billie Holliday, Charlie Parker, Wynton Marsalis, Dr. John and many others. He composed hundreds of songs, and became known as a premier rhythm-section guitarist. He also became a one-man archivist, a keeper of interviews, notes and oral histories about all the great musicians he had known. Much of this he committed to memory, or sketched out in songs he sang to amuse and teach. As author Jason Berry tells us, for Barker "'Jelly Roll' Morton became a prototype, if not a role model: the swaggering storyteller, insisting that people hear him. Danny the raconteur had a comedian's timing, telling his tales in a sly, deadpan manner more effective than Morton's swagger." Anyone who has heard Barker's New Orleans-styled version of "St. James Infirmary" (filled with allusions to his home town, therefore "Touro Infoim'ry") knows how Barker could have fun with the jazz.

When bebop and rock 'n' roll made their appearance, and Miles Davis and John Coltrane became the new progenitors of cool jazz, Barker returned to the Crescent City for a final time. As a member of

Fairview Baptist Church, the older musician brought along a lot of talented young musicians he had winnowed out to play in the Fairview Baptist Church Brass Band. And when he died at the age of 85, in March 1994 (the City of New Orleans had declared 13 January Danny and "Blue Lu" Barker Day), a giant second-line jazz funeral with thousands of people attending stretched out into the streets. "You rejoice when you leave the world, and you cry when you enter it," Barker had said on an ABC TV special called *The Anatomy of Pop*. That, in essence, sums up the prevailing New Orleanian attitude toward

death. The leadership of the Barker's Jazz Hounds passed to Gregg Stafford, a young trumpeter who had been properly "trained up" under Barker's tutelage. Memories of Barker live on in the spirit of the jazz, just as he felt it.

So when people go to dancing in an impromptu parade, or a young kids' brass band goes by, or there is a music festival in town (the French Quarter Festival, Satchmo SummerFest), and people start waving kerchiefs and bobbing umbrellas up and down, it is well to remember what Barker said about the importance of music and the people of New Orleans: "You see the music's effect on the people... foot patting, finger snapping, head and body bouncing to the beat... that's a great pleasure for me and the people... jazz will live on, because it digs down inside the body, the brain, the heart, the nerves and the muscle."

Chapter Two

RIVER AND RIVERFRONT: "PARIS ON THE MISSISSIPPI"

*"The first thing a visitor to New Orleans should look at is the river...
the French Quarter can wait."*
—Irish novelist Sean O'Faolain

*"The Mississippi River in North America, when the first Europeans
discovered it, became from the start what it has remained: an established route of continental intercommunication, or a street... In the
lower valley of this river, in the region where New Orleans was set,
countless lesser streams (called by the Indians bayuks, and by the
white men bayous), together with lakes and the great river itself, all
formed a useful and well-used system of intercommunication. To the
Indians, the explorers, the voyageurs, and the intrepid coureurs de bois
these were streets."*
—John Churchill Chase

It has been called the "Great Father" of rivers, the American Nile, and
aptly so for its mythic "flow" through American history. There is a
custom that says when travelers first come to the Mississippi's edge, they
should crouch down and plunge their hands into the muddy water to
be baptized in the South. After that ritual a voyager should look out
across the river's expanse—it is at its widest (2,200 feet) and deepest
(212 feet) at New Orleans. One sees an impressive stretch of shiny,
placid brown water, with some fast currents making herringbone
patterns in places; there is short tangled vegetation on the shores,
interspersed with wharves and docks and other such landings. It is not
especially pretty as world rivers go...

But at New Orleans you observe that there is a hush, a thickening
of sound, like a damper held down over the water. And if you press the
imagination into service, the churning, chugging, swashing sounds of a

steamboat bearing down on the Port of New Orleans become just audible. Moments like these conjure up images of nineteenth-century New Orleans, the wild riverboat days of the sternwheelers, when "sports" and gamblers debarked, according to one *fin-de-siècle* madame, "shaved, perfumed, in their best duds and flawed yellow diamonds", ready for gaming and more.

Maybe the waterway's coordinates should be turned around: New Orleans is not settled on the Mississippi, rather the Mississippi settles in on it. An evocative literary account of the river's powerful wend is that of Mark Twain, or Samuel Clemens, credited as the master of American literary realism. His travel journal as a 21-year-old "cub" pilot aboard a steamboat headed to New Orleans, where he hoped to secure passage on a ship to South America, is documented in his *Life on the Mississippi.* The 1857 account supplies an authentic picture of what life must have been like when settlers depended upon a river to be a liquid "four-lane highway" of commerce and adventure. The Mississippi's first steamboats had appeared in 1812, only five years after Robert Fulton built the first commercial vessel, which was called the *New Orleans.* By 1840, there were more than 400 steamboats on the river. Approaching New Orleans, "Metropolis of the South", on a sternwheeler, Twain observes:

> *In high-river stage, in the New Orleans region, the water is up to the top of the inclosing levee-rim, the flat country behind it lies low—representing the bottom of a dish—and as the boat swims along, high on the flood, one looks down upon the houses and into the upper windows. There is nothing but that frail breastwork of earth between the people and destruction.*

Twain relates how he must, as a boat pilot-in-training, memorize each feature on the shore and in the water down to New Orleans, so that he may navigate future voyages and avoid "hang-ups" or dangers lurking in some of the faster-running water. The young navigator duly stores each remarkable feature in his mind—a fallen tree here, an abandoned building there—but it is not until he reaches the Crescent City that he realizes that he is going to have to remember them all again going back, only backwards! This throws the cub pilot into disarray, but he perseveres. Even today, Mississippi River pilots perform an important function, and all captains of vessels heading upriver must hand over navigation of their craft to a seasoned group of pilots who are specially trained and positioned in a station at the mouth of the river for precisely this purpose.

The golden age of the riverboat is portrayed in Twain's novels. Their sumptuousness and the "sporting life" they supported were certainly worth writing about. The riverboats were also vehicles that carried new musical styles, articulated by many a New Orleans musician, throughout the Midwest and beyond. The first minstrel shows, then Dixieland, found their expression aboard packet boats such as the *S.S. President*, which was built in 1924 and purchased by the Streckfus Company in 1929. Louis Armstrong played on the Streckfus steamers with Fate Marable's band between 1918 and 1922. Because riverboats could accommodate so many people, many big bands played floating concerts out on the Mississippi.

River Excursion
Twain's first impression of New Orleans was, like many seeing the city for the first time: "What a beautiful old place." In a distant way, it is possible to see what the young author saw with a voyage on a faithful recreation of those luxuriously outfitted vessels, such as the steamboat *Natchez IX* with its steam-powered calliope (moored right at the riverfront, not far from Café du Monde, behind Jax Brewery), the *Paddlewheeler Creole Queen* or *Riverboat Creole Queen* (both depart from the dock at Riverwalk Marketplace, along the riverfront at the foot of Canal Street). When the sun is low and light is saturated, the effect is always the same. The burnt sienna, coral, salmon, ochre, pale pink and verdigris are just as compelling a century or more later:

> *[The French Quarter's] buildings' chief beauty is the deep, warm, varicolored stain with which time and the weather have enriched the plaster. It harmonizes with all the surroundings, and has as natural a look of belonging here as has the flush upon sunset clouds. This charming decoration cannot be successfully imitated; neither is to be found elsewhere in America...*

Across the river from where the steamboats and commuter ferries depart lies the neighborhood of Old Algiers, on what is called in New

Orleans "the West Bank". Algiers evolved from plantation lands that developed around the shipbuilding and railroad industries. This causes a lot of confusion for everyone, residents and visitors alike, as the West Bank is not actually west, but, rather, east or slightly south. To picture it correctly in the mind's eye, one can think of the snaking Mississippi River as perhaps a long cottonmouth slithering from the north and emptying into the Gulf of Mexico. It twists this way and that, so direction seems impossible to discern, but if the snake (or river) were straightened out, all locations on the right side of the river would be on the east bank, and those on the left would be on the west bank. Whether one is on foot or in an automobile, it is possible to take the Canal Street Ferry (free for pedestrians) across to the historic town of Algiers—and many do commute back and forth from work.

As in Twain's time, there are people who work the river in all different capacities. No matter what they do, however, they must see everything differently from the landlubber's vantage point—they can be out on the river and look back at the shore, and upon themselves. The view is ever changing. Capt. "Doc" Hawley, for twenty years the majordomo of the eighth-generation steamboat *Natchez*, can testify to the hold the river has had on him: "I've had a wonderful life... met a lot of wonderful people... seen a lot of river." Hawley came to New Orleans as a boy from the West Virginia hills who thought on his first journey down the Mississippi towards New Orleans that "somehow we turned the wrong way down there and we'd ended up in Europe! I've been in love with New Orleans since 1957." Speaking of the two-hour-long excursion run that he has made every day for twenty years on the *Natchez*, he recalls, "People would ask, 'Don't you get tired of goin' from Toulouse Street to Chalmette (scene of the Battle of New Orleans), and up to the Huey P. Long and back?' And I'd say, 'No, no. Every trip is a new adventure! All the traffic out there! And in the spring the river cuts up... high water...,'" he trails off dreamily.

The contemporary dockworkers doing the considerably harder job of unloading container ships have their maritime union contracts, Workman's Compensation, and personal injury lawyers well versed in maritime law to mitigate their sufferings. Stevedores of the city's colonial past did not have these advantages, just the hard-core diversions of longshoremen in a riverfront town. And this was part of the life we can only imagine today.

Indeed, historian John Churchill Chase paints us a vivid picture of the life of the rugged keelboatmen, who rode their large skiffs up and down the river both before and during the steamboat "invasion". For keelboats, going downriver was not so difficult—merely a push with a pole to glide along—but going upriver involved a strenuous maneuver called "bushwhacking" that entailed the crew's grabbing at bushes and trees along the riverbank, then literally hauling the boat upstream. They were a wild bunch, these muscle-bound boatmen:

> *Life on the keels consisted of much hard work, and long periods of ease and idleness. On each trip the ease and idleness came first, as the current swept the boat down to the warm ports of Natchez Under-The-Hill, and Journey's End at New Orleans.*
>
> *There was ample supply of food and music and whiskey and women, and all of it was bad… Each keelboat had its barrel of Monongahela rye whiskey secured in plain sight amidship. No keelboater would sign up on a boat without it, and the privilege of taking a nip with or without a reason.*
>
> *The music was a type of mountain music that had lost altitude; and the women were the Lorelei who waited in New Orleans to lure them to The Swamp, back-of-town on Girod street…*
>
> *Perhaps the keelboater's most enjoyable of off-duty pastime was fighting. Each boat had its champ, or bully, who wore a red turkey feather as an insignia of his pre-eminence—literally, a chip on his shoulder. The ambition of each boat's bully was to fight another boat's bully. So when several hundred keelboats tied up at Tchoupitoulas street, there were duels of the champs, and then whole crews jumped rival crews. The results were frequently fights with nobody left to watch.*

This was just one of the notorious riverfront "attractions". One night in 1817, fifty drunken "Kaintock" keelboatmen decided to carry out a prank and at the same time terrorize some of the local Creole population [there was ongoing antipathy between the two cultures]. The rabble descended upon a circus staged by a Señor Gaetano in the Faubourg Ste. Marie—the keelboatmen bearing knives and clubs set upon the Creole circus-goers brandishing their cane swords. Confusion reigned, there was blood and mayhem, and in the end all the circus

animals escaped into the streets. After the mêlée, it was no wonder that Gaetano returned to his native Havana. The small street one block off of Philippa Street continued to be called Circus Street until the Civil War. Today it is South Rampart.

Gallatin and People of the Port

If one stands near the foot of Esplanade Street, near the curbs of the French Market at North Peters, the ghosts of the night people of Gallatin Street may be heard, partying hard after a hard day on the river. For in the early nineteenth century, two blocks of Gallatin were the "bawdiest, filthiest, wickedest two blocks in any community anywhere", says John Churchill Chase. Barrelhouses, dance halls, gin mills and brothels kept rowdy keelboat men, rafters, sailors, stevedores and every other description of seafaring ruffian occupied. He adds: "Historians nod their heads in sad agreement that the harlots of Gallatin established new lows to which human beings might sink, and the male habitués there were more skilled in mayhem, murder, and robbery than ever heretofore known."

The riverfront flotsam and jetsam are no longer there (today you might find their modern counterparts holed up in holes-in-the wall along

Tchoupitoulas Street, farther upriver, or perhaps buying a fifth at the Hit and Run Package Liquor Store). So, Gallatin's raunchy secrets will have to die with it, because the buildings are all gone, and the street has been paved over with another, called French Market Place. Memories float downriver and are awash upon what we know about the importance of the waterway to the City of New Orleans in the twenty-first century. Shipbuilding at Avondale Shipyards (supplying the city with 6,000-plus jobs) and a major defense contract with the federal government are the current priorities of one Senator Mary Landrieu. New Orleans is the Mississippi River's southernmost terminus for any craft either headed downriver, or for seagoing vessels wishing to load or unload inland off the Gulf of Mexico. To see just the riggings of the freighters and container ships regally gliding by—all you can see sometimes peering over the levee—is a poetic suggestion of the heft of these craft the size of floating football fields, and the berth that they require.

Economic Imperative

The stretch of riverbank from the contemporary Port of New Orleans all the way upriver to the capital, Baton Rouge, comprises the country's second-largest port, second in size only to the Port of New York. The wharves and terminals flanking the river, the Industrial Canal, and the Mississippi River Gulf Outlet—22 miles of those facilities in total—handle as much as thirty million tons of bulk cargo annually (commodities such as coffee, rubber, steel and forest products from countries in the Far East, Latin America and Europe), representing roughly $700 million worth of water-born commerce and providing more than 60,000 jobs for the Metro area.

The city's fathers, then, knew what they were doing. They chose the present site for New Orleans (precarious though it is, built on alluvial silt washed from the Missouri and Ohio rivers and more than 250 other tributaries) precisely because they recognized its strategic geographic importance as a gateway to the riches of North America. Situated at the end of an old Indian portage that led to a stream called the Bayou St. John (Bienville named it after his patron saint; it is extant today as it winds through Mid-City), and emptying into Lake Pontchartrain, the bayou allowed vessels to sail into the lake from Biloxi or Mobile (of Louisiana Territory), head up Bayou St. John to the back of the levee, and unload cargo—thereby avoiding treacherous open

Gulf waters. Biloxi and Mobile had also posed the difficulty of anchoring far offshore due to the shallow waters all along the Gulf Coast, which prevented ships with a deep draft from coming ashore to dock and necessitated taking trips in smaller boats to make the landing. One can appreciate the wry appropriateness of historian Pierce F. Lewis' remark (*New Orleans: The Making of an Urban Landscape*) that "The Mississippi River demands a city at its mouth, but fails to provide a place for one."

In fact, so water-locked is New Orleans, the city could only truly grow and prosper when, at the turn of the twentieth century, new large-scale pumps enabled the drainage of swamps flanking the city, allowing development to fan outward toward Lake Pontchartrain. Now a vast public drainage system can pump rainfall at one inch per hour, and creates miles of canals rivaling those of Venice. So much water has also meant that many parts of Louisiana were hard to reach until such modern-day structures as Huey P. Long Bridge (1936), the Greater New Orleans Bridge (1958) and the I-10 (through the 1970s) were built. The river and the old River Road were, until the 1950s, the only means of moving goods and passengers—and they were the way that people were able to travel to a city to find out about everything they heard it had to offer. It also explains, to some extent, New Orleans' insularity, keeping it distanced from the influence and trends affecting the rest of the state and, indeed, the rest of North America.

Jazz Journey: Louis Armstrong

"Jazz is played from the heart. You can even live by it. Always love it!"
　　　　　—Louis Armstrong

Mulling over the idea of what should be considered New Orleans' most famous exports to the world, one thinks of the city's port history. Perhaps it is New Orleans food that immediately comes to most people's mind (or stomach, as the case may be). There are oysters Rockefeller, bananas Foster, pralines (that oversweet Creole confection made with sugar and butter, then studded with pecans), grillades and grits, gumbo, jambalaya—even the entire "brunch time" meal (created by Madame Begué, who at her restaurant at 823 Decatur St., which is now popular Tujague's, fed French Market merchants who did not have time to eat their morning meal). One may even include the invention of the cocktail (see Chapter Three, Bourbon Street: Shots and Hot Spots).

There is only one export that New Orleans has sent out to the rest of the country—indeed the world. It is the one "commodity" that can be considered history changing, and of international import, affecting the greatest number of people. It is the birth of jazz. And what serendipity that its best-recognized and faithful ambassador was also born here. Known simply as "Pops", he is none other than spectacular, avuncular Louis Armstrong. The river, which took Armstrong away from home the first time in 1919, also afforded him the opportunity to join "homeboy" Fate Marable's band in St. Louis, and it floated him upstream to play with him on the Streckfus Mississippi Riverboat Lines. It is appropriate, therefore, that the Jazz National Historic Park, where a regularly scheduled assortment of musicians performs, is located right on the brink of the river at 916 North Peters St.

"Ambassador Satch" sailed into the history of jazz: he recorded hit songs for over five decades, appeared in more than thirty films, composed countless jazz standards, performed in hundreds of concerts a year, including state-sponsored tours and broadcasts (to such countries as Ghana, where he entertained a crowd of 100,000), and set the standard for the way jazz could be played with what one critic calls the "utter fearlessness of his groundbreaking solos" and scat singing. Fellow horn man "Dizzie" Gillespie admits, "Louis Armstrong's station in the history of jazz is unimpeachable. If it weren't for him, there wouldn't be any of us."

Armstrong came from one of the poorest part of town, what used to be called "The Battlefield". He was an earnest, hardworking boy who supported his mother and sister by singing on street corners for coins (the boys singing and tap-dancing with pop bottle tops in the bottoms of their shoes are still there), selling coal from a cart, selling papers and unloading boats. One New Year's Eve, after firing off a pistol at midnight (a dangerous practice still carried out with great glee on New Year's Eve today), Armstrong was brought to the Jones Home for Colored Waifs, spending about 18 months in its care. There, he took his first formal music lessons and played in the brass band. His early days were also spent listening to music at the "Funky Butt Hall" (the

forerunner of today's incarnation on North Rampart), soaking up lessons from his mentor and early jazz great Joe "King" Oliver. Oliver was one of a handful of New Orleans musicians, including the legendary "Jelly Roll" Morton and Sidney Bechet, who were creating a unique new band music out of blues and ragtime. It was just the beginning of a career for Armstrong that would thrust him into the limelight with many great bands, headlining in New York, Chicago and around the world.

When all was said and done, Armstrong held close to his roots in New Orleans. And although the official Armstrong website (www.satchmo.net) and Armstrong House and Archives are maintained in Flushing, NY, Satchmo's true comfort may well have been left back home, in New Orleans, in the jazz cradle. He admitted late in life: "I'm always wondering if it would have been best in my life if I'd stayed like I was in New Orleans, having a ball. I was very much contented just to be around and play with the old timers. And the money I made—I lived off of it. I wonder if I would have enjoyed that better than all this big muck-muck traveling all over the world." Armstrong returned often to his hometown and was pictured on the front of *Time* magazine as "King Zulu" in 1949, when he came specifically to accept and carry out that very exceptional role of honor for Mardi Gras (see Chapter Ten, Mardi Gras Mocked).

Armstrong's humble, loving, and exuberant spirit will always be remembered. There is a park named for him, filled with ponds, fragrant magnolias and willows. It borders a significant length of North Rampart Street, from Toulouse to St. Philip streets and contains the Mahalia Jackson Theatre for the Performing Arts as well as the headquarters of New Orleans' favorite radio station dedicated to the indigenous sound, WWOZ FM. Armstrong's bronze figure stands erect holding his trademark cornet and handkerchief. Satchmo is always thought of as a mentor here, and there is not a young New Orleans trumpeter alive today who does not readily credit Armstrong and send up praises for his playing—among them Wynton Marsalis, Nicholas Payton, Kermit Ruffins, James Andrews, Jamil Sharif, and many others. The airport in recent years has been named after him: Louis Armstrong New Orleans International Airport. And in order for people to have something to do in the worst of the summer heat, a festival has been created in his name: Satchmo SummerFest. It brings out the brass to blow away the humidity for visitors and locals to enjoy during the most trying of dog days.

Rue de la Quai/Decatur Street

Since New Orleans is settled along the river, with the French Market, St. Louis Cathedral and Jackson Square together the visual and social focal point of the city, it is natural to find many people convening there. This has been true for many years: New Orleans was always flanked by a market, a cathedral and an old square. They are sites that have served as the city's *loci* for physical and spiritual nourishment. For two hundred years, people have worked or played here, and people have come to gather and see one another, or stroll the environs on what used to be called Rue de la Quai. That thoroughfare, running beside the river, was eventually renamed Levee Street, and finally Decatur Street in 1870, when, due to the river's alteration of course, city fathers realized that it no longer closely skirted the levee. Decatur today wends alongside the riverfront and its most popular attractions, and it is therefore usually thronged with tourists day and night, especially during a special event, such as Mardi Gras. More and more activities are being held at the waterfront Woldenberg Park, such as the Zulu Lundi Gras Golden Nugget Festival that draws crowds of people anticipating Tuesday's abandon.

The Old Mint

Exploring the riverfront appropriately begins at the far end of the French Market, where, at 400 Esplanade, the Old US Mint, just one facility of the multi-venue Louisiana State Museum, shows "New Orleans Jazz". It interprets the reasons why New Orleans' special historic, economic, and social circumstances at the end of the nineteenth century allowed for the creation of entirely new American art form, now listed as a National Treasure: "The Jazz". Photographs, instruments, recordings, sheet music, archival papers and other objects date back to the early days of what was once called "jackass" or "jass" music. The cornet and bugle on which Armstrong was taught to play is housed there, still burnished but now mute.

A short distance from the museum, at the foot of Chartres Street, are the expansive, expensive ($23 million) new facilities of "the Julliard of the South", a regional, "pre-professional" arts complex called New Orleans Center for the Creative Arts, or NOCCA. Alma mater of eight-time Grammy winner trumpeter Wynton Marsalis, as well as young lions Harry Connick Jr., Terrence Blanchard and Nicholas Payton, NOCCA continues to keep the jazz tradition alive. This is one of the educational facilities (complementing grassroots training supplied by family mentorship) that has gained a national reputation. It has served students from all of Louisiana's 64 parishes. NOCCA Riverfront's student body cuts across boundaries and socio-economic backgrounds, and approximately half of its students come from families living below the poverty line.

It is programs like NOCCA's, along with other important initiatives such as the Jazz Studies course at the University of New Orleans, stewarded by jazz patriarch pianist Ellis Marsalis, Clyde Kerr, Jr.'s program at Southern University at New Orleans, and the New Orleans Jazz & Heritage Foundation's Heritage School of Music under the baton of saxophonist Edward "Kidd" Jordan that ensure New Orleans talent is still being nurtured and sent out to the world.

Danny Barker, one of New Orleans' best-loved musicians and a contemporary of Satchmo's, speculates that the Mississippi River is more than muse to musicians, but actually lends a special effect that amplifies a person's playing. He quips in his inimitable jazz raconteur's style:

> *The Mississippi bends in a crescent here, so that water, the vapor from that water, sort of was an enclosure with sound. If you know about decibels of sound. An' the river, sound carries on the river, and it circles. An' you got the lake, which is a huge body of water on ya north, ya dig? Up above ya got bayous and swamplands. That's water. So when the sound hits, it's an enclosure an' it bounces around.*

No doubt musicians have heard the sounds of the river resounding—foghorns moaning, wharves creaking, motors humming, waves lapping—and incorporated them into their syncopated tunes, knowingly or not.

Barker is not the only one to put forth this theory. Jazz historians recall the oral histories that claim when Buddy Bolden practiced his trumpet from the front yard of his home at 2309 First St., where he lived from 1887 to 1905, you could hear him all the way across town. The story may be apocryphal, but the house is still there. Just listen to the riffs of street musicians and pick-up bands of the riverfront and French Quarter whose notes punctuate the steady stream of tourists moving upriver. On a quiet morning in the French Quarter, from the vantage point of Jackson Square, you can indeed hear a horn from a long distance away.

While on the French Market end of Decatur, it is wise also to stop and hear the jazz (i.e., not the more formulaic "Dixieland" version) at Nina and George Buck's excellent Palm Court Jazz Café (1204 Decatur St.). This British couple (many music lovers and jazzophiles from Britain have made their home here) collect rare jazz recordings and sell them in the café setting. A recent foray during the Tennessee Williams Festival's music programming ("Jazz with a Foreign Accent") turned up an event that explored the way many young European musicians came over to New Orleans in the 1960s and decided to stay.

Lars Edegran, a Swede, headlined the band of musicians that included clarinetist Jacques Gauthé, of France, and Clive Wilson and Les Muscutt of England. Dr. Bruce Raeburn, jazz curator at Tulane University's Hogan Jazz Archive, moderated a discussion that intertwined commentary by local vocalist, "Big Al" Carson. To the delight of everyone, especially the proprietress, who, during a moment of pure abandon got up to shake a leg to the "Opelousas Strut", Carson concluded: "You can't be a part of the music unless you live the lifestyle. Listening to records only takes you so far…" To add to the club's own jazz history, Danny Barker, who played there in his waning years with his Jazz Hounds, wrote a well-loved local anthem for "the Bucks" establishment: "Do the "Palm Court Strut"/Shake your butt/Shake it to the East, shake it to the West/Shake it to the one that you love best…"

Hooked on Caffeine

> *"First thing in the morning, after a sleepless night, the Creole gentle-man stands before a coffee woman's stall in the Market:* Pitti fille, pitti fille, pitti fille *(Little girl, little girl, little girl), he sang. Then, maybe doffing his hat, he launches into an extemporaneous tribute to the deftness with which she combines water and coffee grains:* Pitti fille qui couri dan dolo *(Little girl who ran in the water)..."*

Ethnographer Lyle Saxon provides many such stories in his seminal collection of Louisiana culture, *Gumbo Ya-Ya*, particularly about the coffee women of the Old City of New Orleans. He writes about the "Negro women" whose businesses were found on Canal Street, in front of St. Louis Cathedral and in the French Market. How their melodious cries of *Café noir!* and *Café au lait!* rang out. Then, as now, a day without coffee was not worth starting, and when you reach the French Market (a cupola-topped edifice designed in 1913 by architect Joseph Tanesse called the Halle des Boucheries) find the famous sidewalk coffeehouse, Café du Monde, straight across Decatur from St. Louis Cathedral. It is certainly worth stopping for some frothy New Orleans coffee and chicory, as well as the confectioner's-sugar-dusted *beignets* (donuts). Then it is easy to appreciate how coffee percolated through Creole life and still continues to lift the spirits.

Witness the florid lament of a *Daily Picayune* staffer who in the late nineteenth century praised the beauty of his favorite coffee woman, Rose Gla, and mourned her untimely death: "...one of the comeliest of her race, black as Erebus, but smiling always and amicable as dawn." Her coffee was "the essence of the fragrant bean", wrote the reporter in a fit of elegiac ardor, "and since her death the lovers of that divine beverage wander listlessly around the stalls on Sunday mornings with a pining at the bosom which cannot be satisfied."

According to Saxon in his compilation of Louisiana lore and custom, Manette, a quadroon woman, operated a popular French Market coffee stand in the 1840s. She sold java, homemade pastries and *bière du pays* (beer brewed from pineapple). Children sent to market would keep a *picayune* (a small-value Spanish coin) ready in their pockets for a sip of Manette's "delicious and fragrant brew" before starting home. Taken internally, coffee provided nineteenth-century

New Orleanians with a morning kick-start. But Creole women also managed to find an external use for it, darkening their hair with coffee grinds at the first sign of gray. Coffee even found its way into the language, as when a blend of dark and light family colors produced people euphemistically called *café au lait*.

In the nineteenth century, coffeehouses such as the Empire, the Gem and the Ruby served caffeine devotees. Liquor was not on offer, but lingering encouraged. "No gambling, no theatricals," read a sign in Lawlor's Coffee House. Coffee was for everyday consumption, but it was also for feast day: Christmas Reveillon feasts traditionally concluded with steamy brandy-fortified, orange-laced *café brûlot* ladled from a Sheffield *brûlot* bowl. The after-dinner *brûlot* is described in Stanley Clisby Arthur's *Famous New Orleans Drinks* as "liquid fruitcake".

Brokers of the green bean lined the wharves all the way up to Magazine Street, Uptown. In 1852, one Henry T. Lonsdale, Coffee Broker at 89 Gravier St., recorded the market price of coffee in his Weekly Coffee Statement. That artifact, kept on file in the archives of the Historic New Orleans Collection, listed coffee at nine cents a bag. Such low prices are far removed from those familiar to the clientele of contemporary neighborhood coffeehouses who pay upwards of three dollars for just one cup of specialty coffee. In return, New Orleanians only ask that the coffee be good.

As one of the city's contemporary purveyors of coffee-by-the-cup, "PJ's" president and chief executive officer Phyllis Jordan points out, caffeine is an asset the city has always enjoyed. Despite the early-1960s nationalization of coffee production by commercial roasters such as Folger's and Nestlé, and in spite of a general decline in coffee quality when high prices meant commercial roasters bought less expensive, lower quality beans (Brazil's freeze of 1973), New Orleans has always been able to enjoy the products of local roasters.

Coffee-and-chicory blends such as Union, Blue Plate, CDM, French Market—"The Kind New Orleans Likes"—and Luzianne have helped generations of New Orleanians greet the morning. An advertisement, circa 1945, for Blue Plate pictures a young man in uniform tilted back in a kitchen chair with Mama in apron and the dog wagging his tail: "Gee Mom! It's Great to Get Home to You—and Blue Plate Coffee." Though strong coffee and dark roasts (preferably slow-dripped in the favored French white porcelain pot) are associated with New Orleanian tastes, coffee-drinkers have developed exceptionally sophisticated palates for coffee beverages that in former years were considered exotic.

Looking out over the river from "the Moonwalk" (a boardwalk maybe a mile long named after former mayor "Moon" Landrieu), the day perks up. While a big ship is off-loading coffee at the Jourdan Road Wharf, the smell of beans roasting wafts all along Tchoupitoulas Street, where piles of brown jute bags in the warehouses of Neeb-Kearney & Co., Inc. (with one and a quarter million square feet for coffee storage), exude that peculiar, pungent, malty-green aroma. Joseph Logsdon, professor at the University of New Orleans, has observed the coffee phenomenon from vantage points both as a historian and aficionado: "It's into everybody's rhythm... coffee is part of what I call the public culture, or the shared culture of New Orleans, its food, music, architecture." Logsdon attributes the strength of New Orleans' public culture to what he points out was, historically speaking, the "tremendous hold of the French, Roman Catholic host culture, which was there a hundred years before the Americans." Unlike cities to the North that kept immigrant communities at arm's length, he says, New Orleans experienced the inclusiveness of French culture—a pulling of cultures toward the center.

Café du Monde

In an interesting example of cultural synthesis, Café du Monde is more strongly modeled on the Spanish version of a coffeehouse—serving no liquor (as French coffee bars would). And the *beignets*, which one might think of as a French sweet, more closely resemble Spanish *churros*. Hubert N. Fernandez, now deceased, bought the company in the 1940s; it is not known whether a Spanish pedigree goes as far back as the coffee shop's founding in 1862.

In another cultural coup, Café du Monde has established a strong Japanese following, with as many as forty locations opened in that country after a successful debut at the Osaka World's Fair. And CDM may yet capture another market sector. The Vietnamese, who love their coffee strong with sweet, hot milk poured in slowly, make up much of CDM's local workforce. When management found out that the Vietnamese employees were sending the Café du Monde's

Original French Market Coffee Stand brand to friends and family both at home and abroad, it did not take long to have Vietnamese grocers stocking their shelves with the New Orleans coffee-and-chicory blend.

Another reason that coffee continues to be shipped by so many New Orleanians is its plentiful supply. The Port of New Orleans is, and has been since the 1700s, a prime destination for importation of the commodity arriving from Central and South America, as well as for goods from the Caribbean Rim. As the "backdoor to the continents", says Logsdon, it was far easier to ship to New Orleans. Neither Florida nor California was as well-developed or well-equipped to handle shipments.

Today, Latin America leads the world in the production of coffee, and America is the largest consumer. New Orleans lies in the middle of that profitable configuration and is, according to recent Port of New Orleans figures, the number-one Gulf/Atlantic coffee port. Millions of pounds of coffee (measured in short tons) arrive in the Crescent City from top-five export markets, including Guatemala, Brazil, Colombia, Honduras and Mexico. Coffee is the third-largest import through the port, after steel and natural rubber. Making their stately way up the sinuous curves of the Mississippi, ocean carriers from as many as twenty shipping lines call at the Port of New Orleans direct from coffee-producing nations. But all of that may not be of interest to writers, artists, or politicians, who may just want to gather at New Orleans coffeehouses for socializing. Customers make their way to coffeehouses for poetry and music, as reading series and performances are regularly scheduled at most venues, and people attend dressed in New Orleans' own version of haute couture, what might be called vintage "shabby chic".

In coffeehouses ideas are born; through ideas, events take place, and the seeds of revolution are sown. But this particular evening it is just a peaceful poetry reading at a café almost directly across from the French Market. New Orleans' unofficial "poet laureate", Arthur Pfister, or Professor Arturo, is reading from his homage to the city, "My Name Is New Orleans", reminiscing about the can he kept his marbles in as a child: "I'm a Luzianne Coffee & Chicory can fulla chinees. I'm a chiney. I'm a boley. I'm a cat-eye. I'm a crystal. I'm a knuckle fitter." New Orleanians add coffee—and the coffee culture—to their local mythology. Even a youth organization devoted to promoting positive images of the city, the Young Leadership Council, chooses a java-inspired motto paired with a blue fleur-de-lis for its civic-awareness campaign. "Wake up and smell the café au lait," reads the lapel buttons, signs and bumper stickers produced for the purpose.

Market Day

"The dresses are varied as the faces; the baskets even are of every race, some stout and portly, others delicate and adorned with ribbons and ornaments; some, again, old, wheezy and decayed, through whose worn ribs might be seen among solemn and melancholy cabbages, turnips and potatoes, crammed and jostled together in ruthless imprisonment. The butchers scorn to use all those blandishments that the lower grades of market society use to attract purchasers. Like Mahomet, the mountain must come to them. From the ceiling hang endless ropes of spider webs, numberless flies, and incalculable dirt. The stalls are deeply worn by the scraping process; in some yawn pits, apparently bottomless; and lastly, the floor of the market is not at all clean, but covered with mud and dirt from the feet of its patrons.

Through the crowd lurk some skeleton-dogs, vainly hoping, by some
happy accident, to secure a dainty morsel."
—Will Coleman, writing in his 1885 diary

The French Market today is nothing like the very first one, whose vendors were Indian hunters, fishermen, and German farmers from outlying towns such as Des Allemandes. That structure received skiffs downriver loaded with pecans and peppers, and it was probably somewhat rough around the edges. Today the market might even be said to err on the other side: too neat, too commercial, with its ever-pristine piles of brilliant-colored fruits and vegetables, ropes of garlic, and kitsch-oriented booths of indigenous foods and comestibles—say, alligator sausage on a stick. Neither is New Orleans' French Market like the impressive food markets in some larger North American urban centers, where you can procure either a local farmer's blueberry pie or a tender truffle imported all the way from the Dordogne. The French Market cannot rival Seattle's Pike Market, for instance, for its sheer size and selection, nor either of Toronto's St. Lawrence and Kensington Markets for ethnic offerings, or even a small back street market in Paris' Montmartre for charm. In short, it is too much like a grocery store.

As far as indigenous or unusual items go, the better bet for merliton in season (a small yellow squash ideal for stuffing with seafood), or okra, or local *chèvre* is the weekend Crescent City Farmers' Market in the Warehouse District on Magazine Street, which draws the crowds who wander over from the Quarter. For that reason, from Esplanade all the way to the sidewalk amphitheatre across from Jackson Square, where the mule-drawn carriages and their drivers line up for passengers, it most resembles a giant social "scene", bustling with buskers of every kind, magicians, dancing street kids looking for a tip, European backpackers, people hawking time-shares, mothers pushing strollers, French Quarter employees, overpriced ice-cream sellers, and so on. Perhaps it is the same sort of street scene that you might see on the Champs-Elysée, prompting travel writers to dub New Orleans with the sobriquet "Paris on the Mississippi". It is what prompted Russian traveler Aleksandr Borisovich Lakier in 1857 to say, "New Orleans more than any other city [in America] recalls the outdoor street life of southern Europe."

Levee Lore

The Mississippi River levee, though much changed from former days because shipping has moved to modern wharves farther up and down the river's curves, remains full of pedestrians who navigate the walkways to reach shopping venues and entertainment to be had all along the riverfront from the downriver part of the Quarter to the enormous upscale Riverwalk shopping complex and the Ernest N. Morial Convention Center at the foot of Canal Street. There is a shiny red trolley with stops all along the river's edge and now big-time casino gambling with Harrah's New Orleans Casino nearby.

Gone is the levee of a different time, with its wharves mooring rafts and flat-bottom boats and paddle wheelers. Donald MacDonald, a Scotsman headed from Havana to Charleston, South Carolina, wrote in 1826:

> *During the first half of the year trade is very brisk, the Levee being covered with bales of cotton, casks of sugar & tobacco, coffee & rice, carts driving in every direction with goods, and shipping of all descriptions lying on the riverbank. While I remained in New Orleans, there were never less than 12 or 15 steamboats lying there, and several times in the course of the day, the guns of those arriving and departing were heard in every part of the town.*

From the levee it was possible to watch all manner of activity, with burly stevedores unloading hogsheads of sugar and handling those doubtless thousand upon thousands of bales of cotton that were unloaded there because, as the saying goes, in the nineteenth-century South, "Cotton was King." But oyster boats from the Gulf Coast waters also unloaded their wares there, and the quay hummed with conversation and people seeking distraction as ladies promenaded. The frontier geographer William Darby noted: "There are few places where life can be enjoyed with more pleasure." Visitors were coming to the levee to see the whole panorama of New Orleans spread out before them. "The ladies wear no headdresses in fair sky," wrote Arthur Singleton in letters to his brother, published as *Letters from the South and West* in 1824, "but modest becoming white or black veils. There are some beautiful brunette girls here; and the French *mademoiselles* have a peculiar soft drawling, but rather insinuating tone of voice. The negresses wear checked turbans, or gay colours… as to the morals of this city, the word is obsolete."

Singleton goes on to describe the fashionable trend, at the turn of the nineteenth century, for duels—and one recalls the fact that duels were more popular in New Orleans during the first half of that century than in any other American city. There is a spot farther inland, at City Park, called "Dueling Oaks", where settling vendettas (a veritable sickness at that time, with the first symptom being death) took place. Singleton observes facetiously, "Duels are very fashionable, if they can contrive an affront; such as—'How dared you to spit as I was passing?'—'How dared you to pass as I was spitting?' or, 'You shall not sneeze where I am!' This would make a pleasant duel. There is a corner called Cadiz [Cadiz Street is in the Faubourg Bouligny, Uptown] a rendezvous for assassins, and no inquiry made."

The Riverbend

For a glimpse of the levee as the land form that it is, built to hold back the river, one needs to go farther upriver and away from the French Quarter to where the levee is accessible (because most of the riverfront is heavily industrial). Once on the levee Uptown, the person promenading gets the feeling that everything is far, far away, even during Mardi Gras season when tourist areas and local neighborhoods are full of excitement (see Chapter Ten); and in the Riverbend part of town, in the district called Carrollton, which used to be a summering spot for New Orleanians when it seemed far away, it is possible to feel truly hidden from the world. The trip can be made by car, or via river on an excursion to Audubon Zoo aboard the *John James Audubon*. The landing for the zoo is located in the Riverview park, fondly called "The Fly" by locals for a piece of modern sculpture by which people picnic. The levee here is undisturbed, and on the *batture* one views the battered, rusty freighters with Russian and other strange alphabets marking their sides slide by with tugboats right behind them. A little farther along, at the actual river's bend (debark the St. Charles Streetcar where St. Charles turns into Carrollton Avenue, in front of the Camellia Grill), walk back to the levee. It closely resembles what one imagines of the levee of old—"covered with shells and small stones and made into a hard terrace, behind which runs a wide road, separated from the first street or row of houses by an open space of a

mile in length but only two or three hundred feet wide."

At night, the passing boats sound off in their maritime language of foghorn blasts, as this is one of the most treacherous turns in the river. Samuel Clemens/Mark Twain describes a terrible steamboat accident in his personal narrative *Life on the Mississippi*, and even incorporated them into some of his novels, as we see in *Adventures of Huckleberry Finn*, when the runaway boy Huck and his friend the slave Jim espy a foundered steamboat:

> *The fifth night below St. Louis we had a big storm after midnight, with a power of thunder and lightning, and the rain poured down in a solid sheet. We stayed in the wigwam and let the raft take care of itself. When the lightning glared out we could see a big straight river ahead, and hick rocky bluffs on both sides. By-and-by says I, 'Hel-lo Jim, looky yonder!' It was a steamboat that had killed herself on a rock. We was drifting straight down for her. The lightning showed her very distinct. She was leaning over, with part of her upper deck above water, and you could see every little chimbly-guy [wires used to steady the chimney stacks] clean and clear, and a chair by the big bell, with an old slouch hat hanging on the back of it when the flashes come.*
>
> *Well, it being away in the night, and stormy, and all so mysterious-like, I felt just the way any other boy would a felt when I see that wreck laying there so mournful and lonesome in the middle of the river. I wanted to get aboard of her and slink around a little...*

Steamboat accidents, particularly explosions of their massive boilers, were, as they say in New Orleans, "nuthin' nice". These were frequent, and frequently they were tragic.

Chapter Three
THE FRENCH QUARTER: "SPLENDID BEDLAM OF A CITY"

"Once this house was alive. It was occupied once. In my recollection, it still is, but by shadowy occupants like ghosts. Now they enter the lighter areas of my memory."
—Tennessee Williams, *Vieux Carré*

"...that foreign city and paradoxical with its atmosphere at once fatal and languorous, at once feminine and steel-hard,... a place whose denizens had created their All-Powerful and His supporting hierarchy-chorus of beautiful saints and handsome angels in the image of their houses and personal ornaments and voluptuous lives... a place created for and by voluptuousness, the abashless and unabashed senses."
—William Faulkner, *Absalom Absalom!*

Imagine 27-year-old Thomas Lanier Williams (a.k.a. Tennessee Williams) arriving in the Vieux Carré of the 1930s, grandson of an Episcopalian minister escaping the conventional mores of his upbringing and the unhappiness of his family life he would later portray in the Pulitzer-winning memory play *The Glass Menagerie*. As he wandered the streets of the French Quarter, remarking them "alive with antique and curio shops", with "relics of Creole homes that have gone to the block", he may have wondered, "What would it be like to live here?"

Then he would find that he had begun a four-decade-long relationship with New Orleans, and the French Quarter in particular, a place that he had come to call his "spiritual home". In this down-on-its-luck sector, once inhabited by middle-class Creoles (but in Williams' time largely a working-class, predominantly Sicilian, neighborhood) the young man found a comfortable place in which to live and work, away from the rest of the world he perceived as inhospitable.

Throughout his life, Williams would move between his creative *loci* of New York City, Key West, Florida, and New Orleans. In the latter he said he could "catch [his] breath," and feel what he called "the liberating effect" of its ambience. It allowed his "whole personality to feel free" and gave him what he called inner security. Moreover, New Orleans was the tolerant, open setting for his coming out. It was where a proper young man from St. Louis could experiment without censure, and where he took the courage to realize his potential as a writer. When there were difficulties in his life from which he needed to retreat, New Orleans was usually the place he would choose: "Each time I have felt some rather profound psychic wound, a loss or a failure," he once wrote, "I have returned to this city. At such periods I would seem to belong there and no place else in the country."

Williams was grateful to the French Quarter because it was in those days a "vagabond's paradise", he said, a stopping place "for fugitives from economic struggle" (in other words, it was cheap). He enjoyed his ten-cent breakfast at Morning Call in the French Market (the café has since moved to the suburbs in Metairie), where he watched the merchants' early-morning preparations before getting to work writing; in the late afternoon he relished eating fresh, inexpensive seafood.

Budgetary considerations aside, New Orleans and the French Quarter took on a sensual, emotional texture for Williams. Its rather shabby ease (still evident on the edges of the Quarter), its soulfulness, seem to have appealed to the writer and carried within the mood a certain bitter-sweetness. In a passage of the production notes for *A Streetcar Named Desire*, describing the home of Stanley and Stella Kowalski, Williams sketches it for the reader/audience: "The exterior of a two-story corner building on a street in New Orleans which is named Elysian Fields and runs between the L&N tracks and the river…" Then he sets a tender tone, the sad spirit for the drama that will not only be a background for Blanche DuBois' psychological undoing but a poetic suggestion of this "broken world" (the play's epigram quotes American poet Hart Crane):

> *It is first dark of an evening early in May. The sky that shows around the dim white building is a peculiarly tender blue, almost a turquoise, which invests the scene with a kind of lyricism and gracefully atten-*

uates the atmosphere of decay. You can almost feel the warm breath of the brown river beyond the river warehouses with their faint redolences of bananas and coffee. A corresponding air is evoked by the music of Negro entertainers at a barroom around the corner. In this part of New Orleans you are practically always just around the corner, or a few doors down the street, from a tinny piano being played with the infatuated fluency of brown fingers. This 'Blue Piano' expresses the spirit of the life which goes on here.

For Williams, New Orleans offered up fodder for the creative process. The decadent, "crazy broken-down city" in large part created his oeuvre, contributing powerful metaphors, complex characters, and a unique setting he hardly needed to dramatize for such full-length works as *A Streetcar Named Desire* (considered his masterpiece), *Suddenly, Last Summer*, and *Vieux Carré*, as well as one-acts such as *The Lady Larkspur Lotion* and *Lord Byron's Love Letter*. In later years he himself estimated New Orleans to be the source of "more than half of his best work". Williams became emotionally involved with the city. One can see in the short story "Angel in the Alcove", with the tenderness with which he describes it, that the city is personified, and *female*: "New Orleans and the moon have always seemed to me to have an understanding between them, an intimacy of sisters grown old together, no longer needing more than a speechless look to communicate their feelings to each other…"

While Williams lived in the French Quarter, he explored its underground with his lovers and friends, and had his places, among them Lafitte's Blacksmith Shop (941 Bourbon St.—an ancient-looking Creole cottage about which many dubious stories abound), Victor's, or Napoleon House (500 Chartres St.), where he would sit with poet and Tulane University professor Oliver Evans and friend Marion Vaccaro, who later would become models for Billy and Cora in the short story "Two on a Party".

Williams found the seedy French Quarter (which, as Holditch notes, was then "little more than a slum", a "shabby but gentle old village") spiritually renewing. Its quirkiness is still evident, as is the peculiar way that the profane (bars, nightclubs, strip clubs, rowdiness) mixes with the sacred (the cathedral, Ursuline Convent, the cemeteries, and Roman Catholic traditions in general). Perhaps this is what prompts Blanche DuBois to cry in *A Streetcar Named Desire*, "Those cathedral bells—they're the only clean thing in the Quarter."

Colonial Crescent

"The Quarter"—or "the Quarters" to many locals—is New Orleans' old town. It is also called the Vieux Carré ("Old Square") because that is how it started: a settlement of 66 squares laid out by French engineers Blondel de la Tour and Adrian de Pauger, who worked under the direction of the Scotsman adventurer-entrepreneur John Law. It was Law to whom the Duke of Orleans, regent between the monarchies of Louis XIV and Louis XV, had granted a monopoly on commerce in the new colony. Law's "Mississippi Scheme" was designed to encourage investment in what he claimed was a land of great financial promise, particularly rich in minerals.

De la Tour and de Pauger charted the land, laying out the first row of T-square-and-triangle lots along the river: the squares were 260 feet deep with a frontage of 130 feet, surrounded by a drainage ditch. Law also ordered that a church, an administrative building, governor's mansion, two barracks, a prison and a general shop be built. He entrusted all of this to Bienville; "… and call it New Orleans," are the words, attributed to Law, who wished to establish firmly in people's minds the fact that the settlement was a French crown colony. According to historian John Churchill Chase, "coupling the colonial capital with the Regent's name was the proper association. No more Indian names, such as Biloxi, Mobile, and Natchitoches, which would not sell a share of stock to Parisians."

The streets were named for princes, dukes and counts of the court of Orléans (Bourbon, Burgundy, Conti, Toulouse, Du Maine), or for popular saints (St. Ann, St. Peter, St. Philip), and for the functions they played ("Barracks", where troops lived; "Esplanade", where they marched; "Rampart", for the surrounding fortifications; "Canal", for a moat at the southeast boundary of the city). In 1724 the first levees were built as primitive dykes; and the gates keeping the city safe closed at 9 o'clock each night. (Today we think of the French Quarter as the Downtown neighborhood bounded by the river and Rampart Street and by Canal and Esplanade—some 90 blocks in all, one of the largest areas listed as a National Historic Landmark.)

New Orleans became an official Crown colony in 1731. Still, it was not easy to attract pioneers to come and rough it in the bush, and Law had to engage recruiters who were instructed to round up immigrants for the purpose of shipping off for a crossing which, on average, took as long as five months. The first boats were filled with contraband salt dealers, who joined paupers and ex-convicts with nothing to lose on the long sea voyage to the squat settlement at the mouth of the Mississippi. Law must have been a great promoter. He ran an advertisement in the Paris *Mercure* in 1719 showing the first map of New Orleans, along with drawings of attractive Louisiana landscapes and, according to Churchill Chase, "views of docile Indian braves kneeling before happy Frenchmen, and dreamy-eyed Indian maidens lounging around."

Mississippi Myths
Maybe it is the same for all the mythic cities of the world. It is often difficult to separate empirical reality from legend, and, as is particularly the case today, from spurious marketing rhetoric. Even William Faulkner, while he lived in the French Quarter, was once pressed into service by friends as a tourist guide—and by all accounts did a pretty good job of it, embroidering and creating convincing "build-up stories", according to New Orleans literary historian Kenneth Holditch.

The editorial staff of a now-defunct magazine in New Orleans once decided to get even with some of worst perpetrators of bogus travelogue: the motley crew of city buggy drivers. The tour operators became the target for a humorous feature written by a couple of "undercover" correspondents who wanted to see if they could pose as tourists, hear the various patters, and see what would happen in their experiment to separate fact from *faux*. Though a few of the drivers were ultimately commended, it was revealed (surprise!) that commentary was 99-percent sales pitch, with drivers driven to outdo one another while subsidized by local businesses featured in the patter. And so it was confirmed, they said: "the widespread suspicion that the drivers spread more shit than the morose mules that pull them."

You always find the drivers draped against the black cast-iron fence alongside *banquettes* in front of St. Louis Cathedral, "shoo-shooing" clutches of visitors, honeymooners, and small groups of teens or conventioneers as they pass. The mules slink, heads down low under their silk-flowered hats, as though embarrassed by it all. It is ironic that the buggy drivers have never fallen victim to the "Clean up the Quarter" campaigns that have plagued the Vieux Carré. Residents and city officials have instead set their sights on ridding the streets and squares of performance artists, buskers, palm and Tarot readers, and the like, claiming they are a public nuisance.

At least one thing continues to remain true about the Quarter— there is probably no other place in the US with a like range of structures and architectural styles in such a confined area: from grand plantation homes to the simplicity of raised shotgun cottages and cramped storefronts; from townhouses with spacious European-style courtyards to hidden Creole patios twined with ivy, confederate jasmine and bougainvillea, backed by slave quarters and alleyways which are tucked around them. The overall effect of these structures fitted artfully together, surrounded by lush vegetation and wide flagstone *banquettes*, finished with a flourish of curly wrought- or cast-iron, is extremely pleasing. The pre-eminent architect Benjamin Latrobe wrote in 1819, "New Orleans has at first sight a very imposing and handsome appearance beyond any other city in the United States in which I have been."

The largest number and oldest examples of New Orleans architecture are concentrated in the original city. An excellent panoramic aerial view around the Quarter down to the river can be had from April to November from the rooftop bar of the Royal Orleans Hotel (621 St. Louis St.), between Royal and Chartres streets on Orleans. From the seventh floor and large parapet one floor higher, one sees the Quarter's variegated rooftops, a view pierced by the graceful spires of St. Louis Cathedral. The Royal Orleans is built on the site of the former St. Louis Hotel, a gathering spot for nineteenth-century Creole High Society. It was also the site of a slave auction block on a dais near the hotel's grand entrance, for New Orleans was a key center for the Southern slave trade. "The principal scene of slave auctions is a splendid rotunda, the magnificent dome of which is worth to resound with songs of freedom," noted Swedish traveler Fredrika Bremer in her 1850s diaries, recoiling from this aspect of the city. Ironically, the same site would eventually house a Reconstruction-era black-dominated legislature. The original building was torn down in 1916.

It is especially in terms of adaptation to subtropical living, says Samuel Wilson in his *Guide to the Architecture of New Orleans, 1699 to*

1959, that New Orleans, and the French Quarter in particular, shows its character: "Architecturally, the New Orleans tradition is revealed far more in attitude toward building than any persistent set of forms." According to Wilson, three forces stand out as influencing New Orleans' architecture: a dominant French ancestry reflecting Renaissance refinement; the region's humid climate, which required architects to adjust their European building methods; and the changing levels of the Mississippi River. In both the Creole French and Spanish construction, architects dealt with oppressive heat and humidity by encouraging the use of patios for *al fresco* living. French Quarter townhouses incorporated airy galleries for use as corridors—and for eating, sleeping and simply relaxing. Full-length windows, along with shutters, grilles and jalousies, allowed easy access to, and maximum circulation of, breezes when there were few to be had.

There are several buildings open to the public that can give a close approximation of Creole life, among them: the Beauregard-Keyes House (1113 Chartres St.), a raised cottage that once was the home of Confederate Gen. P. G. T. Beauregard in the years following the Civil War and where novelist Frances Parkinson Keyes wrote *Dinner at Antoine's*; Gallier House (1132 Royal St.), home in the mid-1800s of the respected New Orleans architect, and rated one of the nation's best small house museums by *The New York Times*; Hermann-Grima House (820 St. Louis St.), which has the only remaining stable and open-hearth kitchen in the French Quarter; and the Williams Residence, which is part of the massive Historic New Orleans Collection (533 Royal St.), a treasure trove of archives, maps, documents and ephemera of New Orleans history.

Still, it is walking the Quarter and peeking into the courtyards, the quiet corners, and leafy bowers that remains the chief joy of exploring this area. As Oliver Evans promises:

> … *what is most beautiful in the Quarter is not what you see imme-*
> *diately; the excitement of wandering about these streets is partly a*
> *matter of discovering the various angles from which, at your leisure,*
> *you can admire the houses and the courtyards. And there are delight-*
> *ful surprises in store for you: narrowly avoiding a giant ashcan set*
> *squarely on the sidewalks of a particularly disreputable-looking alley,*
> *you may suddenly glimpse, through the grille of a massive iron gate,*

a patio more beautiful than you have seen anywhere else in New Orleans—a miniature paradise sparkling with flowers, shaded by fig and banana trees, and murmurous with the sound of water plashing in a fountain.

Though the Vieux Carré Commission was established in 1936 to protect the beauty of the French Quarter with stringent rules as to how the buildings may be used, re-used, restored, or expanded (i.e. signs must be of a certain size, paint must be of a certain color), it is interesting to note that there is only one structure left that is from the French colonial period. Fire engulfed much of the old city in 1788, destroying St. Louis Cathedral (that structure had replaced another destroyed by a hurricane in 1723), along with more than 800 other buildings. Another great fire in 1794 consumed 212 structures but spared the cathedral. The oldest building in the French Quarter, in the whole of New Orleans—and, indeed, east of the Mississippi River Valley—is the Ursuline Convent at 2635 State St., which was completed in 1794 and modified between 1845 and 1851.

In comparison to the European veneration of historical personae and events, it may also seem strange to travelers that in the French Quarter not one statue or monument exists dedicated to colonial French and Spanish eras. Adding to this notable absence is the neighborhood's misleading name. As most of the remaining architecture in the Quarter is not French but rather Spanish in design, it should be perhaps called the "Spanish Quarter". Two notable examples are the stately 1790s Cabildo, seat of Spanish colonial power and site of the Louisiana Purchase Transfer, and the Presbytere (designed in 1791 to match the Cabildo and house the city's Capuchin monks), both part of the Louisiana State Museum complex flanking St. Louis Cathedral. Also, much of the seemingly "antique" wrought-iron balconies and scrollwork that people associate with the French Quarter is, in fact, the more commonly reproduced cast-iron, which has been added in the interest of preservation and the overall integrity of the Quarter's appearance.

Saints. . .

All things considered, French Quarter residents' moral rectitude may have been of more concern than architecture to "preservationists" over the centuries—in fact, even back to the very beginning. One Sister Madeleine Hachard de Saint-Stanislas wrote a letter home in 1728, dealing what she viewed as her parishioners' wrongheaded priorities:

> *The women are careless of their salvation, but not of their vanity.*
> *Everyone here has luxuries, all of an equal magnificence. The greater*
> *part of them eat hominy but are dressed in velvet or damask, trimmed*
> *with ribbons. The women use powder and rouge to hide the wrinkles*
> *of their faces, and wear beauty spots. The devil has a vast empire here,*
> *but that only strengthens our hope of destroying it, God willing.*

This was written only ten years after the city's founding. The Ursulines had come to New Orleans in 1727 in answer to Governor Bienville's call. They knew that the governor recognized, says an historical account on the order's contemporary website, that "education was of vital importance if the fledgling colony were to grow and prosper."

Under the direction of then-prioress Mother St. Augustine, the nuns saw to the spiritual and educational development of the parish— to those enrolled, as well as to boarders, day students and orphans. The convent took in children from the colony as well as homeless children who survived the 1729 Natchez Indian rebellion and the subsequent massacre. African-American and Native American girls of the colony were educated by the Catholic Church, predating the national standard for public education by almost a century. Today, forty percent of African-Americans living in New Orleans are Roman Catholic. And there are three times more Catholics citywide than all other denominations combined.

Indeed, Roman Catholicism sets New Orleans apart from Protestant north Louisiana, and informs most of its customs and traditions. It is important to remember that the city was considered a spiritual extension of the European motherland, and that the French monarch was always referred to as "His Most Christian Majesty" and the Spanish as "His Most Catholic Majesty". The strength of the Church in New Orleans can be seen in its people's still-fervent veneration of saints. All Saints' Day is a civic holiday (at one time cups of coffee and gumbo were even sold in the cemeteries as families cleaned and whitewashed the monuments of their ancestors). The city closes down entirely on Ash Wednesday. St. Patrick's Day and St. Joseph's Day are also celebrated with vigor by the entire city (see Chapter Ten, Saints Alive!), so that it seems, even to the non-Catholic celebrants themselves, that these figures have become a part of their own culture. One middle-aged woman in filmmaker Neil Alexander's video documentary entitled *Island of Saints and Souls* confesses: "[The saints are] places to go when you're in trouble, just like your family." (Even the New Orleans NFL franchise is called the Saints—and in the past many have thought it would be a miracle if the team could win for once. The team was then derisively called "The Ain'ts".)

Our Lady of Guadalupe Chapel at 411 North Rampart St., on the edge of the French Quarter, shelters the international shrine to St. Jude, patron saint of hopeless causes. It was most likely to St. Jude that New Orleanians prayed in times of yellow fever epidemics that would hit the colonial city. This place of worship was, in fact, called "the Mortuary Chapel" because during outbreaks of contagion people perished more quickly than they could be buried, so bodies had to be piled in the sanctuary. Our Lady of Guadalupe is the oldest surviving church in New Orleans (predating the present St. Louis Cathedral) and is the official chapel of the New Orleans police and fire departments.

The grotto at the Shrine of St. Anne on Ursulines Street is also a sacred site and national shrine. As well as being the mother of the Church Mother, Anne, it is said, is the patron saint of childless women, and it is to her, say many New Orleanians, that an unmarried supplicant must enjoin, "St. Anne, St. Anne, send me a man…" Another instance of the influence saints have: when in 1932 Russell Long won his senatorial race in Louisiana, capturing ninety percent of the vote, he had a billboard erected reading, "Thanks be to St. Bernard for services rendered," a reference also to the working-class parish that had contributed largely to his victory.

It was during the Battle of New Orleans, in 1815, that serious supplications were offered to the Holy Family and intervention sought at this defining historical moment from Mother Mary, "Our Lady of Prompt Succor". To this day it is believed by many that Mary sent the required miracle to deliver the city from attack by British troops. On 8 January 1815, as a pitched battle was being waged on the Chalmette Battlefield, the Ursulines and their faithful were huddled in St. Louis Cathedral, praying to Mary for a favorable outcome. When Gen. Jackson's victory was assured, a solemn *Te Deum* mass was said in the cathedral. It is a now a national shrine, and the cover of the order of service reads: "Novena to Our Lady of Prompt Succor (Every Wednesday) at the Daily Masses at St. Louis Cathedral, a Minor Basilica)—Established as a Parish in 1720, Oblates of Mary Immaculate, 615 Père Antoine Alley."

St. Louis is the spare but stately church built in the late baroque style by French architect Gilbert Guillemard, but financed by a Spanish colonial philanthropist, Señor Don Andrés Almonester y Roxas, a native of Andalusia who had made a fortune in New Orleans real estate. Nowadays, if it seems that there is an impossible problem to solve—as was the critical battle against the British—New Orleanians can continue to say their novenas at St. Louis Cathedral on Wednesdays, or they may turn to St. Jude at Our Lady of Guadalupe. If St. Jude is busy, there is yet one more addition to the New Orleans hagiography. In the same church is a statue of "St. Expedite", the patron saint of people who need speedy answers to legal matters. People are still not sure if this saint is only legendary, but, in any case, his services rendered could prove useful to some New Orleanians.

. . .and Sinners

> *"... this is a flagrant vice capital of the civilized world... This city is famous for its gamblers, prostitutes, exhibitionists, anti-Christs, alcoholics, sodomites, drug addicts, fetishists, onanists, pornographers, frauds, jades, litterbugs, and lesbians, all of whom are only too well protected by graft."*
>
> —Ignatius Reilly in John Kennedy Toole's *A Confederacy of Dunces*

> *"Here is a list provided by the Jefferson Parish Sheriff's Office of those arrested in this week's raid of Airline Highway motels:*
> *S.R., 29, 4231 Airline Highway, No. 29, Metairie, crime against nature.*
> *L.J.G., 20, 1536 Stumpf Blvd., Gretna, crime against nature.*
> *L.C., 27, 256 Carolyne, Destrehan, prostitution, crime against nature and resisting arrest..."*
>
> —*The Times-Picayune*, Friday 3 August 1990

How does a city so strongly associated with saints and Catholic devotion —one that also happens to be situated in the middle of the Southern Baptist Bible belt—come to such a pass? Historian Oliver Evans explains the contradiction this way: "A Latin morality is the city's heritage, and Latin morality was originally a pagan morality. . ." It might seem excessive, if not a violation of constitutional rights, that the local organ would actually list the names and addresses of citizens given a police shakedown at the sleazy motels that line Airline Highway. It is a shame— literally, but all is fair in vice and the public domain. The more sins, it may be reasoned, the more souls need salvation. The greater the salvation, the farther yet again to fall... "New Orleans is as vile a place as any under the sun, wrote one nineteenth-century British traveler, remarking on the city as a Gomorrah of Gaming, where "the renegades of all nations... make violence and bloodshed indigenous." And "there is a strong atmosphere of sexuality overhanging the entire city," complained General Andrew Jackson in a letter to his wife Rachel, "Great Babylon is come up before me... Oh, the wickedness, the idolatry." Walt Whitman, the great American poet who visited New Orleans in 1848, simply concluded: "[It is] the wickedest city in Christendom."

New Orleans has been thought of a city that has been in need of forgiveness, as well as the promise of redemption that the Church provides, for a very long time. As the editors of *Louisiana Sojourns: Travelers' Tales and Literary Journeys* suggest, "Stretching at least as far back as the 1803 Louisiana Purchase, New Orleans was identified with such sybaritic pleasures as food, music, dancing, gambling, and illicit sex. Its pestilential climate bred the undying spirit of *laissez les bontemps rouler*. It was a pagan city whose spirit of revelry, invoked annually at Mardi Gras reigned throughout the year."

Much has also been made of New Orleans' "dark side"—which might well include (depending upon the individual's own perception and tastes) not only indulgence in drink and other stimulants but also an emphasis on sexuality and any other kind of sybaritic pleasure, obsession with and celebration of death, the secreted presence of *vodou* and other exotic cultural expressions, in addition to such gloomy realities as poverty, racial strife and police and political corruption. Even before New Orleans was ranked nationally in 1994 and again in 2001 by the FBI "Uniform Crime Report" as national murder capital (Washington, DC, Chicago and Detroit often share that dubious distinction), people said the place was dangerous. But then again, what is dangerous? The real danger in New Orleans, some might say, is that one can so easily fall into an all-engulfing swamp of hot weather, indolence, and pleasure—never to re-emerge.

Bourbon Street: Shots and Hot Spots

"Let's fly down,
or drive down
to New Orleans.
That city,
so pretty,
historic scenes.
I'll take you,
I'll parade you,
down Bourbon Street.
You'll see all the hot spots,
you'll meet all those big shots,
down in New Orleans."
　　　　　　—Paul Barbarin, "Bourbon Street Parade"

The mood of the French Quarter at just about any time seems to exude expectation. It is somewhat surreal, this constant feeling of anticipation; there is a notion that people here are just waiting for a party to break out, perhaps to meet someone fascinating. This feeling has persisted for some time, and New Orleans author John Kennedy Toole captures the tone of the Quarter, and Bourbon Street in particular, in this passage from *A Confederacy of Dunces*:

> *Twilight was setting around the Night of Joy bar. Outside, Bourbon Street was beginning to light up. Neon signs flashed off and on, reflecting in the streets dampened by the light mist that had been falling steadily for some time. The taxis bringing the evening's first customers, Midwestern tourists and conventioneers, made slight splashing sounds in the cold dusk.*
>
> *A few other customers were in the Night of Joy, a man who ran his finger along a racing form, a depressed blonde who seemed connected with the bar in some capacity, and an elegantly dressed young man who chainsmoked Salems and drank from frozen daiquiris in gulps..."*

Genevieve Pitot, matriarch of an old-line New Orleans family, in an interview with Kenneth Holditch about her life in the Quarter, admitted: "everyone of us in those days [during Prohibition] had a sense of life, of joyousness; we were all looking forward to something, and we celebrated that."

People who live and work in the French Quarter must be tolerant of one salient factor: it often seems that many people come to New Orleans with the need to escape, whether from conventional morality, from too much rigidity in their lives, from the humdrum, or simply to satisfy a need for something new. On a television "reality show" recently, New Orleans Police Department officers are shown carting off a couple during Mardi Gras for public indecency (outdoor recreational sex of *Kama Sutra* variety is not an unusual sight during Carnival), and several celebrants are charged with urinating in public. "Would you do this in *your own* city?" demands the cop of his bleary-eyed captives, and they shake their heads no. "Then why would you come here and do it *in mine?*" New Orleans' liberal liquor laws (viz. drink liberally) have largely contributed to its well-deserved reputation as a wanton renegade of order. As one Quarter resident puts it: "It's not the 'City That Care Forgot', it's the 'City That Sanity Forgot'."

That New Orleans continued a wet city even during national Prohibition was of particular benefit: "For the artists and writers the availability of liquor, albeit of questionable quality, seems to have been a consideration of some importance," writes historian Holditch, "surely one of significance for Faulkner, who arrived in the Vieux Carré and wrote his first novel *Soldier's Pay* at 624 Pirate's Alley (formerly Orleans Alley). From the family plantation he brought his own supply of corn whiskey," Holditch adds, "'just in case'." Throughout this period the sale of liquor was kept vital under the table by such local characters as "Papa Joe" Joseph, who dispensed bottles from his grocery store at Royal and St. Peter streets. As lore goes, Papa Joe would sit in his chair outside his storefront in fine weather and, when he had a customer, bade the tenant upstairs to lower a bottle in a basket, in which money was deposited in exchange for the precious liquid.

From the days when flatboat men and stevedores frequented the saloons of Gallatin at the riverfront, until today, the Crescent City has supported drinking pleasures. Today many bars are open "24-7" (as the Southern colloquialism has it), and liquor is sold in most grocery and convenience stores, every day of the week, at any hour of the day (compared with many totally dry rural counties in, say, Mississippi, or even a big city such as Atlanta, whose laws dictate that liquor aisles be roped off on Sundays and that bottles may not be sold after midnight). When bar patrons cannot finish a beverage, or may have somewhere else to go, in New Orleans they can say to the bartender: "Put it in a go-cup," and that means they want to take the remainder out onto the street. As long as the alcohol is decanted, police do not bother perambulating drinkers, who wander the streets of the French Quarter (at Carnival time in droves), plastic go-cup in hand. But drivers should avoid the "DWI ("dee-doubleyah-ah" on a Southern tongue), or "driving while intoxicated" charge; the punishment for this infraction comes with a hefty fine, along with other corrective measures such as a several-weeks-long community work. Despite disapproval concerning drinking and driving, there are actually drive-in daiquiri bars around town, such as the ones you see on Airline Highway. Can it be true, as they say, that if the paper wrapper is still on the straw, police won't write you a ticket?

If a traveler does finds him- or herself up on a charge, then there is only one thing to do. A good stiff one cures anxiety. Lafcadio Hearn, the Irish-Greek author who lived in New Orleans and documented the lives of Creoles, lists in his *Creole Cook Book* recipes for *pousse café, café brûlé* (or *brûlot*) and "many confections and delicacies for the sick, including a number of mixed drinks." The pouring of alcohol accompanies almost every social event in New Orleans, and creates mayhem on feast days, Mardi Gras being the greatest libation-powered spectacle of all.

"Mixology" has become an art form—and that is appropriate, since good food (viz. Creole-French, *Nouvelle* Creole, Cajun, soul and other ethnic cuisines) must be accompanied by good drink. Creoles in the old days distilled their own Muscatine wine, cordials and brandies to take with their meals. Or perhaps some took a mixed drink: New Orleans lays claim to being the place where the first cocktail was served, by one Antoine Amedée Peychaud. Peychaud ran a pharmacy in the French Quarter at 437 Royal St., and he liked to add his own bitters to a dram of cognac. The idea caught on and became a popular drink in coffeehouses citywide. The liquid was then served in an egg-cup-like piece of crockery called a *coquetier* (forerunner of the jigger), which was mispronounced "cock-tay."

The Sazerac is one of those "cock-tays", or cocktails. Known around the world and still a favorite of New Orleanians, the Sazerac combines bitters (instead of the old-time and now-illegal absinthe), rye whisky (instead of the original Sazerac-de-Forge et fils cognac) and a bit of lemon to create its unique taste. It was first mixed at 13 Exchange Alley in 1859 at the Sazerac Bar, which later made its reincarnation at Gravier and Carondelet streets in the old Roosevelt Hotel, and which now can be found in the Fairmont Hotel's lobby (the Fairmont is on Baronne Street in the Central Business District). A Sazerac is the royal drink of Rex, King of Carnival. But one can be made other days of the year with a Sazerac mix, available at many locations around the city, including the well-stocked Martin's Wine Cellar in the Quarter.

The Ramos gin fizz is also a Crescent City specialty. During Mardi Gras, in 1915, barkeeper Henry C. Ramos hired 35 shaker boys to mix the drink for which he has become known. Gin is mixed with lemon and lime juices, orange flower water, white of egg, cream and seltzer and is shaken "long and deliberately" so that it will "taste like a flower," according to Stanley Clisby Arthur, the New Orleans cocktail expert. There has long been a raging debate as to whether two drops of vanilla extract should be added: but Ramos staffers who lived, after all the agitation, to tell their story insist that there was no vanilla in the drink.

The Real Beat

Of course, drinking goes hand in hand with entertainment. In the Vieux Carré there is no end to available diversion, but there are some who take enjoyment very seriously, and that is the thrust behind a new event in town. The two-day intensive "retreat" called Tales of the Cocktail, is hosted at the French Quarter's Monteleone Hotel (214 Royal St.) and is sponsored by Southern Comfort distillers. Bar owners, managers, bartenders, chefs and waiters are invited by invitation only to attend seminars and "cocktail clinics" with industry experts. For the mere layman, cocktail hours are spent schmoozing with authors, and restaurants whip up their themed dinner nights pairing highlighted dishes with special drinks (www.talesofthecocktail.com).

For those who come to New Orleans and the French Quarter, in particular, to discover the city's nightlife, and the clubs, there are plenty of resources to consult, among them *The Times-Picayune* and *Gambit* newspapers, *OffBeat* magazine, WWOZ FM Radio and its website of club listings, and an interesting new digest called *Beat Street*. Unfortunately for some, staying on the well-beaten path in the French Quarter is determined by some ill-informed tourism representatives or fearful locals. Visitors find themselves moving within an imaginary, safely "cordoned" area for the best clubs playing indigenous music but find, instead, either nothing or—worse—inauthentic talent.

This was, no doubt, the experience of Simone de Beauvoir and American novelist Nelson Algren (*A Walk on the Wild Side*), who in the 1950s were caught up in an affair and met in New Orleans, and during one notable instance sought out New Orleans music. De Beauvoir had responded enthusiastically to the French Quarter and once wrote in her journal of seeing a square "as pure and simple as the Place des Vosges in Paris", sketching out her impressions in detail:

> ... there we were in the French Quarter of New Orleans. The old colonial city was built as if by architectural planning, like a modern city, but its streets are lined with one- and two-storied houses which

remind one of France and Spain; they have the serenity of Anjou or Touraine, and the beautiful, green, wrought-iron balconies remind one of the balconies of Cordova or the iron window grilles of Arab palaces; and Andalusian warmth pervades the silence.

One evening, de Beauvoir and friends go looking for "authentic" New Orleans music. Perhaps this means "in the place where jazz was born" or "with the passion of Louis Armstrong"—or any such understanding a traveler may have. As de Beauvoir puts it, "We did not want to miss the spirit of New Orleans nor the secret of its nights." After a few false starts, it seems, the author and her party stumble upon the Old Absinthe House where, as a result of their spirit of adventure, they encounter a pick-up band whose impromptu energy is what they have really come to hear:

> They took us to another bar in the Vieux Carré where there was a good Negro band with saxophone and trumpet: the trumpeter was young and played with youthful zest. He had a natural gift, so complete in itself that his whole being seemed to be concentrated on each note. It is here in these unostentatious nightclubs and among these unknown players that jazz attains a real dignity, far more so than in Carnegie Hall or the Savoy...

Then the author seizes on the very essence of music in New Orleans—that its unbounded energy depends on the collective human experience, and especially on the African-American history of suffering and privation, which is part of this country's racial legacy. Also, that the proximity of life and death, the possibility of life through death, is at the heart of New Orleans' unique jazz funerals and a whole musical oeuvre:

> If these men's lives are often so tormented it is because, instead of holding off death at arm's length like other artists, they are conscious at every moment of the marriage of life and death. It was against this background—the background of death—that the inspired music of the young trumpeter rose up. You could not listen to him merely with your brain, for he conjured up an experience in which you felt you had to let yourself go utterly.

That is just it. Those who simply must walk the length of commercial Bourbon Street, the strand Erskine Caldwell called a "Southern gentleman's Skid Row," will find that today's Bourbon Street offers up few surprises and has the overall feeling of a boozy-smelling theme park. In order to find the best bars in the city to hear "the New Orleans sound", where the audience can have an authentic New Orleans music experience, one must generally seek out the "joints" that are at least on the periphery of the French Quarter, if not in more far-flung neighborhoods. Such venues as Donna's Bar & Grill (800 Rampart St.) for New Orleans brass bands, Snug Harbor (625 Frenchmen) for contemporary jazz, the Palm Court (1204 Decatur St.) for traditional jazz, Café Brasil for world beat (2100 Chartres), or The House of Blues (225 Decatur St.) for big-name acts are certainly good places to start. However, it is as well to remember that in this city and the surrounding region that nurtures so much talent, "big name" does not always mean best. As it turns out, many bars on Bourbon do not exist to showcase or support indigenous talent and are, rather, tourist-geared with neon, Day-Glo colors, foolishly named drinks, souvenir T-shirts, karaoke and the like. There are still some strip joints, but compared to other cities' titillations—or even the days of Storyville brothels—they are really quite tame.

"Sahara of the Bozart"?

In terms of the South's lack of high-brow stimulus, in his famous essay of 1917 entitled "The Sahara of the Bozart," Baltimore *Sun* journalist and critic H. L. Mencken wrote about the world of the arts in the South and, in so doing, savaged it as having literary pretensions. He derided a region he perceived as being rural, devoid of culture, "a cesspool of Baptists, a miasma of Methodists, snake charmers, phony real estate operators and syphilitic evangelists", he said. Ever since this scathing assessment, the South's cultural establishment has been on the defensive, and the caustic comments have continued to outrage artists, scholars, historians, ethnographers and the like. They are still at pains to show the region south of the Mason-Dixon Line is not a cultural backwater, but, indeed, a place with a voice and tradition all its own.

Musing on New Orleans as a literary and cultural entity, Lewis P. Simpson thinks that it "was never in the cards" for the city to claim a national artistic presence, pointing out that compared to New York or

San Francisco, there is not even a significant number of publishing houses (Louisiana State University Press in Baton Rouge and Pelican Publishers in Gretna are the only two publishers of note). Simpson concludes that, unlike Boston in the north, New Orleans could never become an "Athens of America" because, according to him, commercial concerns have outweighed the value of culture:

> One reason, possibly the overriding one, that New Orleans did not like Richmond and Charleston at least take on the semblance of a literary center is that in the critical years of the city's first great expansion, between the War of 1812 and the Civil War, literary aspiration was completely obscured by the city's obsessive ambition to become a great national and international marketplace.

Simpson's observation is well taken. "Nouvelle Orléans" may, as an early settlement, have proven to be a miserable failure, but that was all reversed when steamboats and river traffic secured its role as an important port, indeed as an agricultural market for the entire Midwest. Then-President Thomas Jefferson had boasted: "There is no spot on the globe to which the produce of so great an extent of fertile country must necessarily come."

On Royal Street in the 1850s you could find any sort of luxurious frippery. Remarked a *Times-Picayune* reporter in 1858, "One was given the idea people on Royal lived on perfume, soaps, cigars, lottery tickets, toilette articles, furniture, cakes, candies, ladies' shoes, fancy groceries, wines and toys. Tasteful exhibits by mercers, milliners, mantua-makers and modistes, in Royal, Chartres and Canal, were well worth a stroll within." Even then, traffic in the Quarter was slow going. The writer further complains, "Furniture carts on narrow Royal stood close up to the curbs... traffic sometimes was impeded annoyingly." During the first half of the nineteenth century the city bustled so that it moved young governess Kate Conynham to write in a letter home to her family that New Orleans was a "splendid bedlam of a city".

It may not have been a literary capital, but it was the sophisticated cultural heart of the South. The French Quarter was the birthplace of the first internationally recognized American artist/composer, Louis Moreau Gottschalk, born in 1829; it was home to the first opera staged in North America, André Grétry's *Sylvain*, performed in 1796;

and it was home to North America's first opera house, a handsome building erected in 1859 on the corner of Bourbon and Toulouse streets, which was later razed in a fire in 1919. New Orleans was also the birthplace of the Negro Philharmonic, formed in the 1830s, comprising more than a hundred members. There were numerous theaters, the oldest being Le Cap Français, which presented Louisiana's first professional performances in 1792. But the grandest was the Théâtre d'Orléans (no longer extant), built in 1813 between Royal and Bourbon on Orleans. It featured four operas weekly and on other evenings presented vaudeville and musical comedies. The Théâtre d'Orléans was a favorite night out for the *demi-monde* of New Orleans until the French Opera House was constructed in 1859; in the late nineteenth century, New Orleans' opera and theatre seasons rivaled those of Europe and New York City, with such performers as Jenny Lind, Adelina Patti and Lola Montez arriving for extended engagements. And who can forget the fabulous water-bound thespian Caroline Chapman (1819-80)? She traveled up and down the Mississippi reciting her lines "on the boards"—on the boards of a flatboat, that is.

The life and times of colorful characters of the French Quarter come alive in the imagination while just walking its shadowed lanes, side streets and back ways, and occasionally through the creations of contemporary New Orleans artists and literati. For example, a new opera entitled *Pontalba*, performed by the New Orleans Opera Association during the Louisiana Purchase bicentennial, drew its key inspiration from Tulane University history professor Christina Vella's biography *Intimate Enemies: The Two Worlds of the Baroness Pontalba*. Published by Louisiana State University Press, this biography became a *New York Times* "Notable Book" for its lively depiction of quixotic, beautiful baroness Madame Micaela Leonarda Antonia Almonaster y Roxas y Broutin Pontalba.

Pontalba, a native Louisianan and heiress to a sizeable estate, married the son of a French baron at the age of 16 and bore him three sons; but this marriage between scions of two wealthy families was unhappy. Madame Pontalba's father-in-law insisted that the young couple move to France, and that the young woman should sign over her fortune to her husband's control. She refused. Later, during a trip to France, the greedy father-in-law arrived surreptitiously in her bedroom armed with a pistol ready to shoot her. Thinking that he had indeed killed her, he then shot himself dead. But Madame Pontalba managed to crawl downstairs for help, received medical attention, and ultimately lived. She took her fortune back to New Orleans and built a structure on Jackson Square that is known today as "The Pontalba" or Pontalba Apartments. Tourist patter states that it is "the first apartment house in North America", but it is actually a form of architecture that was prevalent in the mid-1800s. The baroness' large townhouse would shelter many famous artists and writers, such as author Sherwood Anderson, and is now considered an exclusive address in the French Quarter, though shops below cater mainly to the tourist trade.

Sherwood Anderson and *The Double Dealer*

Most of the writers we associate with the French Quarter were not actually born in New Orleans, but are those who would come and go— or come and stay. They were people who felt somehow deeply drawn to the place: Sherwood Anderson, born in Camden, Ohio, William Faulkner, born Oxford, Mississippi, and Tennessee Williams, also born in Mississippi (Columbus). All felt the Quarter exert a pull on their lives—partly because of its exotic appeal, partly for its easy-going and affordable lifestyle.

Sherwood Anderson, author of the American classic *Winesburg, Ohio* (1919) and mentor to both William Faulkner and Ernest Hemingway, likened Chicago in the north to a "hard fist"; the South was an "open hand". He referred to New Orleans as that "half-foreign city at the southern 'lip of the continent'." And from his first place on the third floor of the LaBranche Building, essentially an inexpensive rooming house at the intersection of Royal and St. Peter streets, Anderson wrote to his brother in 1922, entreating him to come for a visit: "[This is] surely the most civilized spot in America," he urged. During his time living in the Quarter, and throughout his involvement with the literary journal *The Double Dealer* (subtitled "National Magazine of the South") Anderson came to redefine his notion of what "culture" meant—not "the high life" or "society", but rather, as he characterized it, "the enjoyment of life, leisure and a sense of leisure… time for a play of the imagination over the facts of life… time and vitality to be serious about really serious things and a background of joy in life in which to refresh the tired spirits."

Anderson spent time roaming the French Quarter watching with great interest the athleticism of stevedores unloading their cargo at the riverfront. He conducted what he called an "ambulatory relationship" with a young woman by the name of Adaline Katz, and they dined together at Guy's, a restaurant (long gone) near his boarding house. In his essay "A Meeting South" we see the ease that attracted Anderson, and also get a glimpse of the life of Quarter residents at the beginning of the twentieth century, quite different from today's rhythm:

> *We walked slowly... through many streets of the Old Town. Negro women laughing all around us in the dusk, shadows playing over old buildings, children with their shrill cries dodging in and out of hallways... Families were sitting down to dinner within full sight of the street—all doors and windows open. A man and his wife quarreled in Italian. In a patio back of an old building a Negress sang a French song.*

Again, this is the same Vieux Carré that appears in Williams' notes for *A Streetcar Named Desire*:

> *Two women, one white and one colored, are taking the air on the steps of the building. The white woman is EUNICE, who occupies the upstairs flat; the colored woman a neighbor, for New Orleans is a cosmopolitan city where there is a relatively warm and easy intermingling of races in the old part of town.*

As is revealed in the passage above, Anderson particularly responded to what he considered New Orleans' unique blending of francophone and Afro cultures. This he may well have romanticized— but in any case, most travelers considered New Orleans' diversity different from that of other cities. Says Temple University's Richard S. Kennedy in *Literary New Orleans, Essays and Meditations*: "The Spanish and French cultural presences had mingled with the American frontier thrust and the legacy of Negro slavery to produce something exotic."

A charmed circle of friends formed in the French Quarter—think of a Southern version of Gertrude Stein's expatriate Paris *salon*. They were such people as Lyle Saxon (who rented and renovated 18 rooms at 536 Royal St. throughout the 1920s and hosted Thomas Wolfe,

Edmund Wilson, Sinclair Lewis, John Steinbeck and John Dos Passos); Lafcadio Hearn (who liked to document the lives of the city's Afro-Americans, renting rooms at 516 Bourbon among other places); and New Orleans-born novelist Hamilton Basso. Basso used to meet Anderson and the rest at 407 Royal St., site of the Pelican Book Shop. The writers who stewarded the *The Double Dealer* would meet for a "tea", including rough sandwiches made of salami and hunks of crusty bread, and literary conversation. That building is now occupied by Raymond H. Weill and Co., one of the chic antiquarians that line the top of Royal Street. Basso, a New Orleans native, called the Vieux Carré "the Creole version of the Left Bank" and later remembered, "If I never much hankered after Paris in the 1920s it was because… I had Paris in my own backyard."

William Faulkner, "Count No-Count"

He arrived in the French Quarter on Sherwood Anderson's suggestion. At the time, Anderson was living in the Pontalba, and Faulkner took up residence at 624 Pirate's Alley with illustrator William Spratling, who taught architecture at Tulane University. They collaborated on a book capturing the spirit of the time, called *Sherwood Anderson and Other Famous Creoles*. Next-door lived John McClure, then-editor of the *Times-Picayune* book review section and the man who was to publish Faulkner's first fiction (so far, Faulkner had published a collection of poetry called *The Marble Faun* in 1924, and a series of sketches including "Mirrors of Chartres Street"). Looking out of the fourth-floor window at St. Anthony's Garden and living beneath the great cathedral's heft of shadow, Faulkner found a place that touched the part of him which recognized beauty:

> *The violet dusk held in soft suspension lights slow as bellstrokes, Jackson square was now a green and quiet lake in which abode lights round as jellyfish, feathering with silver mimosa and pomegranate and hibiscus beneath which lantana and cannas bled and bled. Pontalba and cathedral were cut from black paper and pasted flat on a green sky…*

And as it was for Tennessee Williams, New Orleans' French Quarter was also the place where Faulkner's literary transformation took place. This brilliant writer and complex man, whom hometown Mississippians called "Count No-Count" (alluding to his heavy drinking, as well as—to them—his inscrutable manner), found a milieu much more to his liking and ken. Says Joe DeSalvo, owner of Faulkner House Books, which now occupies the space where Faulkner lived, "Faulkner came here thinking he was a freak, but found out that he wasn't." Living in New Orleans, and enjoying the mentorship of Anderson was affirmation to Faulkner. During the years 1925 and 1926, the writer shed the romantic traditions in which he had been working and began to write about the little patch of earth he knew, rural Mississippi of a dying Old South, a place he would call Yoknapatawpha County, the locale of his imaginative world.

While living in the Quarter, Faulkner wrote for *The Times-Picayune* and *The Double Dealer*. One reporter recalls regular parties in the Quarter to which Faulkner was invited, and one in particular: "I remember Bill was having a big time that night, observing. He used to love to stand in the corner and oversee. He was a people watcher." Another contemporary remembered instead an "unhappy poor drunk". Whatever the truth, Faulkner was able to portray keenly some of his literary peers in a satirical novel called *Mosquitoes* (1927), upbraiding some of the members of the literary society of which he had become a part. This book he dedicated to Helen Baird, a young woman with whom he had fallen in love while living in New Orleans (probably the inspiration for the characters Patricia Robyn in *Mosquitoes* and Linda Snopes of *The Mansion*). When the novel debuted, Faulkner invited some of the unsuspecting people whom he had satirized to a lavish meal in the century-old Galatoire's dining room (209 Bourbon St.). Its bright lighting—as well as the novel's arch subtext—perhaps helped some of the subjects see themselves clearly. No harm done, as far as Faulkner was concerned...

Now the author's former dwelling is a bookstore named in his honor, selling new and rare titles, by and about him, as well as works about the South in general. It is also home to the William Faulkner Literary Society. Annually, the society's "Words and Music Festival, A Literary Feast" calls Faulkner devotees to remember the brilliant writer whose works remind us that "to endure is all." It is the worn glory of New Orleans that Faulkner helps us to see and appreciate.

Tennessee Williams: "The Bird" Alights

His creative output was prolific: some thirty full-length plays, numerous shorter dramatic works, two volumes of poetry, and five volumes of essays and short stories. He was a two-time Pulitzer Prize-winner (for *A Streetcar Named Desire* in 1947 and *Cat on a Hot Tin Roof* in 1955); he won the New York Drama Critics Awards four times, the Donaldson Awards three times; and he was conferred a Tony Award for his 1951 screenplay of *The Rose Tattoo*. Among many other distinguished attainments, Williams was also awarded an honorary doctorate from Harvard University (1982), and was fêted by President Jimmy Carter at the Kennedy Center in 1979.

All of this acknowledgement was for a writer who for most of his life considered himself an outsider—a wanderer. In his literary works, Williams took on the banal world of convention and celebrated, instead, the imagination. His territory became the eternal conflict between tyranny and freedom, and the dichotomy between spirituality and sexuality. New Orleans was an ideal place for such dramas to take place, because, geographically, form seemed to fit content—so much went on before the playwright's eyes. This is articulated in *Vieux Carré* when the play's protagonist declares: "God, but I was ignorant when I came here! This place has been a—I ought to pay out—tuition."

Graduating from the University of Iowa, Williams took leave of his less-than-perfect family life and turned his back on St. Louis, Missouri. In December 1938, he imagined himself soaring out of the binds that had pulled him down, flying "like a migratory bird going to a more congenial climate." From that year until his death, Williams would touch down off and on in New Orleans. He occupied various rooming houses and apartments throughout the Quarter, but his favorite apartment was at 632 St. Peter, where he wrote *Summer and Smoke* under the skylight, as well as *A Streetcar Named Desire.*

It is somewhat ironic that the directions Blanche followed in the opening scene of *Streetcar* ("that rattletrap streetcar that bangs through the Quarter, up one old street and down another") would have actually taken her right into the graveyard itself. As one critic notes, the run-down setting at the edge of the French Quarter and into the Marigny foreshadows Blanche's breakdown: "In view of what happens to Blanche, one of Stella's lines earlier in the play—'New Orleans is not like other cities'—takes on an ominous and foreboding tone."

Now that an extension of the Canal Street line exists, there actually is a line called "Cemeteries" that takes the rider all the way to City Park. And New Orleans residents know that the Elysian Fields to which Blanche refers is no golden utopia but rather an area of scruffy industrial warehouses and other neglected properties. In a sad irony, Tennessee Williams actually died at the Elysee Hotel in New York City, after having swallowed a pill bottle cap. It is sad that he could not have had his wish, which was to pass quietly away in the city that he loved: "I hope to die in my sleep, when the time comes, and I hope it will be in the beautiful big brass bed in my New Orleans apartment." (He had purchased a townhouse at 1014 Dumaine St.)

Williams knew the kind of freedom and daily beauty that he needed to ensure his creative potential and to give him personal contentment. New Orleans also happened to be his muse, and many of his great works are informed with New Orleans' essential spirit, a spirit Williams inhabited: "Writers are, as you know, the purest spirit of all vagabonds," he told New Orleans journalist Don Lee Keith. "Especially young writers, those whose creative shapes have not yet been molded by their muses. They have trouble staying still. I did. And it isn't by chance, I think, that so many end up here in New Orleans, for short stays, at least. Then they go somewhere else and bide their time until their New Orleans seed begins to sprout. Meanwhile, this place just waits for more of them to come and go. And they do."

French Quarter Fêtes

Each year in March the Tennessee Williams/New Orleans Literary Festival pays tribute to the brilliant playwright who, many will agree, still haunts the Vieux Carré in quiet moments, when his presence can be felt. That seems to happen particularly when, during the staging of his works, there is a sense of déjà vu, a *frisson* of knowing that moves through the audience. During a recent production of Williams' *Small Craft Warnings*, which brings to life and the stage the kind of lost, oddball, fringe "barfly" characters Williams likely knew well in his ramblings about the Quarter, the candles flickered simultaneously on the tables ranged about Le Chat Noir. It was as though "the Bird" had flown in and hovered at just above shoulder level in the intimate setting, watching the actors and listening to his realization of human foibles. In another production, *Lament for the Moths: the Lost Poems of Tennessee*

Williams, another persona appeared—the obscured incarnation of Williams as bard—in a carefully scripted dramatic monologue weaving his early and later verse. One production company, the zany NO Running With Scissors theatre troupe even takes a satirical swipe at Williams' *Cat on a Hot Tin Roof* with their double-entendred *Pussy on the House.*

Williams would probably be surprised if he were here today to see such an elaborate event devoted to him. The five-day festival is geared to even non-academic or non-literary types—maybe those with an interest solely in New Orleans and the South, or those who just wish to be entertained. For this sort of festival-goer there are culinary events, focusing on local foods, and a popular wine tasting called "Tennessee Sips", attended and "curated" by connoisseurs and experts of varied backgrounds. There are dinner gatherings that pair festival-goers with some of the visiting authors from around the world, and there is a citywide "dine-around" with restaurants posting ingenious Tennessee Williams-inspired fare—starters, entrées and desserts. After a meal such as those specially presented there are also "walk-arounds" (group or private), literary walking tours of the French Quarter interpreted by historian/Williams expert Kenneth Holditch.

The heart of this gathering, however, which is soon to enter its third decade, are the plays and performances themselves (usually at least two to three works staged by local and visiting troupes), as well as seminar discussions and master classes. Panel topics may range from discussions about aspects of writing, the modern-day memoir genre for instance, or making books into film. Or the forums are historical in nature, a history of the old River Road that parallels the course of the Mississippi perhaps, or a peek into the art of burlesque and prostitution in New Orleans.

Reminiscences of Tennessee Williams are proffered each year by friends, guests and acquaintances of the author, as well as by Williams' younger brother, Dakin, a colorful character in his own right. Le Petit Théâtre du Vieux Carré, on St. Peter Street, is Festival headquarters, but additional bars, restaurants, theaters, museums and courtyards host various events. Drummer & Smoke highlights a musical program each season—perhaps an aggregation of musicians performing the works of "Jelly Roll" Morton—and there is also a variety of literary events, the staging of the winners' works from the Festival's One-Act Play

Competition, and the rousing finale, a "Stanley and Stella Shouting Contest". The loudest "Stanley", performing amidst a host of bellowing contenders and passersby shouting their support, is adjudged and crowned.

Then, in April, another round of performances begins—and another reason to party arrives. The annual French Quarter Festival pulls in some 300,000 people to a street fête that represents probably the best showcase of New Orleans talent aside from the New Orleans Jazz & Heritage Festival (many think of it as the better event, since prices are lower around town, and the music line-up is just as varied and plentiful). Each year, French Quarter Festival is presented on a large number of stages erected throughout the Quarter. Royal Street is closed

for a good stretch so that it functions as a pedestrian mall in which people mingle, listen to great music, dance in the streets, and experience sporadic outbursts of pure, unadulterated joy.

On one occasion, Doreen Ketchum, a young black woman, belted out on her jazz clarinet a rousing program of standards and popular tunes. She had her audience in rapture as she held one note with circular breathing for what seemed like five minutes—then released it, and the audience's breath it seemed, to thunderous applause. On another occasion, at the Gold Nugget stage on the riverfront, during a rousing cover of the Commodores' R&B classic "Brick House" by Donald Harrison, Jr., two NOPD officers were seen dancing—not together, or obtrusively in the middle of a crowd, but visibly moving the hips supporting the holsters. Music in New Orleans, if nothing else, is a socially inclusive, strata-leveling phenomenon. . . .

The French Quarter Festival is now into its third decade, and it remains popular for the fact that people can wander peacefully about Jackson Square—once a place made for troops to gather—and sample New Orleans cuisine from reasonably priced food kiosks, listen to indigenous music for free, sit on the grass of Woldenberg Park

watching each other or the ships gliding by, or stroll the length of Royal Street in the dusk as confederate jasmine scents the night air. It is an event engineered each year by French Quarter Festivals, Inc., as well as a phalanx of local volunteers, and the teamwork of Orleans Parish Parish Prison worksuited inmates, who are duly selected to be part of a Community Service Program to support such public work projects.

So Many Lives

People who love both the real and surreal quality of the French Quarter and spurn its theme-park image propagated by local and state tourism officials wonder if the depiction of the city's Old Square will always be manipulated by marketers. Residents grow weary of romantic, superficial stereotypes, ersatz references to French heritage, phony four-color photos depicting second-line jazz funerals at the riverfront and other unheard-of places, and depictions of the Old South as innocent, gracious days of plantation life, mint juleps and overstuffed furniture—minus the dehumanizing atrocities of slavery. The Zeitgeist of the twenty-first century impinges on the French Quarter of today: keeping all surfaces squeaky clean and the entertainment upbeat for tourists seems to be top priority. For a while, a tide of chain of national "theme" restaurants threatened the individuality of the Quarter, i.e., Planet Hollywood, or the Fashion Café, owned by a triumvirate of fashion models. ("Ours is not a theme restaurant," one owner sniffed, "it's a restaurant with a theme!") Kenneth Holditch believes—and it is unfortunate in a way: "The cheap, walk-up attic flats or roach-infested rooms of the early part of the [twentieth] century have been replaced by time-share condos or low-ceilinged efficiency apartments where up-and-coming young lawyers and stockbrokers and art gallery owners lead a life that would no doubt seem to the struggling scribblers of Sherwood Anderson's day luxurious and lavish and *sterile*" [my italics].

What one wants to feel walking the streets and lanes of the French Quarter is the past. As Walker Percy saw it, the decay is just part of the appeal in the lower Quarter: "the ironwork on the balconies sags like rotting lace. Little French cottages hide behind high walls. Through which sweating carriageways one catches glimpses of courtyards gone to jungle." Here one finds evidence of time's passage. Oliver Evans describes this urban metamorphosis well:

The whole neighborhood, of course, is a shell—a shell which has been inhabited by so many lives that those of the moment seem only of a relative and temporal consequence. It is rare that one feel this in an American city; it is a common enough experience in London or Paris or Rome, but one is not prepared for it here. And the natural restlessness of American life exaggerates it...

Here is the restlessness that must have attracted peripatetic playwright and poet Tennessee Williams. It seemed to satisfy the temporal sensibilities of a man who needed movement in his life. Perhaps this sense of dislocation appealed to him; in any case he understood it. For as Williams wrote in *The Glass Menagerie*, "time is the longest distance between two places." Between past and present, time in the French Quarter covers vast territory.

Chapter Four

Faubourg Tremé, Faubourg Marigny and Bywater: Goin' Downtown and "Backa Town"

"The period of Reconstruction in Louisiana is the most tragic part of its story. New Orleans had been one of the richest—if not the richest—city in the country. It became one of the poorest."
—Lyle Saxon, *Fabulous New Orleans*

In the year 1860, New Orleans' population had exceeded 700,000 and reflected a social order determined by Louisiana's plantation-based economy and supported by slave labor and yeoman farming. During the American Civil War, the Crescent City was coveted for its strategic position on the river—and for its wealth. Unfortunately, as a result of this tragic conflict and the years of occupation it would experience, New Orleans would be devastated economically. Speaking of the Old City, Kenneth Holditch remarks:

In two centuries the old French Quarter of New Orleans has undergone incredible changes. From a small walled village, it grew to one of the wealthiest cities in North America, glistening brightly among American capitals during its golden age, then enduring federal occupation through the years of the Civil War and Reconstruction. By the start of the twentieth century it was well into a serious decline, which has never been truly reversed.

As far as heroic battles go, the Civil War period for New Orleans was not, relatively speaking, a momentous one, due to the fact that it was annexed by the Union army. According to Oliver Evans:

No important battles were fought in or around it, and in this respect
it differs from other large Southern cities like Atlanta or Richmond.
The reason, of course, is that it was occupied by Federal troops early
in the war and remained so occupied until hostilities ended. And
yet, because of its size and importance, New Orleans stood to lose
more from a Southern defeat than most cities: when Louisiana ceded
from the Union on January 16, 1861, New Orleans was the fourth
largest city in the nation, and her total commerce (forty-five per cent
of which was in cotton) stood at $324,000,000. She was never to
recover this prestige.

During the war, the US government prudently decided to blockade
the Gulf ports and positioned cruisers at the mouth of the Mississippi
River, thereby shutting off any ocean-going trade. New Orleans grew
more and more isolated. The North sent General David Glasgow
Farragut to Ship Island in the Mississippi Sound, where 20,000 soldiers
prepared to seize the city. As fate would have it, New Orleans was
poorly guarded at only two forts—Jackson and St. Philip—and within
the city there were only 3,000 regular soldiers plus a few militiamen.
Most of the troops drawn from the area had previously been sent to
fight with the Confederate army elsewhere.

On 24 April 1862, Farragut led his men past the forts and forged
up the Mississippi River to New Orleans, where General Mansfield
Lovell had evacuated Confederate troops and set about burning surplus
cotton and tobacco stores. When Union soldiers landed, the sky was
obscured by the conflagration and by thick black smoke it created—but
the city was taken regardless.

Although President Lincoln had, before his assassination, argued
for a liberal reconstruction following the North's victory in the Civil
War and had encouraged the slow integration of blacks into the life and
government of the South, radical Republicans demanded, instead, that
the South be treated as a conquered foreign region. Thaddeus Stevens,
who led the radicals, was uncompromising in his views: "Settle the
Southern states with new men, and exterminate or drive out the present
rebels as exiles." Andrew Johnson, who succeeded Lincoln, advocated
the confiscation of southern estates as the best way of dismantling the
old "slaveocracy". Then, by the strict Reconstruction Act of 1867,
southern states were divided into military districts overseen by a

collection of majors-general. By ratification of the Fourteenth Amendment, enfranchisement of "the Negro", as well as the disenfranchisement of white leaders, was made a condition for admission to the Union.

In New Orleans, the population began to swell with northern adventurers who arrived wishing to play a major role in state government. They became known as "carpetbaggers" (for a type of suitcase popular at mid-century), and they were reviled for what was perceived as their plundering, "get rich quick" mentality. The carpetbaggers, along with newly empowered blacks and "scalawags" (southerners who had sided with the radical Republicans), comprised the new government. Due to the large proportion of blacks in Louisiana, many of the top positions in legislature were held by them, including that of lieutenant-governor (Oscar J. Dunn) and governor (P. B. S. Pinchbeck). But Republicans began to quarrel among themselves, and a band of racist rebel southerners calling themselves the "White League" began to take matters into their own hands.

It was a period of disruption, political corruption, violence—and lynchings—as those who opposed the Reconstructionist government in Louisiana acted out their frustrations. Resistance came to a head in a pitched battle in the streets of New Orleans between the members of the White League (radical white southerners) and the new "carpetbagger" governor William P. Kellogg's metropolitan police force, most of whom were black. Forty people were killed and hundreds wounded in that skirmish. A *Chicago Times* article commented: "The rebellion in the city of New Orleans is one of the full-grown fruits of that most unwise and short-sighted statesmanship which, refusing to deal with human nature as it is, proceeded upon the assumption that it is possible to reconstruct human nature by force of Congressional enactments."

By 1872, it was obvious that radical reconstruction would not work. Eventually, however, the South won back self-government, and a Democratic alliance known as "the Solid South" formed. In 1879, a new state constitution was constructed that restricted the black vote by increasing appointive powers of the governor and by tightening the qualifications for blacks to gain admission to the legislature. Following this move, a convention was put in place imposing impossible educational and property requirements on black voters—and, as a result, they were once again disempowered.

Shades of Difference

Against this backdrop of changing political fortunes for blacks in the South is set New Orleans' unusual racial situation. The African-American makeup of the city struck many travelers as the most palpable aspect of the local essence; indeed, during the time of slavery, blacks constituted one-half of the population of Louisiana. Before the Civil War, visitors, many of whom were northerners or Europeans and considered themselves opposed to slavery, were simultaneously horrified and fascinated by the institution of slavery itself. They believed it to be an abomination. The account of Solomon Northup in *Ten Years a Slave* (1853) was proof, should anyone have required it.

A free black man, Northup was kidnapped and sold into slavery. Before ultimately being rescued, he was forced to work on a Louisiana plantation and kept a journal detailing his terrifying ordeal. Northup labored like all the rest of the slaves on the plantation, save for the few days of Christmas festivities that the slaves were allowed before returning to the fields. He wrote: "Such is 'southern life as it is,' three days in the year, as I found it—the other three hundred and sixty-two being days of weariness, and fear, and suffering, and unremitting labor."

In contrast to the status of southern slaves, in New Orleans there existed a large population of an entirely different class. They were termed "free people of color," or *gens de couleur libres*, descendants of slaves and their French or Spanish masters. Many *gens de couleur libres* arrived in New Orleans from St. Domingue (present-day Haiti), after the slave revolts of the late 1700s and early 1800s, and many came also from Cuba around 1809. The "Creoles of color" formed their own caste, and in many cases experienced a kind of acceptance accorded to them by southern whites who, based on bigoted notions of white supremacy, thought of the mulattoes as "more intelligent". As is noted in *Journal of Southern History*: "Many southern whites preferred mulattoes to darker Negroes and provided them with better opportunities in slavery and freedom." Studies have shown that blacks with lighter skin, straighter hair, and Caucasian-like features were often favored on plantations as slaves and in southern towns as free people. Mulattoes were granted freedom more often than blacks of darker skin tone.

Indeed, in New Orleans many *gens de couleur libres* sometimes maximized their freedom to make fortunes, were well educated or skilled in a trade, and sometimes were employers or even slaveholders themselves. For instance, the affluent cigar manufacturers George Alcées and his uncle Lucien "Lolo" Mansion (also a poet of note) employed as many as 200 workers in the mid-1800s to capitalize on their knowledge of cigar making, an art that originated in St. Domingue and Cuba.

The free people of color made up a community that was disproportionately much better off financially than those of darker complexion. Through their social life and organizations (such as self-help clubs called "social aid and pleasure clubs"), *gens de couleur libres* sought to distinguish themselves from the larger masses of blacks and to assure their own well-being and independence. One's station could be determined and controlled by many influences—most of them out of the average African-American's hands. In his intriguing study *People of Color*, which deals with the complicated social status of mulattoes in the South, James Oliver Horton, concludes: "In the upper South, where mulattoes were likely to have resulted from unions between blacks and nonelite whites, their status was lower than that of mulattoes in the lower South, where they were generally the product of unions between slaves and the planter aristocracy."

In New Orleans, indeed throughout Louisiana, there was a careful distinction made between the terms "mulatto" (the child of a white parent and a black parent), "quadroon" (or *quateron*, the child of a white and a mulatto, "one-quarter black") and "octoroon" (someone considered "one-eighth black"). These citizens were noted as *hommes* and *femmes de couleur libres* in public records. Some Creoles could seize the opportunity to *passer blanc*, crossing the color divide to pass as whites, and very likely they often did. This might have occurred, say, at dancehalls in town where "the paper bag test" was employed, i.e., if a guest could show that he or she was lighter than the paper bag, admittance could be gained.

With the perspective of history, these designations seem ludicrous. Today, many of the old-line Creole families of New Orleans—one thinks of such family names as Morial, Bagneris or Glapion, for example—hold public office, are prosperous businessmen, and are respected leaders in the community. Thankfully, Greater Metropolitan New Orleans' diversity propels it into the twenty-first century. Yet there still exists a very real divide between the races, despite the fact that New

Orleanians like to think of the city as different (i.e., successfully integrated) from the rest of the South in terms of race relations. When *The Times-Picayune* published a fascinating series of articles on the legacy of miscegenation in New Orleans, it was reported that some Caucasian family members went so far as to vandalize City Hall and library records in order to expunge from the records evidence of their African-American heritage.

Tremé's Territory

> *"I am softdrinks and hard times, magnolia trees and second lines*
> *My name is New Orleans..."*
> —Arthur Pfister

Today in New Orleans there is a patchwork quilt of neighborhoods, Uptown and Downtown have historically been considered predominantly "black neighborhoods", and the Tremé is one of them. But ask the average African-American citizen where he or she lives and the answer will most likely be one of the city's 17 municipal wards (a raucous recording by one of the new-generation brass band demands, "Where ya from? Where ya from? Where ya from?" and the call-and-response answers are "Uptown", "Downtown", or "Backatown" wards). For instance, the "Backatown" neighborhood called the Faubourg (suburb) Tremé is in the 6th Ward. The Tremé not only lays claim to being the oldest black neighborhood in the country, but it is rich in economic, cultural, political and social developments that have affected African-American history. But in recent years there have been efforts toward gentrification of the neighborhood, and locals are known to refer sardonically to some newcomers' relocation as the "Invasion of the White People".

Flanking the French Quarter to the northeast and stretching between North Rampart and North Broad Street, from Canal to St. Bernard Avenue, the neighborhood takes its name from Claude Tremé, who migrated from Sauvigny, in Burgundy, France, to settle in New Orleans in 1783. A hat seller by trade, Tremé immediately began to make connections with wealthy landowners, but shortly after his arrival found himself in jail for killing a thief on his own property; the thief, allegedly, was an escaped slave from a plantation across the river.

Ultimately released from prison, Tremé then became a member of the militia and, in March 1793, petitioned for permission to wed Julie Moreau, the daughter of a wealthy New Orleans family. After proving the "purity" of his blood in a notarized document, according to Spanish regulations, the two were allowed to marry. The bride's grandmother died that very same year, and the former prisoner found himself owner of one of the largest plantations in the colonies. Its great house stood near the city ramparts from about 1739 until shortly after the First World War.

Tremé began selling off much of his property before the Louisiana Purchase, and a large chunk went in 1812 to the city for subdivision by surveyor Jacques Tanesse—the result being the creation of Faubourg Tremé. Its settlement developed outward from the city ramparts, metamorphosing from small habitations and country seats to city blocks with town homes in the Creole tradition. A cut-through to Esplanade Avenue across Bayou St. John helped the area to develop even further. Free persons of color and eventually slaves who had won, purchased or otherwise made agreements for their release from servitude were able to own property in the Tremé. There are public records to support the fact that hundreds of African Americans in the eighteenth and early nineteenth centuries bought real estate when the rest of the country was still mired in slavery. John Blassingame in his study *Black New Orleans* asserts, "The strongest economic base of the free Negroes rested on ownership of real property. By 1850, a decade before the outbreak of the Civil War, free blacks held $2,214,020 in real estate, with much of that in the center of the city."

Within the boundaries of the Tremé are the 1829 Meilleur-Goldthwaite House at 1418 Gov. Nicholls St., and St. Augustine Church. "Villa Meilleur", originally belonging to Simon Meilleur, a jail keeper, and home also to prominent bookseller Franklin Goldthwaite, then painting conservator Alonzo Lansford, is the finest remaining *maison de maître* (master house, a large Creole cottage) in this historic neighborhood. It is a center-hall raised villa with a large dormer window, and it retains its outbuildings, original interior and much of the large lot on which it was built. After a recent renovation this beautiful old house has been chosen to house the holdings of the New Orleans African American Museum of Art, Culture & History. "Louisiana/Congo", a permanent collection of African art from the

Democratic Republic of Congo, shows as a tribute to New Orleans' Afro-centric roots examples of beadwork, costumes, masks, textiles, musical instruments and *objets* for healing and divination. Actors portraying important New Orleans African-American personages actually lead the interpretive tours.

The Voodoo Queen

"More than 'the hoodoo capital of America,' New Orleans becomes a neo-African Vatican in which elements of Roman Catholic belief and ritual have been incorporated into a vibrant, traditional black religion. It is a holy metropolis, sacralized through folk rituals and various forms of traditional speech by which leaders regularly and confidently invoke the power of the spirit world into the lives of ordinary people."
—Louisiana Sojourns

One turbaned actress-tour guide who walks the halls of the African American Museum of Art, Culture & History is the woman who plays New Orleans' most famous (or infamous?) hair stylist, Marie Laveau (1801-81). Called the "Voodoo Queen of New Orleans", Laveau was not only sought after by countless New Orleanians for her skills as a beautician, but she gained a popular reputation as a healer with effective powers of divination. As a practitioner of *vodou*, or voodoo, it was thought that there was no one else who could wield a spell or employ *gris-gris* (charms, fetishes and curses) like Laveau.

Voodoo is actually very much misunderstood; it is a true religion, a synthesis of many Roman Catholic, West Indian and even Native American Indian traditions combined with nature-based belief systems that originated in Africa. *Vodou* is not nearly as sinister as it has been portrayed in movies and such but, still, its existence in Laveau's time depended on "the traditional African American belief in conjurers' ability to influence human lives and to control the course of events on behalf of their clients." Laveau's hold on the public imagination was great (and it was carried forward by her daughter, also called Marie, a quadroon, a hairstylist and a woman of great beauty). A popular tune about the conjurer, called simply "Marie La Veau", was composed by Robert Gurley and performed by Oscar "Papa" Celestin's New Orleans

Band in her honor: "There lived a conjure lady not long ago/In New Orleans, Louisiana, named Marie LaVeau/Believe it or not, strange as it may seem,/She made a fortune selling voodoo and interpreting dreams."

Anthropologist/ethnographer and writer Zora Neale Hurston, who is best known as a founding member of the Harlem Renaissance of black artists of the 1920s, was interested in New Orleans as a repository of African-American folk customs and as a spiritual center. At the urging of her publisher, Hurston inserted a section on voodoo into her best-selling book *Of Mules and Men*, published in 1935. Hurston visited New Orleans for six months in 1929 and found what she called "a folk culture influenced by its African origins and the city's cultural history." For a time she visited the Tremé, and also lived in Belleville Court in Algiers (reputed home of the "Seven Sisters of Hoodoo"). Then, she made her way across the Industrial Canal into the Lower 9th Ward, where she interviewed working-class blacks who lived in suburban neighborhoods there. She includes in *Of Mules and Men* an interesting interview she conducted with one Luke Turner, himself a "hoodoo doctor", who claimed to be Laveau's nephew:

"Now, some white people say she hold hoodoo dance on Congo Square every week. But Marie Leveau [sic] never hold no hoodoo dance. That was a pleasure dance. They beat the drum with the shin bone of a donkey and everybody dance like they do in Hayti [sic]. Hoodoo is private. She give the dance the first Friday night in each month and they have crab gumbo and rice to eat and the people dance. The white people come look on, and think they see all, when they only see a dance.

"The police hear so much about Marie Leveau that they come to her house in St. Anne Street to put her in jail. First one come, she stretch out her left hand and he turn round and round and never stop until some one come lead him away. Then two come together—she put them to running and barking like dogs. Four come and she put them to beating each other with night sticks. The whole station force come. They knock at her door. She know who they are before she ever look. She did work at her altar and they all went to sleep on her steps."

Another Tremé personage represented at the African American Museum is Thomy Lafon, son of French architect/surveyor Barthélémy Lafon (see Chapter Five, Lafon's Lower Garden District). He was a longtime resident of the Tremé, an *homme de couleur libre*, and offspring (through the tradition of *plaçage*, see "Marigny Remembered" below) of Lafon Sr.'s relationship with Modeste Foucher, a third-generation African-American and onetime slave. Thomy was a prominent businessman, philanthropist and community benefactor, donating funds to many associations to benefit New Orleanians of color and the disenfranchised among them.

Gumbo Ya-Ya

As for daily life in the residential parts of Tremé in the twenty-first century, economic hard times and minority disadvantages have taken their toll. For those enduring life below the poverty line, public assistance is often the sole option for dealing with privations that take the form of substandard housing, inadequate health care and under-funded public school education. Leisure activities often are (or must be) family- and community-oriented—simple pleasures. In the evenings in the Tremé people sit on the stoops of rustic double shotgun houses and Creole cottages, visiting with neighbors. Some of the dwellings are painted traditionally in white with dark-colored batten shutters, or others are stained worn pastels shades reminiscent of the Caribbean.

The Church holds sway here, as people busy themselves with its activities and dinners. Roman Catholic formal services—at St. Augustine or St. Peter Claver—interweave with the simplicity and evangelism of Baptist traditions. The African-American custom of "making a joyful noise" through worship is expressed, and the music is joyful as brass and rhythm sections are now part of church ensembles getting "in the spirit", with the choir's ebullient, close harmonies spilling out of the door into the sultry air. The juke joints, or "jukes", such as Joe's Cozy Corner, the Candlelight Lounge or Little People's Place, are where people go for a cold beer on a hot night, and when the music starts up, so does the dancing.

Someone strolling into the neighborhood may immediately be recognized as a stranger, because living in the Tremé (as in other smaller New Orleans neighborhoods) means that most residents know one another, or know one another's "people". Yet when introductions are made, and especially during Carnival or other feast days, a bowl of red beans and rice with "a portion" of smoked sausage is a welcome offering to anyone crossing the threshold. And food is definitely a bond that brings people together. As local poet Arthur Pfister's epic poem to New Orleans proclaims:

> *I am food*
> *I am good food*
> *I am good New Orleans food. . .*
> Cuisine
> *I am a plate of red beans, rice, smoke sausage*
> *And a potion of berled shrimp*
> *I am a hot sausage sandwich (dressed)—to go*
> *(My church havin' a supper, girl)*
> *I am soft-shelled crawfish, rabbit sausage (with Creole mustard*
> *sauce), crabmeat piquant, Pasta Jambalaya, pecawn candy, pecawn*
> *pie, smothered chicken, Oysters Bienville, raw oysters, fried oysters,*
> *berled oysters, and Oysters en Brochette. . .*

As a native New Orleanian, Pfister has an ear for the accent, and an appreciation of the local traditions that in many other cities are now long gone—the street vendor, for instance, who is still seen in certain parts of town, singing as he does in Pfister's verse:

> *I'm the veggitibble man:*
> *"I got ba-na-nas, watermell-on, sweet patoo-oo-oo-ty!*
> *"I got ban-na-nas, watermell-on rade to dee rind!*
> *—so goo-oo-oo-ood it keep the ba-a-aby from cryin'!"*

Pfister shows that the vendor is still singing, just as he did before the turn of the century, when Lafcadio Hearn captured the same hawkers' accents and dialects—whether black, Italian, or French:

> *"Chick-EN, Madamma... Lemons, Ap-Pulls, Straw-BARE-eries*
> *Lagniappe-y..."*

Hearn even devoted a book to the rich language(s) of the city, calling it *Gombo Zhebes*, and subtitling it a "Little Dictionary of Creole Proverbs Selected from Six Creole Dialects." These dialects he translates into English and Standard French, supplying careful notes, indexes to various subjects and brief remarks on the Creole idioms of Louisiana. It makes for fascinating reading.

Hearn was a writer who wholly dedicated himself to a process of, as literary historian Hephzibah Roskelly in *Literary New Orleans* terms it, "translating for the majority culture the cultures of the other populations of the city at the fringe of a newly progressive South: the Creole, the Cajun, the black." Born of Irish/Greek ancestry, in 1869 Hearn ran away from a harsh convent school in England and landed in Cincinnati, Ohio. He was mentored by a printer called Henry Ward Watkin, and taught the journalist's trade; in later years Watkin helped Hearn to make his way to New Orleans, where he lived for a decade, writing essays, editorials, sketches and features that explored cultures of the city. He was employed for a time at the New Orleans *States-Item*. Ultimately, Hearn would leave the US for the Orient. He became immersed in Japanese folkways and is well known for his Japanese stories. He became a respected professor at the University of Tokyo.

But during his time in New Orleans Hearn was an effective cultural translator; as Roskelly notes, "his dual role of participant and spectator made his observations rich and accurate." He chose to live on the Creole side of town, "Backa Town" and away from the mainstream. He was not just a local colorist but an ethnographer, she says, because "through Hearn's eyes, the majority group became aware of the strangeness and beauty in familiar sights: gypsies singing on the levee at night, children reciting charms to ward off the evil eye, white chalk marks on pillars to signal a death from fever."

Hearn must have cut something of a peculiar figure as he made his way among people who were so different from him—and especially in view of his own eccentric ways and appearance. His editors called him "the distorted brownie" because of his strange, small figure (he had lost his left eye in an accident, the other bulged badly with eye strain) and—ironically—extreme shyness. Getting by financially was a struggle for Hearn while he stayed in the Crescent City, and he sought out those nickel plate-lunch restaurants in the Quarter. He worked hard at what he loved doing, and his creative output while living in New Orleans also includes a novel called *Chita: A Memory of Last Island*. It is the "best nineteenth century novel dealing with Louisiana," says Oliver Evans. The plot of this story is based on a killer hurricane of August 1856 that totally destroyed Last Island off the coast of Louisiana ("a strange land of winding waterways... where all things seem to dream"). Hitting the high-class Trade Wind Hotel, which fronted the beach, the devastating result of this terrible storm is captured in the novel, which pictures the scene. According to Evans:

> *During the storm a ball was in progress... but the gaiety of the dancers changed to panic as they saw water seeping up through the ballroom floor; soon the entire building was inundated and swept away. Approximately three hundred persons lost their lives in this hurricane. When the waves at last receded, looters came in droves but there was very little left of value on Last Island. Bodies contin-ued to be washed ashore for days, some of them grotesquely attired in ballroom finery.*

All in all, we remember Hearn particularly because he was so adept at depicting the people of Louisiana, and especially for the affectionate portraits of the people among whom he lived. One short story entitled "Creole Character" attempts to paint an amusing vignette showing the gulf between what he perceived as Creole idleness contrasted with American industry. With gentle wit Hearn depicts two Creole carpenters who will abandon their assigned task at any provocation—a lovely woman who crosses the street, slight rain, a mad dog they feel compelled to chase. The journeymen stop to talk to anyone passing. As Hearn has the character in "A Tale of Fan" confess: "Bah! It is too hot to write anything about anything practical and serious—let us dream dreams." This is the spirit of New Orleans.

Armstrong Park

In order to make New Orleans' civic dreams a reality for the development of Louis Armstrong Park and Congo Square (traditional New Orleanians call it "Beauregard Square" after Civil War hero General P. G. T. Beauregard) it was, ironically enough, part of the historic neighborhood of Tremé that was sacrificed. In 1974 the development of this memorial site to the legacy of New Orleans' jazz great involved the annexation of parts of the Tremé and the building of a park on land cleared of the bars and houses where other musicians once lived. This area is now a placid 32-acre space of greenery located in the Downtown area and outside the French Quarter, surrounded by the somewhat seedy streets of the Tremé on its periphery. Grasslands, walkways, bridges and lagoons can be found bordering Rampart Street between St. Peter and St. Philip streets, where from the 1940s to the 1960s popular clubs such as the Astoria, the Dixie Bell, the Downbeat, the Dog House, the House of Blue Lights, the Hot Spot, 700 Club, Talk 'o the Town and Tick Tock throbbed with the sound of New Orleans R&B.

Situated inside the park is the original site of Congo Square, a big field at Orleans and Rampart approximately, where slaves before the Civil War were permitted by law to have dances on Sundays. "Congo Square was a place to test a set of bones," says artist-historian Stephen Longstreet, attempting to capture the sensuousness, the free spirit of that long-ago time and place:

> ... *the tom-toms—dancing and playing, shouting* 'Bamboula! Danser! Bamboula! Badoum Badoum! Bamboula! Bamboula *was*

the drum covered with cowhide, made of a length of bamboo. Before
the brass, before the valve horns, they used a jawbone of the jackass,
his teeth making a light rattle when it hit tempo.

Only a distant echo of this folk expression can be heard today, perhaps when a drumming group makes its way to the grounds of the park to practice or perform for those who pass by and might put a bill in the jar, or when you see a troupe such as Bamboula 2000 shake and undulate their bodies with the wild, rhythmic, synchronized syncopations of the old dances. In the dancers' place this century, and in the heart of Louis Armstrong Park, is the headquarters of listener-supported, volunteer-operated radio station WWOZ FM (90.1). A seemingly ubiquitous source of information and a New Orleans Jazz & Heritage Foundation organization devoted to the sound of Louisiana, "double-yuh, double-yuh oh-zee" is well loved by most New Orleanians and is an institution when it comes to supporting local music, local musicians and the local entertainment scene. WWOZ's mission is to keep the music culture alive by broadcasting an eclectic range of styles that mirrors the city's diversity.

Musicians make regular stops by the radio station in the park, dragging with them friends and colleagues, offering their new releases for airplay, or waiting to be interviewed, regaling listeners with stories and the local music gossip, with which many people who consider themselves local-music-savvy try to keep up. WWOZ's website streams live feeds of tremendous Louisiana roots programming that covers traditional and contemporary jazz, brass band, zydeco and Cajun, R&B (old and new school), gospel, Celtic, Latin and Caribbean genres all over the world. Also located by Armstrong Park are the Backstreet Cultural Museum (1116 St. Claude St.) and the Mahalia Jackson Center for the Performing Arts (in Louis Armstrong Park adjacent to the Municipal Auditorium), each doing its part to keep New Orleans music happening and heard. The Backstreet Museum presents permanent exhibits on Mardi Gras Indians, jazz funerals and second-line parades and is located in the old art deco Blandin Funeral Home Building.

While traditionally it has been the African-American neighborhoods that have had to endure the pressures of urban expansion, we now see the long-overdue homage to African-American culture in New Orleans taking place. It should have taken place a long time ago, but it took even New Orleans—a city more racially mixed than perhaps any other North American city—many years to emerge from the deadening influence of Jim Crow laws and segregation, when whites and blacks of New Orleans were kept separate. John Steinbeck astutely wrote about the challenges of public school desegregation that he witnessed in 1960 in his travel book *Travels with Charley in Search of America*. Accompanied by pet poodle Charley, and aboard an outfitted pickup truck dubbed "Rocinante" after Don Quixote's horse, Steinbeck tilted at the follies he perceived in his country.

Only now is the African-American contribution to New Orleans' culture being fully recognized—the very birth of jazz, the development of 1950s and 1960s R&B that put rock into rock 'n' roll, the mysterious Mardi Gras Indians, brass bands drawing countless thousands to second-line jazz funerals, gospel music with the likes of its diva Mahalia Jackson. African-American music and culture has been the lifeblood of the city.

We hope that gone are the days, when, as in the 1970s, city and state officials rode roughshod over the Tremé community, heedlessly pushing completion of their civic improvement project—as when the I-10 overpasses with cement support beams formed dismal arches to span a stretch of Tremé's backyard, bordering Claiborne Avenue. People were displaced from their homes (lengthening the already great distance from affluence), and hundreds of trees were cut down into the bargain. New Orleans' "poet laureate" Pfister wrote:

> *I am dirty rice and dirty politics*
> *I am crabs in a barrel*
> *I am Gentilly Woods, Smallwoods, Amazing Technicolored Mayors*
> *and a Project named Desire*
> *I am modernity*
> *I am treeless strips of Claiborne Avenue in the name of progress*
> *(making the city safe for tourism)*
> *—que pasá, señorita?*

Cities of the Dead

> *"In a New Orleans cemetery*
> *the tombs are crowded together,*

whitewashed, sculptured,
spidered with cracks,
magnolia-shaded, guarded by angels,
and epitaphed;
marbled, moss-grown, with crosses crowned,
and, strangest of all,
above ground."
    —Len Gasparini

Tremé is a neighborhood in which music seeps up from the sidewalks, but so does water. A sudden storm in many of the lowest parts of the city—and that is most of it—covers streets in a matter of a few hours. Flash floods make for thigh-high water on a monsoon afternoon. A hurricane like Katrina proves disastrous. Though there are now high-tech pumps and canals for drainage, if it rains more than one inch per hour, the rain cannot be pumped away fast enough.

In colonial times, long before the city's advancements in drainage, settlers realized that burying their dead would present a very real problem in view of the high water table and the region's frequent heavy rains. Burying bodies in shallow graves, as they had always done, resulted in the contents of the graves being washed away or exposed to the elements. (In addition to the yellow fever epidemics, maybe this explains New Orleans' preoccupation with death—or, at least, its conspicuous presence.)

The only answer was to bury the dead above ground. Now the "Cities of the Dead", as New Orleans' cemeteries are referred to, are an artifact of the past, with the dead living in their own houses among the living. They are "little cities filled with miniature houses," writes Evans; he notes that they are arranged in blocks, just like real communities, with Protestants separate from Catholics, and white from black. "The city of the dead seems as real and important as the living city, of which it appears to be merely the microcosm," he says.

The tombs themselves are cement over brick, some with iron railings and decoration. Designs reflect the neoclassical taste that was so prevalent in the day they were built (the oldest tombstone in St. Louis No. 1 dates from 1789, earlier graves no longer exist), with columns, arches, ornate pediments, statues and elaborate cast-iron décor. The cemeteries are bordered by high walls that are whitewashed and thick enough to contain a coffin's length, and that is where the poorer families were laid to rest; the wealthy had their own sarcophagi. (In fact, there is no room left now in St. Louis No. 1, as these above-ground plots sold out in the 1820s.) In vaults resembling windowless houses (called *fours* by the French for their oven-like appearance) there would be two tombs per family: upper and lower. A coffin was sealed in the upper tomb for a period of time prescribed by law, the bones then placed in a crypt.

There are several cemeteries in New Orleans, the best-known and most-visited being St. Louis No. 1, bordered by Basin Street, St. Louis, Tremé and Conti streets. It is the oldest of the cemeteries and the eternal resting place of Etienne de Bore, who perfected the process for refining sugar, Paul Morphy, the chess champion, Homer Plessy (of landmark 1892 case Plessy vs. Ferguson, which sanctioned Jim Crow laws in the South) and Ernest "Dutch" Morial, the city's first African-American mayor. Marie Laveau is said to rest here, too, although there are some conflicting accounts concerning the whereabouts of her burial place. Visitors pay homage to her gravesite and place candles, trinkets and other memorial objects there; they mark the tombstone with an "X" to keep off evil spirits. Her daughter, the other Marie Laveau, resides in St. Louis No. 2 (bounded by Claiborne Avenue and Canal Street, St. Louis and Robertson), as do nineteenth-century mayors Pitot and Girod, and pirate captain Dominique You, who assisted General Andrew Jackson in defeating the British in the final battle of the War of 1812.

There are many other lovely cemeteries: Lafayette Cemetery

Uptown, St. Patrick's I and II, Cypress Grove, Odd Fellow's Rest (for the use of that benevolent society), Metairie Cemetery, but perhaps St. Louis No. 1 and No. 2 are the ones most often pictured in the imagination. One thinks of the famous scene in the film *Easy Rider* where counterculture protagonists played by Peter Fonda and Dennis Hopper hang out among the crumbling tombs. "Save Our Cemeteries, Inc." is one organization devoted to preservation of these "outdoor museums", and for those visiting the

Cities of the Dead for the first time it is a trustworthy group that gives accurate information—not ersatz history. It was founded in 1974 with a mission to preserve the Cities of the Dead. Graveyard-related merchandise funds maintenance of the graveyards in a city that can barely maintain its living population. Emblazoned on the 100-percent-cotton shirts supporting the cause is the slogan "Tomb It May Concern."

Street Sound

"Man, I really had a ball in New Orleans—five funerals!"
—Cartoon in British music magazine *The Record Changer* in 1950, showing an exhausted traveler, valise in hand

"When I die, you better second line,
When I die you better second line,
When the angel meets me at the gate,
Be so happy to see my savior's face
When I die you better second line."
—Kermit Ruffins

On a fine spring morning, all dark thoughts of death should be put aside for welcoming the day ahead. But someone somewhere may come to the door and shout, "We're going to a second-line." Soon you are loaded in the back of a pickup truck and approaching Our Lady of Guadalupe, where a crowd of two hundred people or more is milling about the steps of the church, some wearing "memory T-shirts" with a pictures of the deceased on them, or cooling themselves with cardboard fans, also graced with a picture of the deceased. Everyone waits for the coffin to emerge, carried with great care and dignity to a glass-mounted carriage pulled by the shiny black horses of Charbonnet-Labat Funeral Home.

The pallbearers and the people who have gathered know what to do next on the long walk—the final walk—to the loved one's resting place in New Orleans No. 3 on Esplanade Avenue. "Fleet as a Bird", the mournful dirge, is played by the Tremé Brass Band (there may certainly be more than one brass band for the jazz funeral, especially if the deceased is a musician or otherwise important community member).

The funeral procession, as it commences, takes on its iconic look, as author Jason Berry aptly describes it:

> *Two grand marshals center-scene rivet the eye; white gloves holding dark hats; the somber dignity of their faces; the stately body language as they move beneath arched flagpoles; the Zulu Social Aid and Pleasure Club banner behind them as [the carriage] advances. The dark glistening street seems like a platform, while two long trombones jut in from lower left, conveying anticipation in the sweeping space.*

When the body is "cut aloose" from this world, and the family has paid its final respects at the cemetery, the procession of mourners then begins to celebrate. The parade-goers sing and dance and follow the brass band's "first line" in what is known as a "second line". They are joyous because the deceased has truly moved on to a better place. Lionel Batiste of the Olympia Brass Band explains: "The New Orleans jazz funeral is about celebrating life from the beginning to the end." And says Danny Barker, jazz-raconteur: "A jazz funeral is a celebration of entering a new world—one that people don't know about—as they are trying to understand death."

There need not necessarily be a death to precipitate a second-line parade. Whether it is for Mardi Gras or an impromptu neighborhood march, when the first few bars of the brass band anthems "Didn't He Ramble" or "Oh, It Ain't My Fault" strike up, New Orleans' second-liners (and "third line" of photographers and ethnographer-types) follow a drill. They fall in behind the band, just for the sake of dancing through the streets for miles. A full-fledged parade on a humid summer afternoon may take hundreds of sweating celebrants through dozens of neighborhoods, causing everyone to throw open their windows. People in the neighborhoods join in, or they dance on top of cars and rooftops, and climb up street signs. They are either absorbed into the ranks or go on inside after the parade passes by.

This unique brass band expression is a home-grown New Orleans sound with a legacy that pre-dates the jazz era and can be traced back to the military band tradition of the Civil War. In a complex handing down of musical heritage (in name, song, custom and costume), one generation informs the next, the Young Tuxedo of the 1990s drawing on the music of the 1930s Young Tuxedo, which had reached back and

drawn on the traditions of the late nineteenth-century Tuxedo Brass Band. These bands are credited with being an important influence on the development of jazz. Today, such ensembles as Harold "Duke" Dejan's Olympia Brass Band, the Onward Brass Band or Tremé and PinStripe are keeping traditional sounds alive, while youthful newcomers such as the Dirty Dozen, ReBirth and Coolbone are bringing about a whole new brass band genre, adding funk, reggae, pop and even rap riffs into the mix. The brass bands are revered at festivals and events around the world, and are just as popular back home, regularly playing such local clubs as Donna's Bar & Grill, the Maple Leaf and Vaughn's.

Those who wish to experience a brass band in the streets, for either a second-line funeral or a second-line parade, watch for obituaries and announcements in *The Times-Picayune*. The *ne plus ultra* of second lines would be the funeral of a beloved New Orleans musician. At drummer Paul Barbarin's funeral, as many as 5,000 people came to pay their last respects and be part of the second line. This is when musicians really turn out to honor "one of their own". And so do the historians, ethnographers, photographers, artists, writers, journalists and international visitors who are fascinated with this form of "linking" cultural expression so lacking in the contemporary North American life. Jason Berry writes that it is a ceremony marking "the exaltation of ordinary people, seed-carriers of a folk culture who remain anonymous to the larger world... during the 1969 funeral of clarinetist George Lewis, the sadness and stoicism etched on the brows of the pallbearers leaving the church [had] a timeless quality, as if the death of one jazzman incorporates the sorrow felt for all members of the church who have gone before."

Of late there are grumblings among some traditionalists about how today's second-line funerals are not what they used to be; some regard the "artificial element" of what has become known as buck-jumping as unnecessary. This semi-competitive dance form of young African-American males, performed in camaraderie throughout the march, is certainly an eye-catching part of the parade. Traditionalists say that the buck-jumpers are just show-offs "cutting up" for the cameras; they say the dancers detract from the solemnity of the occasion. Be that as it may, the jumpers have become a part of this complex, energy-infused ritual. Without doubt, there is no other place on earth where the backbeat of the tuba rises quavering in waves with the heat of the street, and the infectious call to celebrate both life and death is answered.

Marigny Remembered

A second line might make its way down the entire length of Esplanade Avenue, to St. Louis Cemetery No. 3, almost to the Bayou St. John. This is the area that Bernard Xavier Philippe de Marigny de Mandeville developed as the first suburb of New Orleans. Creoles imagined it to be their version of the Champs-Elysées, and it was Downtown's St. Charles Avenue. Some people still think of the Marigny as the far edge of the French Quarter, wedged as it is on the down-river side of Esplanade Avenue and stretching past Franklin. Here, on a high ridge between the river and the bayou where Esplanade stretches, town homes and carriageways are not as densely packed as they are in the Quarter. Close to the Quarter there are bars, nightclubs, restaurant and commercial buildings all around the Frenchmen Street area, but along Esplanade these soon give way to Creole cottages and elegant Victorian homes.

The neighborhood's namesake is yet another eccentric New Orleanian. Marigny (1785-1868) was heir to a vast fortune and when he finally acquired his legacy, he quickly squandered it (in the early 1800s in his twenties, he began selling off the family estate). His predilection for a game learned while in London helped the young man to empty his pockets. It was a diversion that would soon become popular with *les Américains* who were arriving in droves. It was called "Johnny Crapaud's game"—later just "craps"—after their derogatory name for the Creoles, who consumed frogs' legs, or *crapaud.*

They may have derided the Creoles, but the Americans competed with them in building what they thought of as homes of surpassing loveliness (see Chapter Five). An interpretive tour focuses on the Reconstruction era in New Orleans and includes a walking tour to explore the neighborhood's Creole past.

Degas House is an example of the elegant architecture of Esplanade Avenue; it is located at 2306. It was home to Impressionist master Edgar Degas for two years in the 1870s. This mansion, built in 1854, is the only studio or home of Degas open to the public in the world. It was here that Degas resided while visiting his maternal relatives, the Mussons. He painted more than twenty works during this sojourn; in fact, one image shows a scene painted from the back door of the Musson house, looking out to the garden.

Degas House is actually a bed and breakfast (rated five stars by Fodor's) and does double-duty tours as a small house museum. One can actually stay in the house and/or arrange for a guided tour (by appointment only). The museum has produced a special film about the artist produced by the Edgar Degas Foundation, filmed on location and partly funded by the Louisiana Endowment for the Humanities. The film chronicles the artist's sojourn to the city while staying with the maternal side of his family and simultaneously gives an intimate look into the habits of a Creole family of Reconstruction New Orleans. One of the film's commentators is Dora Miller, the great-granddaughter of Estelle Musson Degas.

Esplanade Avenue is also known for another reason, as the site of many gracious old homes where the tradition of *plaçage* was secured. *Plaçage* referred to the formalized custom of a white man taking a free woman of color as a mistress. On a very interesting website, www.gensdecouleur.com, which posts genealogies, history links and other publications to read, the definition of *plaçage* goes as follows:

Plaçage was an arrangement between a free woman of color and a white "protector." As it was illegal for a woman of color to marry a white man, these arrangements benefited both parties involved. Noted as women whose beauty was renowned, they were presented at "Quadroon" balls, similar to today's debutante affairs. Highly chaperoned by the girl's mother and other relatives these balls allowed meetings between potential protectors and the lovely women. After dancing with a man, if the girl was attracted to the gentleman, he would be allowed to speak with her mother to see if a suitable arrangement could be made. He had to be able to provide her a home, which she would own. The home would be furnished and supplied with servants. All children of the union would have to be well provided for and educated. Male children would often be sent to France, while the daughters were educated in local convent schools. Children were often left substantial inheritances from both their fathers and mothers. These unions would often last for the lifetime of both parties or would end upon the marriage of the man. White Creole men would often marry in their '30s to white Creole women, combining the family fortunes. As many of these marriages were arranged by family, the Creole man's relationship with his placée would continue. If it did not continue, the free women of color would pursue other means of support if needed through business ventures, room rentals and occupations such as hairdressing and sewing.

The *plaçage* unions intrigued visitors. The "shadow families" of white men were a cultural curiosity—some would say aberration. In any case, today, even among the people of New Orleans themselves, there is a lack of understanding about these complex race relations and how they differed from the rest of the South. For some New Orleanians it is even hard to admit that their hometown is truly an example of a racially mixed city.

How successful were the wealthy white men at securing their often beautiful, accomplished young Creole mistresses? If it were not for the Bals du Cordon Bleu, or quadroon balls, the arrangements with the quadroon and octoroon young ladies of New Orleans would not have been effected. The major requirement was that he should support the woman well and provide security if he should ever leave her for any reason. The man would maintain his "shadow" family just as he maintained the one with his own wife.

The Duke of Saxe-Weimar visited in the 1830s and remarked that the quadroon balls were "much more decent" than the white masquerade balls, and he noted that attendance at the latter suffered when the quadroon balls were on the calendar. The balls were held twice and sometimes three times a week, and the price of admission was twice as high as any other dance. A building that housed the first quadroon balls was on Conde (now Chartres) between St. Ann and Dumaine streets. Later they were held in the St. Philip Theater and in the 1830s and 1840s, during the zenith of their popularity, they took place at the Salle d'Orléans, which flanked the Théâtre d'Orléans. It was the best dance floor in the US, featuring solid oak on pine.

Creoles eventually began moving to other neighborhoods of the city, and in the first years of the twentieth century a variety of Italian, Irish and black citizens took up residence in the Marigny. It, along with neighboring Bywater, is now experiencing a renovation boom as a desirable inner-city district. In fact, Bywater has developed into an artists' colony of sorts. Glass artists, sculptors, painters, writers and musicians have rediscovered this traditionally working-class neighborhood. Bordered by St. Claude Avenue, the Industrial Canal, the Mississippi River and Press Street, Bywater is another district annexed from plantation lands. Its early residents were *gens de couleur libres* but today it is a diverse mix of just about everybody. The dwellings also represent an interesting blend of early Creole cottages, Victorian gingerbread creations, Edwardian shotguns and 1920 bungalows, all set close to the sidewalk.

A real estate advertisement promoting the key selling points of owning a "fixer-upper" on Kerlerec Street in the Marigny reads, "Precious Creole Cottage in Historic Faubourg Marigny—wood floors, high ceilings, brick fireplace, French doors, inviting pool." Another boasts of a quarter-of-a-million property on St. Claude: "Elegant Victorian Double, mint renovation, 1 block to the Quarter, 2 bedrooms each side." While many people used to think of Marigny and Bywater as run-down sectors of town (more run-down than the rest, perhaps), both *faubourgs* are now considered fashionable places to live.

The Marigny has always had a few very popular clubs: Snug Harbor, New Orleans' longest-running venue for modern jazz, has been open since the 1970s and is still home to some of the best jazz in New Orleans. Snug Harbor was billed by *Esquire* magazine as "New Orleans' Premier Jazz Club" (626 Frenchmen St.). Here one can hear nationally known artists such as Maria Muldaur or Mose Allison, as well as the home-grown talent (jazz patrician Ellis Marsalis, his daughter vocalist Charmaine Neville, the contemporary aggregation Astral Project, jazz scholar Dr. Michael White, and trumpet phenomenon Nicholas Payton).

"Snug", as locals know it, is just the beginning; there is a whole club scene on Frenchmen Street where music is offered practically round the clock. The area continues to draw in more and more devotees of New Orleans music for their baptism. The Blue Nile, formerly the Dream Palace is a cavernous dance hall that experienced several incarnations and name changes while helping to launch the careers of such nationally known bands as the Radiators and the Neville Brothers. In the late 1980s, a Brazilian immigrant took over an old laundromat across the street from the Dream Palace and created Café Brasil, a really hot spot featuring Latin music and reggae as well as jazz, funk, blues and rock. A little while later, the Thai restaurant down the street started booking bands in its opium den-like second floor, dubbed the Dragon's Den. More small clubs and restaurants have sprung up, such as the Spotted Cat, where the real local sound can be found. Frenchmen Street represents the antithesis of Bourbon Street, where the "frat" boys and businessmen gathered to carouse.

By contrast, Frenchmen is avant-garde, the cutting edge of New Orleans music, specially when it came to jazz, funk and "world beat" genres encouraging experimentation. This is where musicians can walk up and down the street and sit in with each other on their breaks, creating a beautiful confluence of sound and a real community feeling. During Satchmo SummerFest, a new music festival dedicated to the life and music of New Orleans' most famous native son, a "Club Strut" allows festival patrons to purchase a special wristband that gives entry to all participating clubs in the Frenchmen sector. The Strut has proven a great success and gives everyone—visitors and locals alike—an opportunity to hear the music scene in an intimate, street-level forum.

Early Jazzers

"Jazz evolved from the talents of many people of diverse neighborhoods in an unusually musically receptive city. If you ask the question, 'Who invented jazz?' the answer has to be, 'The people of New Orleans did.'"

—Sign at Louisiana State Museum, Old US Mint

There is no "convenient" definition of jazz, and, as Louis Armstrong once said: "Man, if you gotta ask, you'll never know." Still, if you do have to ask, most historians agree that jazz was first played in New Orleans just after the beginning of the twentieth century when syncopated improvisations on popular tunes of the 1890s resulted in what was at first derisively called "jass" or "jackass" music—the first jazz melodies. The legacy of traditional or "New Orleans" jazz is also intimately tied to the minstrel music and spirituals that preceded it, as well as to the swing and modern jazz eras that followed it.

The New Orleans sound took root with brass ensembles and usually included such instruments as the cornet, trumpet, trombone and sometimes a tuba. Pressed into service, too, were the clarinet, banjo, guitar and fiddle. Though upright bass and piano were disqualified in many early bands, due to their awkward proportions, the piano was a popular solo instrument in the honky-tonks, bust-out joints and "sporting houses" of a 38-block "red-light" district known as Storyville, whose main drag was Basin Street. The area bordered the Tremé, which in turn contributed many of the early jazz musicians to the cause of serious pleasuring that went on in the lavish houses of the New Orleans' famous Storyville.

In the 1880s and 1890s prostitution was more prevalent in New Orleans than any other North American city. There were brothels all over town, even in higher-class neighborhoods. As crime would get out of hand, it was proposed, in 1897 by Alderman Sidney Story to annex an area for a district to contain the "action". When, citywide, brothel owners opposed the plan, it was upheld in the Louisiana Supreme Court. Basin Street became the district of disrepute, and much to Story's chagrin, locals gave it his name. As many as 2,000 hookers worked the district, and the brothels were known the world over for their luxurious appointments. No expense was spared in such establishments as Josie Arlington's "The Chateau Lobrano d'Arlington", or Lulu White's "Mahogany Hall", where "Jelly Roll" Morton played the big white piano. White and "Countess" Willie Piazza (both octoroons) were known for their rooms bedecked and appointed lavishly with antiques, mirrors on the ceilings, paintings and Oriental rugs. The Countess, it is said, had a music box installed in her mattress.

Of course, it was the women, not the furniture, who were the draw. In 1902 the first guide to New Orleans' bordellos appeared: *The Blue Book*, a publication about six inches square and 50 pages long. It could be bought for 25 cents in railroad stations and steamboat landings, a "Who's Who" of ladies who lounged about in their "cribs" waiting for their "johns". A section read:

Mme. Emma Johnson... better known as the "Parisian Queen of America" needs little introduction in this country... Emma's "House of All Nations," as it is commonly called, is one place of amusement you can't very well afford to miss while in the District... Everything goes here. Pleasure is the watchword... Emma never has less than twenty pretty women of all nations, who are clever entertainers... Remember the name Johnson's... Aqui si hable Espanola... Ici on parle francais... Phone connection... 331-333 N. Basin.

Tom Anderson, Madame Josie Arlington's partner and lover, was the acknowledged boss of the area and owned three large saloons, including Arlington's Annex. Oliver Evans writes: "Anderson was, in effect, the mayor of Storyville, and was recognized as such by City Hall, which passed on to him matters concerning the peace of the neighborhood." In the foyers and salons of the bordellos, which welcomed the entertainment of the "piano professors", the very earliest jazz was played by Buddy Bolden and Bunk Johnson, whose styles had developed as early as 1895 playing in the numerous brass bands to which they belonged.

Storyville was finally closed in 1917 by the Department of the Navy, which, as we have seen, was concerned about the proliferation of sexually transmitted diseases. But the music played on. What came about was a virtual academy of music born of the streets and in dance halls, many of which were found around Perdido Street, where City Hall and other civic buildings now stand. In the dance halls of this district, the new music inspired such sexually suggestive dances as "the bearhug", which invited, as its name would suggest, a lot of close contact, rubbing and hugging. But first and foremost, jazz was an accompaniment to which feet could dance. It was mostly black and Creole musicians who dominated the new music scene. And, as is the case even today, early jazzmen held "day jobs" as laborers and artisans, but played dances, dinners and lakefront parties (see Chapter Eight). Eventually, jazz traveled up the Mississippi River Valley to northern urban centers, such as St. Louis, and then took the world by storm.

Buddy Bolden is considered one of the great "fathers" of jazz, and an excellent biography to consult is Don Marquis' *In Search of Buddy Bolden: First Man of Jazz.* Bolden was born in 1877 and lived in what is now known as the Central City area of New Orleans. A barber by trade, Bolden played his cornet all over town. It is reported that some of his gigs in the early 1900s were at a club called "Big Easy Hall", but where that club was located is hotly debated. Some say that it was in Storyville, others say in the suburb of Gretna. (This is one explanation of the way New Orleans obtained its nickname, the Big Easy.)

In any case, Bolden is remembered for his passion for music. In his own day he was known for his playing (just as Miles Davis sometimes turns his back on an audience), which sometimes became so intense that he would sink himself into what he called "the trance", a full communion with his instrument. At the peak of his career (1890 to 1920), Bolden was playing jazz at Milneburg and other lakefront resorts, and he formed a band with Bunk Johnson to play the honky-tonks and sporting houses as early as 1895.

Another early jazz ensemble was the Olympia Brass Band, led by Freddie Keppard, with Joe Oliver on second cornet and Alphonse Picou, Sidney Bechet and Lorenzo Tio on clarinets, which began playing on and off between 1900 and 1915. Meanwhile, Oscar "Papa" Celestin was forming the Original Tuxedo Orchestra in 1910. It is estimated that there were literally hundreds of seminal jazz bands, and their members were infinitely interchangeable. Again, the main impetus for jazz was that it should be danceable music; it was based on collective improvisation that produced a joyful, compelling sound—and it was the musicians' joy to play it.

Today there is an elaborate music infrastructure that ensures the works of the great jazz pioneers will continue to be played and appreciated. In addition to WWOZ in Armstrong Park and its steward, the New Orleans Jazz & Heritage Foundation, indispensable to the life of New Orleans jazz music is the non-profit Louisiana Jazz Federation (821 Gravier St). Formed in 1980 as a statewide body of educators and musicians in service to the community, the federation fosters jazz, traditional and contemporary, as an original American art form. It does so through innovative programming such as Jazz Awareness Month, which occurs every October and schedules scores of concerts around town, as well as seminars throughout the month. Legislated to receive funding is a new "Linear Jazz Park", which will comprise a walking tour of sites important in the history of jazz, punctuating city streets of communities such as the Tremé with memorial plaques, stages, interactive exhibits and events.

R&B Roots

"Jazz is jazz, but the blues is Mississippi."
—Local saying

The sound of early blues did not develop in the city, as jazz did, but, rather, as is documented, in the rural Delta area around Tunica and Clarksdale, Mississippi. Yet the blues filtered into the Crescent City from outlying parishes and became an influence on jazz, introducing minor harmonies and melancholic lyrics of lost love and struggle born of the African-American experience of slavery and disenfranchisement. It was likely to have been played by the itinerant barrelhouse blues piano players, who passed through the "Big City" of New Orleans as they crisscrossed the country.

Ultimately, blues would shape the sound of nearly every musical genre emanating from this place, rich as it is in Afro-Caribbean culture, including even the spiritual music of hundreds of churches in New Orleans' neighborhoods. Gospel great Mahalia Jackson confessed to loving to hear the sound of blues, and her favorite blues songstress was Bessie Smith. The blues' sinuous rhythms and heartfelt harmonies melded with the energizing movement of brass band music, ragtime, popular turn-of-the-century tunes, and spirituals, which added to the complexity of "The Jazz".

For those who wanted to hear the real down-home bluesmen, such as "Polka Dot Slim", "Harmonica" Al, "Boogie" Bill Webb or "Tuts" Washington, a venture into 9th Ward nightlife was in order. The rawest blues in New Orleans was to be heard in the bars and clubs that lined Rampart Street. Development of the blues into rhythm and blues occurred with the help of intense rhythmical phrasing, which propelled it into yet another form and put New Orleans on the musical map after the Second World War. It was the piano, in particular, that gave New Orleans' R&B its character. Crucial to the style, say, of "Professor Longhair's" (Henry Roeland Byrd) piano playing is the use of the flattened 3rd in the three-chord blues format, a "blue note". That "New Orleans sound" is created by a slide from the flat 3rd to the major 3rd with a rhythmic 2-4 or 4-4 time, often with call-and-response from the bass line, as, for example, in Huey "Piano" Smith's "Rockin' Pneumonia" or Longhair's "Tipitina". Although the 12-bar blues pattern is typical in most other blues, New Orleans musicians pressed into service the simpler eight-bar style. In actuality, many New Orleans favorites are not blues songs at all but, rather, jazz standards—for instance, Louis Armstrong's 1928 "Basin Street Blues" does not really fit in the blues genre.

Considered one of the creators of New Orleans R&B sound, Cosimo Matassa, with his famed J&M Studio at 838-840 North Rampart St., blazed a trail for New Orleans musicians. The studio opened in 1945. This "low-tech" recording studio, much like Sun Records in Memphis which recorded Elvis Presley, was where it all started, helping artists such as Irma Thomas and Aaron Neville burst on the national scene, and reinforcing the city's claim to musical pre-eminence. (Recently Warren Zane, Cleveland Rock Hall of Fame vice-president declared, "New Orleans is the capital of American music.") Matassa was responsible for producing such recordings as Roy Brown's "Good Rockin' Tonight", Fats Domino's "The Fat Man", and Guitar Slim's "The Things That I Used to Do".

Mo' and More Music

"Where Is Beat Street?
New Orleans Beat Street is the home of jazz. It is also the residence
of funk and the blues. R&B and rock 'n' roll live here, too. When
zydeco and Cajun music come to town, Beat Street is their local
address. Beat Street has intersections all over town—from Uptown to
Tremé, from the Ninth Ward to the French Quarter, from Bywater
to the Irish Channel—weaving its way through Mid-City and all
points back o' town. Beat Street is the Main Street in our musical
village. It is where we gather to dine and to groove to live music in
settings both upscale and down home. Beat Street is where we meet
to celebrate life in New Orleans with second line parades, festivals and
concerts in the park... New Orleans Beat Street is a mythical street
in New Orleans surrounded by water and flooded with music."
—New Orleans *Beat Street Magazine*

So reads an epigram inside the new music digest that has recently been championing the cause of New Orleans' music and musicians as it runs up against City Hall. But in a way, it seems wrong to accuse the municipal government of neglecting its city's talent when it proudly puts the cameo-ed silhouettes of three musicians on public garbage cans—i.e., jazz vocalist Charmaine Neville, blues "queen" Marva Wright and Louis Armstrong-look-and-sound-alike Kermit Ruffins.

Beat Street applauds City Hall's new "Mo' Tunes" program, put in place by the Mayor's Office of Economic Development, in conjunction with big-name sponsors House of Blues, Hibernia Bank, Entercom, Abita Beer (beer is served half-price) and *Gambit Weekly*. Furthermore, the editors point out that they in no way take exception to the mission of giving New Orleans artists greater exposure by pairing up-and-coming bands with more established, sometimes nationally known acts, as the program seeks to do. And nor is providing musicians with decent pay for these gigs an issue. But what upsets *Beat Street*, and probably disappoints many concert-goers/club-frequenters, is the fact that the sole venue participating in the program is one of the largest, nationally franchised clubs in town.

It is *Beat Street's* contention that far too many visitors to New Orleans who want to experience "real" indigenous music far too often find themselves steered in the wrong direction and come away having heard only a "homogenized" re-creation of the experience they sought. A recent arrival/exit survey based on ten million visitors to New Orleans showed that eighty percent of people who came to the city planned to hear New Orleans music, and nearly as many said that they had done so by time of their departure. Asks *Beat Street,* "But did they???" Too often, as the editors point out, visitors define the canned zydeco blaring from T-shirt shops in the French Quarter as authentic and leave town without actually experiencing the joys of zydeco; "instead they ought to have worn holes in their shoes at Mid City Lanes [off Carrollton Avenue, Uptown] on Zydeco Night."

Worse than being a victim of plain ignorance (i.e., one just does not know where to go to hear music in New Orleans) is being a victim of what *Beat Street* terms "hostile hospitality". During a stay at a prominent French Quarter hotel, the editorialist remembers, the concierge points in the direction of Rampart Street [in the African-American, read "dangerous" part of town] and says, "There's no reason to walk that way—there's nothing over there." While riding in a cab from the airport, the *Beat Street* writer remembers the words of his driver: "[He] begins a methodical, obviously rote verbal dissertation of the lack of jazz in the home of jazz. He proceeds to deride most of the jazz clubs and musicians in the city before going into lengthy, racist and knowledge-deficient discourse... he [is] going on and on about the crime in New Orleans and why it's best to stay in the French Quarter." Is it necessary to unnecessarily scare visitors with the latest from the police blotter? concludes the magazine in its section called "The Friendly Opposition". The editorial appears beside an advertisement for South Broad Street-based Capasso & Brancato, attorneys at law and criminal trial lawyers who specialize in "DWI, Traffic Attachments, Child Custody, Divorce, Personal Injury", reads the copy, for "when you get off the beat."

But it is possible to go off the beaten path and find the place where New Orleans music lives—and it is the very same music that is linked to the first jazz musicians of the music's inception. It only takes a bit of research, and going into lesser-known parts of town with some common sense. A venue that is tried and true, for instance, is Donna's (800 Rampart St.), known for its inter-generational and inter-racial line-up. The bands that appear often have their youngest members playing out front, so the audience claps especially loudly for the newcomers. Here one might hear the "ever-sunny" "Uncle Lionel" Batiste on bass drum with the Tremé Brass Band and leader Benny Jones; or the Leroy Jones Quintet, a young trumpeter on the road with Harry Connick, Jr., who has achieved international recognition as a sort of contemporary Frank Sinatra with some New Orleans funk thrown in ("a young man who plays with an old man's soul"); or there is the Shannon Powell Quartet—a charismatic drummer leading a whole new generation of drummers who have come out of the Crescent City (he plays with internationally known jazz songstress Diana Krall); pianist Henry Butler (who plays brilliantly despite visual impairment); young Davell Crawford, grandson of R&B great "Sugar Boy" Crawford and a great vocalist/keyboardist in his own right; or Bob French & Friends (where on Mondays free barbecued chicken and red beans and rice is offered up for "the Monday Date"), a drummer who hails from a premier jazz family and who plays his own brand of "border-blurred" jazz-R&B. A feature writer for *The New York Times* found out that in New Orleans music is a living artifact of the past that is not just "fossilized" but lives and breathes among its people:

> *At Donna's I found Funk 'n Horns to be a hard-hitting unit that just blew the hell out of every 20-minute number they played. The drummer was white, but the rest of the players were lean, young black men. To a listener with a historical cast of mind there was something deeply moving in the fact that their jazz-inflected playing was happening on the very ground of the vanished Storyville district where so many of the early jazz greats got their start. Here, I felt, was authentic continuity in a city that prizes it... The happiest face in the room belonged to Donna's husband, Charlie, who was working behind the bar and was clearly proud of the young men up on the stage. "All these boys," he said, nodding in their direction, "I been knowin' them since they was 15, 16 years old. And now look at them go!"*

Chapter Five
UPTOWN HAUNTS

From atop the serpentine lanes of I-10 encircling New Orleans, the aerial view is of a massing silver-white cloud suspended over rooftops, gables and chimney pots, the soft green tops of trees obscuring what is really the village of New Orleans. "It's like a warm, wet spider web," says a young local artist, "everywhere you go you meet someone you know, or someone who knows someone you know."

This strange sight provokes a feeling, evokes even a sound—that taut embouchure of a blown trumpet—Wynton Marsalis ripping off a solo "I Heard Buddy Bolden [Say to Me]", just like he does at the Village Vanguard in New York City. It is a leitmotif trailing through branches of the live oaks. As the traveler drops off the expressway into the streets, ramping with the tune onto St. Charles Avenue, he is dumped into the narrow byways, the tight enclaves of Uptown. What becomes just visible are detritus-filled gutters lining the few remaining cobbled streets, neat and ragged yards, banana tree or elephant ear leaves flopping over the cast-iron fences, the 1940s plate-glass storefronts of Magazine Street's rag-and-bone shops full of dusty Victorian ephemera (bizarre old Hooter's near Sophie Wright Place), as well as chic boutiques and bookstores crammed with wares. Yet Uptown, too, are the green capacious lawns of Tulane and Loyala universities, the crisp blue-and-white awnings of venerable upscale restaurant Commander's Palace (at 1403 Washington Ave.), the classical stone angels of Lafayette Cemetery, and Audubon Park's gracious live oaks and magnolias.

These are sights in the Uptown neighborhoods of New Orleans. Taken together, this sector comprises grid-like blocks lining one big curve of the Mississippi River, with streets such as Jackson, Washington, Louisiana, Napoleon, Jefferson and Carrollton cutting land up into triangular slices. The grid-like streets and the grid-like properties form an overall impression. Roulhac Toledano, author of *The National Trust Guide to New Orleans*, writes: "Houses present files of closely spaced rectangles, those fronted with more rectangles in galleries, windows, and doors: the whole is an ever-repeated sequence of gracious galleries besides supporting columns."

The neighborhoods, all jammed together, projects and palaces alike, exist beyond the mêlée of the Quarter (only a ten-minute car ride or a twenty-minute trolley trip), and a good distance upriver from the old-time Creole sectors. Here is the ramshackle "Central City" neighborhood, running behind chic St. Charles Avenue, which had its heyday in the early twentieth century but still sports a gem or two, such as the iconic R&B palace, Dew Drop Inn, on La Salle Street (see Chapter Six, Saturated with Music). Central City is now the recipient of federal block grants for revival and, it is hoped, its ultimate survival.

Toward the river are the ragged "shotguns" and simpler Creole cottages that comprise the Irish Channel, as well as the fashionable restorations of the Lower Garden District ranged beside Magazine's heaving sidewalks. Magazine, a main thoroughfare that looks like any other city's side streets, with just two narrow lanes and stores pushed right up against them, follows all the way Uptown, past Audubon Park and Zoological Gardens, past the zoo itself, paralleling the river to meet the Riverbend at Carrollton Avenue.

Cheek-by-jowl with the working- and middle-class neighborhoods are the Greek Revival behemoths of New Orleans' famed Garden District, set far back on sun-dappled lawns, where, behind the leaded-glass windows of doors that glint merrily at Christmastime, someone *does* live. And though he remarked on New Orleans' lack of grand, architecturally significant public buildings, describing the US Custom House on Canal Street "as to decoration… inferior to a geometer", Mark Twain once praised the city's domestic architecture as "reproachless". Noting the Americans' "spacious, snow-white" mansions that "rise garlanded with roses, out of the midst of swelling masses of shining green foliage and many-colored blossoms," he concluded that "no houses could be in better harmony with their surroundings, or more pleasing to the eye. . ."

But where do residents access these lavish structures? It seems that not a soul enters or leaves them. Almost half a century ago, the historian Oliver Evans remarked:

Today there is something rather sad about these gigantic antebellum mansions set in their vast lawns: they have a haunted look, and even the ones which have been kept up seem to belong to the past rather than to the present, and to partake of the quality of illusion that pervades the neighborhood. Perhaps it is because these houses look today exactly as they looked a hundred years ago that they seem slightly unreal—the life that is lived in them now is not the same, for better or for worse, and can never be again. It may have been pleasant to own a house with thirty rooms when labor, including slave labor, was cheap and abundant, but today it is more painful than pleasant, and the families who can afford such luxury are few and far between. This part of the city is like an elegant corpse: the polish of the surface only serves to emphasize the decay which is inner and essential. It has been well preserved, but it is still a corpse.

The corpse Evans described is alive and well today, one could say. New Orleans' elite class may hail from around the globe—but its old-line New Orleans families have, as the city's best-known author and doyenne of draculas Anne Rice says, "vintage lifestyles, concealing many mysteries." Tradition-bound, they are the people who send their children to prestigious private schools such as Newman and Dominican, who still have coming out parties and debutante balls in the style people associate with the Old South, as well as belonging to the oldest, most tradition-bound Mardi Gras organizations. The wedding banns of these families are published (politically incorrectly) in *The Times-Picayune* as "Mr. And Mrs. Charles so-and-so proudly announce…" As in other American cities, socialites fraternize among themselves, and the powerful among them are rumored to be able ride a "carpetbagger" or "scalawag" out of town on a rail.

Lafon's Lower Garden District
Following the Louisiana Purchase, Armand Duplantier, former war aide to the Marquis de Lafayette, purchased the Duplessis-Delord-Sarpy plantation and hired French surveyor Barthélémy Lafon to plan a new *faubourg*, the Faubourg de la Course (or "racetrack", for an area dedicated to that purpose). Lafon did so using an oblong grid of city blocks in much the same way that the French military engineers planned the Vieux Carré. And within the new sector he planned a small

but pretty patch of historic homes surrounding an oblong basin; it was called Coliseum Square. It is still found almost in the center of the area bordered by St. Charles Avenue and the river, from Lee Circle up to Jackson Avenue—what is known as the "Lower" Garden District.

Though most of the Lower Garden District had fallen into disrepair by the early years of the twentieth century, frequented by transients and casual laborers, organizations such as the Preservation Resource Center and "Operation Comeback" (in the Bertucci building at 1500-1504 Magazine St.) have stewarded a vital movement to save this once-chic nineteenth-century enclave. Coliseum Square is what is left of the Lafon plan to create what he dreamed of as an idyllic neighborhood in the classic style, complete with a *prytaneum* (the Greek word for school), ergo Prytania Street, a coliseum, a forum for public meetings, and an actual coliseum. The streets were named for The Arts' nine muses, those ancient personifications of the highest aspiration for creative minds: Calliope (epic poetry), Clio (history), Euterpe (flute playing), Erato (lyric poetry and hymns), Terpsichore (dance), Melpomene (tragedy), Thalia (comedy), Polymnia (mime) and Urania (astronomy).

This classical neighborhood would be interspersed with reflecting ponds, basins, fountains and lush gardens. Greek Revival mansions were built on a large parcel of land purchased from the Jesuits, who had planted it as an orange grove. The homes, built in the 1830s style, are pleasing with their symmetrical forms and decorative details, columned galleries, parterre gardens, and balconies with stylized decorative motifs. An advertisement from an 1833 newspaper for the summerhouse of one John Longpré, which faced both Coliseum Place and Prytania Street between Euterpe and Polymnia, gives an impression of how lovely these properties were:

> *The improvements consist of two spacious and well-divided houses with galleries and their dependencies, two brick wells, two large cisterns, a well-cultivated garden enclosed with hedges of orange trees and planted with a variety of fruit trees, shrubs and flower plants. There are, moreover, beautiful rows of orange trees, most of them bearing fruit, pecan trees, peach, plum, fig and plantain trees, two orange groves, several nurseries of sweet orange trees, a fish pond.*

These massive Euro-Caribbean dwellings with high ceilings and breezy galleries were built to offer a cool place as sanctuary from Louisiana heat. They were splendid, but, obviously, not everyone could afford them.

More and more non-French-speaking Roman Catholics began pouring into the city, and many of them were poor. The Redemptorist Order, which came into the Lower Garden District in 1842 to serve poor Irish and Germans, kept rolls that tell the tragic story. Epidemics of Asian cholera and yellow fever hit the immigrants hard. Parishioners who numbered in the thousands at St. John the Baptist Church in 1852 numbered just 800 after the yellow fever epidemic of 1853. St. Ann's Asylum at 1823 Prytania St. was built for the victims of these scourges. This organization dedicated to the welfare of the poor was called "the Society for the Relief of Destitute Females and Their Helpless Children".

As for Coliseum Place, "Lafon's dreams quickly collapsed into a transitional neighborhood," says Roulhac Toledano, because just too many poor people poured into the community too quickly. Ultimately, the large houses were turned into rental units, and when the down ramp from the Mississippi River Bridge was put at the head of the Coliseum Place thoroughfare, it rang the death knell for Coliseum Square. Even so, Operation Comeback, which matches "needy" homes with prospective owners, provides outreach, information, and leads for "user-friendly" financing. The organization has been making great strides, and several old homes of the neighborhood have been rescued.

One resident, a native Texan, visual artist and expert in the art of antique restoration, is Georgia Ross. Over the course of thirteen years, she has single-handedly restored her 1850s townhouse to its former grandeur, and in it she has established a guesthouse doing business as "The Muses", named, of course, for the nearby muse-inspired streets. (Perhaps there is something to the name that is beneficial for writers: George Washington Cable, author of *Old Creole Days*, lived there, and novelist Grace King moved into the neighborhood with her sister in the early 1900s.) Though Ross' art- and antique-filled house has actually served as a set for the movies (Hollywood action hero Claude van Damme shot one here), when she first bought her property it was inhabited by vagrants who slept in its cavernous unfurnished rooms on old mattresses (and inside those mattresses slept the mice).

Facelifts and Jacklifts

Since dry land was scarce at the turn of the century, smaller lots had to be carved from remaining available land, which, in turn, created longer lots and narrower houses, characteristically built with each room following the next and no, or few, hallways. The result is that New Orleans signature form of architecture, its imaginatively painted "shotguns", so named because one could shoot a gun and the bullet would fly straight out of the back door. Shotguns are found all over the city, particularly because drainage systems improved throughout the twentieth century and neighborhoods were able to spread out. As one enters the Irish Channel toward the river, and throughout the Uptown streets that cross Magazine, shotguns can be found trimmed with Victorian scrollwork, and fronted by postage-stamp-sized yards. Sometimes these dwellings are not so pretty, particularly by the river in poorer sectors. According to the author George Scheer III, who visited the city briefly and remarked on some of the more blighted areas:

> … *the salient creation of New Orleans is the shotgun, that frame-and-board archetype of the mobile home: rooms lined up one behind the other in a soldier course, from the front of the lot to the rear, with no hallway, only a series of doors from each into the one behind… I saw a classic of the genre, a dilapidated double shotgun in a bald gritty yard separated from the street by a chain link fence on which climbed only a few hardy weeds. From every window along each side of the house a window air conditioner drooped, and two electric meters were tacked to the outside wall to the rear.*

Yet people love to buy up these quaint old structures, and rip out and replace floors, with the very first improvement usually being the installation of central air conditioning.

Renovation in New Orleans seems like a favorite pastime, and the real estate business is booming, even though the median value of owner-occupied houses in 2000 was just $87,300, compared with San

Francisco's median value of $396,400. Some of the beautiful old homes turn out to be "money pits" for their owners in terms of the constant, large-scale remodeling that often needs to be done—such as frequent and expensive paint jobs, due to the elements. But, noted Scheer: "Paint peels here so quickly it hardly seems worth the bother. Vegetation threatens to reclaim the city. . ."

Moisture, rain, the constant threat of flooding: these factors play havoc with the construction of homes and the maintenance of communities' streets and sidewalks. Because of flooding, New Orleans is ranked second in the world for the most expensive homeowners' insurance: $692 a year on average as opposed to $48 a year internationally. Indeed, while the rest of the North American continent is built on bedrock, New Orleans and its surrounding areas are built on silt, even finer than sand, which is compacting and settling as it shifts. Land is actually falling away; in fact, it is estimated that an average of 25 to 30 square miles of coastal wetlands are being lost per year. This process has been going on for some time. And things may be coming to an impossible pass: in the past twenty years, buildings have sunk as much as six to twelve inches!

Subsidence is all a result of the fact that the levees, built up and down the Mississippi River to prevent flooding, do not allow the river to deposit new layers of soil over the land. As the earth moves, residents have found it necessary to "mudjack" many of the buildings that are tipping or cracking on top of their pilings. Foundations are bored with drills, and the holes are then filled with mud and cement to raise the dwelling's level. From homes and businesses out into the streets themselves, subsidence hampers the everyday lives of New Orleanians by creating monster sinkholes and killer potholes that cost City Hall thousands of dollars to fix. Consequently, New Orleans' streets are among the nation's worst, driving drivers to spend more than $600 a year on average in repairs to their cars. Recently, "Operation Fill-In", a program launched by the mayor, received an infusion of $1 million to mend 60,000 to 80,000 potholes.

Still, all in all—considering peeling paint, crumbling foundations, and even the recent arrival of the voracious Formosan termite—those who choose to purchase historic New Orleans structures rarely rue the opportunity they have taken to connect with the past. By living in dwellings that have sheltered so many others over the years, New

Orleanians perhaps like to fool themselves into believing that they, too, can share in architectural eternity. When the ninety-year-old Roman Candy man clatters his way through pockmarked Uptown streets, sitting atop his hand-lettered, mule-drawn carriage, it is easy to feel that living without history, the beautiful old buildings and their nostalgia, would not be nearly as sweet.

St. Mary's Market Gang and the Rest of the Gangs

It is not known exactly why the area from Delachaise Street to Jackson Avenue between Magazine and the river became known as the Irish "Channel". Some say it is because newcomers employed a nautical term the Irish sailors and longshoreman were very familiar with; others say it was because the streets flooded so often when it rained. In any case, this National Historic District emerged as the designated area where hundreds of Irish immigrants landed when they began arriving in New Orleans in the 1840s, on the heels of the terrible Potato Famine in Ireland. Magazine Street became the area's main commercial strip, and the houses—Greek Revivals, Victorian row houses, shotguns and classic Creole cottages—were built all along the river. There were many multi-family dwellings and, just as today, these humble quarters coexisted, as Oliver Evans notes, "adjacent to the most select" (in the Lower Garden District and Garden District proper). As he also points out, since the Irish Channel is close to the river, one can still find structures that were part of estates long gone: "remnants of the early plantation complexes add to the area's charm and mystique."

The Irish Channel was notorious for its rowdy inhabitants, dockworkers and stevedores who carried on outside such bars as the Bucket of Blood, the Isle of Man, Ocean Home and the Bull's Head. (The next day, the same saloons offered up salutary free lunches at their counters, which has now become something of a New Orleans tradition.) Evidently, even policemen were afraid to venture into the Irish Channel, night or day, for fear of running into members of St. Mary's Market Gang, the Shot Tower Gang, the Crowbars or the Ripsaws. As Evans adds, "it was one of the most colorful parts of the city—a lusty, brawling place, not unlike certain parts of Manhattan's East Side."

Nowadays, Magazine Street is much tamer, but there is still the odd rough corner—indeed one became known by locals as "The

Twilight Zone" (after the 1950s-era horror television show) because of the strange things that go on there.

It is fitting that a street with so many oddities, curio shops, stuffed from sash to ceiling with goods of all kinds, should be on a street named for a warehouse that Spanish Governor Miro built to house Kentucky tobacco and other exports (from the Spanish *almazón,* or French *magasin*). It would take an entire day to walk its length and visit all the antiquarians, retro boutiques, vintage clothing shops, bookshops, bistros and restaurants (Casimento's, at Napoleon Avenue, a tradition for oysters), coffee shops and merchants of specialty items. It is Magazine Street, with its bizarre holes-in-the-wall that conjures up the spirit of comic literary hero Ignatius Reilly, the farcical Falstaffian figure of author John Kennedy Toole's pen. It was Ignatius who, amid the sights and sounds of New Orleans, attempted to reform the modern world as he saw it, taking on bumbling police Sgt. Mancuso as his nemesis.

Pugnacious Ignatius

> *"When a true genius appears in the world, you may know him by the sign that the dunces are all in confederacy against him."*
> —Epigram to John Kennedy Toole's *A Confederacy of Dunces* (from Jonathan Swift's "Thoughts on Various Subjects, Moral and Diverting")

If there were a book that could be called the quintessential "New Orleans novel", it would have to be *A Confederacy of Dunces.* Anyone who has not read it has a great pleasure in store, for many acknowledge that Toole's rollicking story, and particularly the superb creation of Ignatius Reilly, makes them laugh out loud no matter how many times it is read. *A Confederacy of Dunces* is uncanny in its depiction of the Crescent City, with all its peculiarities and peccadilloes intact. Toole tells the ribald tale of Ignatius' misadventures, a saga that one *Kirkus Review* critic called a "mix of high and low comedy... almost stroboscopic: brilliant, relentless, delicious, perhaps even classic."

Historian W. Kenneth Holditch claims that *Confederacy* is a "faithful recreation of New Orleans settings, traditions, characters, and dialects" and, he underlines:

Of all the New Orleans writers, John Kennedy Toole is the most typi-cal of the city. Many came to the city from elsewhere, and those authors who were born there were, for the most part, not typical resi-dents. George Washington Cable was an uptown Presbyterian; Lillian Hellman left the city at an early age, as did Truman Capote, whereas Toole was as irrevocably tied to New Orleans as Faulkner was to Oxford, Mississippi. No other writer, native or otherwise, seems to have known the city as well nor to have been able to evoke its sights and sounds and smells as powerfully as he.

John Kennedy Toole was born on 17 December, 1937, to a father of Irish descent, and his mother was also descended from Irish laborers and early French settlers of south Louisiana. Both of his parents had grown up in the Faubourg Marigny. Thelma Toole was proud of her French ancestry (the family name was Ducoing) and would sometimes take her son "Ken" to the gravesite in St. Louis No.1 of one of the Ducoing forebears, reputedly a gunner in the Battle of New Orleans. The family finally settled Uptown near Dominican College Catholic girls' school, where Toole taught English. Upon his father's cajoling, Toole studied engineering at Tulane University and then did graduate work at Columbia University. After little success with a first novel, *The Neon Bible*, Toole was encouraged when Simon and Schuster accepted *A Confederacy of Dunces* for publication after many rejections elsewhere. The editors, however, required numerous changes to the manuscript, which proved extremely painful to the young author. For the next three years, Toole pursued studies toward a Ph.D. and taught full-time at Dominican. But friends noticed that the young man was becoming more and more depressed.

Finally, Toole committed suicide in late March 1969, driving to an isolated spot along the Gulf Coast and using carbon monoxide poisoning as a means to end his life. Determined to honor her son's brilliant creative work—and his memory—Thelma Toole took the fading mimeographed manuscript to author Walker Percy, who, though resistant at first to read the work, immediately saw in *A Confederacy of Dunces* the author's tremendous talent. The year following its publication by Louisiana State University Press, Toole was posthumously awarded the Pulitzer Prize. As Walker laments in the foreword to a later Grove Press edition: "The tragedy of the book is the tragedy of the author—his suicide in 1969 at the age of thirty-two. Another tragedy is the body of work we have been denied... there is nothing we can do about it but make sure that this gargantuan tumultuous human tragicomedy is at least made available to a world of readers."

Alive in Toole's story of bloated philosopher *manqué* Ignatius Reilly are the things that make New Orleans, well, New Orleans. And locals recognize these elements immediately: there are the bizarre Magazine Street shops as well as the sex shops of the Quarter, there is the spiritual center of the city, St. Louis Cathedral (the sublime), and the vagaries of the Lucky Dog vendor as he pushes his cart through St. Peter Street, Royal, Chartres and Pirate's Alley (the ridiculous—there is even an obscure book inspired by Ignatius' foray into the wiener business entitled *Managing Ignatius: the Lunacy of Lucky Dogs and Life in the Quarter*). There are references to food, "odors of Mediterranean cooking", such as stuffed eggplant, and jambalaya. And there are references to things of the past that only locals now remember, such as the clock at the D. H. Holmes department store, where anyone venturing Downtown might meet a friend. Ignatius' home in the Irish Channel is just the type that one will see today, a "miniature house" on Constantinople Street, near Tchoupitoulas, where Sgt. Mancuso, the antagonist of the narrative, must come on his way up St. Charles to interrogate Ignatius and his mother, smelling the "moldy scent" and seeing the trees over his head "like a canopy".

Toole assiduously copies the New Orleans accent and gets its unusual dialect correct: "chirren" (children), "ersters" (oysters), "wrench" (rinse), "zink" (sink), and the misuse of the preposition "by", i.e. I went by my Mama's. It is the way the characters converse and understand each other that, for locals, makes the book even funnier. Toole's mimicry is part of the great attraction for New Orleans readers, who, across the board, seem to enjoy his poking fun at them. But if someone criticizes your family, he or she had better be *a familiar*, certainly not an outsider. Holditch observes:

> ... *local interest in Confederacy cuts across class and educational lines, remarkable because New Orleanians tend to bristle at any adverse criticism of that favorite topic, their hometown... New Orleanians seem rather to relish the negative aspects of the city*

enumerated in Confederacy... *they are, I believe, amused and
bemused by the author's grasp of and credible representation of local
customs—social, ethical and culinary—and his ability, probably a gift
from his mother, for identifying qualities that distinguish residents of
particular neighborhoods and for capturing their voices.*

An example of the novel's verisimilitude and Toole's clever way
with dialogue is the brief encounter of Ignatius' mother with the clerk
in D. H. Holmes, where she has gone to buy some wine cakes for her
flabby son. The familiarity between the two women is evident in the
way they kibbutz, New Orleans-style. It is interesting to note that Toole
accurately shows how anyone of any age can call a stranger (who is also
of any age) "babe":

*"Oh, Miss Inez," Mrs. Reilly called in that accent that occurs south
of New Jersey only in New Orleans, that Hoboken near the Gulf of
Mexico. "Over here, babe."*
    *"Hey, how you making?" Miss Inez asked. "How you feeling,
darling?"*

When Ignatius is later collared by the indefatigable Sgt. Mancuso,
who is the very portrait of law enforcement's perceived incompetence,
the windy reformer reveals Ignatius'—and Toole's—disdain for the
strictures of officialdom, as well as the New Orleanian "live and let live"
ethos. When Mancuso asks Ignatius if he is employed, Reilly replies, "I
dust a bit... In addition, I am at the moment writing a lengthy
indictment against our century. When my brain begins to reel from my
literary labors, I make an occasional cheese dip."
    In characteristic hyperbole, Ignatius describes a trip to Baton
Rouge in a Greyhound Sceniccruiser, and captures the average New
Orleanian's xenophobia:

*"... that was the only time that I had ever been out of New Orleans
in my life. I think that perhaps it was the lack of a center of orientation that might have upset me. Speeding along in that bus was like
hurtling into the abyss. By the time we had left the swamps and
reached those rolling hills near Baton Rouge, I was getting afraid*

that some rural red-necks might toss bombs at the bus. They love to attack vehicles, which are a symbol of progress, I guess."

Ignatius' acerbic wit tries out modern morality against his cerebral mindset of the Middle Ages. As Holditch explains, Ignatius' religious views represent the peculiar hybrid of Roman Catholic tradition blended with influences of other denominations (i.e. that of the Baptist Bible Belt): "Some aspects of New Orleans Catholicism represent a bizarre, exotic transformation of traditional orthodoxy, quite distinct from the Roman Catholic religion as practiced in any other American city." As we can see, references to "St. Odo of Cluny parish" or Santa Battaglia's mantel shrine to her mother's memory and the statue of "Our Lady of the Television" attached to her set by a suction cup are not too different from the reality of New Orleans' "patron saint", viz. the statue of St. Expedite at Our Lady of Guadalupe Church (see Chapter Four). Local readers may smile, nod their heads in recognition, and think about the St. Charles trolley driver they call "the James Brown" of trolley drivers. This Crescent City citizen, who is regularly voted the best public transportation driver in the poll conducted by *Gambit*, sits at the car's controls with prayer cards wedged into the big windshield. He keeps up a hilarious running commentary all the way Downtown, calling out to vehicles crossing the neutral ground, "Whoa! Watch that buggy! Trolley driver comin' through!"

Toole's characterizations are exquisitely real, and despite the somewhat pared down, comic plot, Toole gets them right. In the black man Burma Jones, according to Walker Percy, Toole "achieved the near impossible, a superb character of immense wit and resourcefulness without the least trace of Rastus minstrelsy." Anyone who wants to get a feeling for "real New Orleans" owes him- or herself a day or two in a big wicker chair, on a capacious balcony (maybe Uptown's Columns Hotel at 3811 St. Charles), Sazerac in hand, reading this book.

Suburb Chic

Next to the French Quarter, New Orleans' Garden District is probably the best-known and most-visited sector of the city, a 65-square-block neighborhood of showplace homes that Creoles once derisively called "Prairie Palaces". It is suggested that the reason the district is named for its gardens is because, before speculation and development, the land was used for truck farms to grow produce; and, while the gardens of the Garden District are certainly attractive, there are more elaborate, historic and rarer ones seen in other cities. In any case, the area bounded by Jackson to Louisiana Avenue, from Baronne Street over to the river, is the ritzy Garden District suburb designed by Benjamin Buisson, a French immigrant and one-time artillery officer under Napoleon Bonaparte.

Beginning in the 1830s following the Louisiana Purchase, the growth of this neighborhood created New Orleans' first real estate boom, as wealthy "Americans" built their mansions along and behind St. Charles Avenue. These wealthy entrepreneurs and professionals had their own architectural preferences, and incorporated then-fashionable Greek Revival, Italianate, Gothic and Second Empire dwellings into the environs, which can now be viewed on a pleasant afternoon's walk through the Garden District. The Americans chose massive mansions and fanciful cottages over European stucco and brick townhouses, grand double-hung windows over louvered French doors, and burgeoning gardens on sizable lawns over the Creole taste for quiet courtyards. According to historian Oliver Evans, there were only two major Creole families who considered moving into the new neighborhood, and they were the family of Michel Musson (a postmaster) and Antoine Jacques Mandeville de Marigny, the son of Bernard who established Faubourg Marigny. By the 1920s, the American population outnumbered the city's Creoles.

Compared with the predominantly working-class milieu that John Kennedy Toole depicted in his novel—the class to which Senator Long said he was devoted—the Garden District set itself apart. It has turned out among its creative residents the flamboyant playwright and diarist Lillian Hellman, who spent her childhood in New Orleans. Her father was a struggling Jewish businessman. Hellman, born in 1905, depicted her mother's Alabama family as the Hubbards in her play *The Little Foxes*. She spent six years of her childhood with family living at her aunties' boardinghouse on Prytania Street, bordering the Garden District, and enjoyed shopping with them for ingredients to make Creole dishes at the French Market.

Also in marked contrast to Toole's blue-collar world is the Gothic landscape portrayed in the novels of Anne Rice. Best-selling creator of the "Vampire Chronicles", Rice moved to Texas with her family when she was 15, lived in San Francisco during the 1960s and 1970s, and then returned to her birthplace. She is now best known as a New Orleans writer. Certainly she is New Orleans' best-known writer, with 17 novels to her credit, including *The Queen of the Damned* (1988), which spent 17 weeks on *The New York Times'* best seller list, and *The Witching Hour* (1990), for which she received a celestial $5-million publishing contract. In the latter book, Rice lovingly sketched her "sad old city festering with secrets in its perpetual Caribbean heat."

Yet it is not only New Orleans as setting (whose history she assiduously researches), but as home to a certain race of people, that for Rice imbues the city with its spirit, and, in turn, gives her novels their Gothic tone. Rice has said that New Orleans' "psyche" owes much to its many cultures' reverence for tradition, "to their mysticism, and resistance to change". She says there is a "fine line between their daily lives and their souls". The city naturally offers up Gothic and grotesque suggestions, which creep into her works. One critic writing of Rice's novels says that in them New Orleans has "a foreign quality, and certain unique facts of its history [make it] a 'haunted city' as an Englishman in *The Witching Hour* describes it, where mysteries abound, some real, many imagined." Into Rice's novels go the habits and manners of clannish nineteenth-century Creoles, the exoticism and seemingly foreign cultural traits of African slaves and immigrants from colonial St. Domingue, as well as the idiosyncratic practices and rituals of New Orleans' Roman Catholics. Rice uses to her advantage certain Gothic flourishes—the element of ever-present architectural decay, simultaneously the proliferation and rot of the city's abundant tropical vegetation, and the presence of hideous insects and scuttling rodents—to act as the backdrop for her supernatural beings.

It is said that, as a child, Rice sought out books to read that featured New Orleans as the setting for ghost stories. Perhaps the Garden District's "haunted" mansions inspired her as a child, as they evidently do today. Rice's passion for the lovely old structures of the Garden District has turned her into an active preservationist for, and champion of, the Uptown area, particularly in view of her battles with developers who would rob the neighborhood of its character. This was evident in her one-time battle with restaurateur-developer Al Copeland over the construction of his new restaurant on St. Charles Avenue.

Rice has been known to take up the cause of the antebellum homes, purchasing buildings that are probably valued in the multi-thousands, and renovating them, as she did with St. Elizabeth's Children's Home (1314 Napoleon Ave. at Prytania Street), a beautiful 1865 structure and early example of the Second Empire style that had had a previous incarnation as an orphanage. She has since sold St. Elizabeth's; however, she still owns 1239 First St., a Greek Revival-cum-Italianate mansion built by James Caltrow and Charles Pride in 1857.

Rice also purchased St. Alphonsus Church (2029 Constance St.), where the author was baptized, attended school, and was parish member until the church merged with St. Mary's across the street. Built in 1855-7 according to the designs of Louis L. Long, a Baltimore architect, and meant to serve the Irish Catholics living in the area, St. Alphonsus is "well-known for its art and architecture... the frescoes and stained glass windows... are some of the most beautiful in the nation," reads the official Anne Rice website (annerice.com). Italianate in style, with arches and pilasters making a rhythmic surface, inside and outside St. Alphonsus is lovely and ornate. Updates on Rice's properties are given on the website, where fans can also access a lot of other interesting information about the author in sections entitled Direct from Anne,

Bookshelf (story briefs), Anne's Chamber, The Anne Rice Collection, Anne's New Orleans, Exclusive Features, and In Her Own Words. Rice's annual Halloween party is always a big event in the city.

Whether one is wandering the neighborhood on foot, past the J. F. E. Livaudais Plantation, or riding the St. Charles Streetcar, the final resting place is Lafayette Cemetery No. 1, which had historically been the focal point of the Garden District. Here at the intersection of Washington Avenue and Sixth Street lie the hundreds whom yellow fever felled in a "well planned and well planted burial ground with the slightly autocratic air appropriate to its location in the heart of the Garden District," says Evans. The cemetery's tombstones show that in this neighborhood, during the worst of the epidemics, a whole family could be killed off in the space of one week. Now stone angels watch over those who R.I.P. in their crypts and tombs, thankfully lying above the rising water table for an eternity.

Saturated with Music

There's nothing quite like driving up Tchoupitoulas, passing the Rock Bottom Lounge, hearing the sounds of the wharves, seeing the masts of the ships, and then walking in the front door and seeing Fess.
    —Jared Zeller, president, Mothership Entertainment

Jockamo fee no un na nay. Tipitina's is the place where the Indians play.
    —Alfred Doucette, Big Chief, The Flaming Arrows

Like floodwaters, music inundates New Orleans' streets. The best-known showcase of New Orleans music is Tipitina's (501 Napoleon Ave.). "Tip's", as most locals call this unpretentious place, most resembles the kind of nightspots that have gained national mythic stature, such as the Village Vanguard in New York City or The Filmore in San Francisco. And Tipitina's is where New Orleans neophytes go for a baptism by music. Though it recently celebrated its 25th anniversary, one would hardly say seeing the venue for the first time that it is an auspicious place for performers. It is not very big, has low ceilings, a low stage, and hardly any ventilation; in essence, like most New Orleans clubs, it could double as someone's garage.

Articulating some of his fond memories of nights at the club, Reggie Scanlan, bassist for the local band the Radiators, recalls: "You could see the humidity and funk hanging in the air from front of the stage. It pushed people over the edge, and there was this real primitive and tribal feeling." "Tipitina's has survived through changes of ownership and management, through barroom brawls and love affairs, through debauchery and drunkenness," remarked entertainment tabloid *Gambit*'s music critic in a special 25th anniversary issue: "... the musicians and the audience keep coming together generation after generation. It shows the deep connectivity of music and art and our community."

"Tip's" opened on 14 January 1977, when 14 partners came together to establish what they called "Tipitina's Piano and Juice Bar". It had been dubbed 501 Club in a previous incarnation and was just a humble clapboard building at the corner of Napoleon Avenue and Tchoupitoulas. Ironically, when the 14 original investors took over the property, the then-landlord wanted to include in his lease a provision that stated there would be no black people allowed in the building.

In fact, the very reason the partners opened Tipitina's was as a forum for a particular black man, an incredibly talented musician called "Professor Longhair" or "Fess" by most, whose unique vocal and piano style drew on the blues and New Orleans rhythms. Henry Roeland Byrd (1918-80), Fess' real name, was the epitome of the New Orleans piano man. Said Hank Drevich, one of the co-founders:

> *That was our intention—to provide a venue for Fess and his contemporaries as well as what we thought should be heard and felt live— like reggae, little known then in the U.S.A. In the '70s, disco ruled. The Nightcap was for blacks and a few white fools like myself. Jed's and the Maple Leaf were it for live music outside of the Quarter and things weren't so happening in the Quarter either.*

There are stories about how the juice bar was named, and these tales show just how New Orleans mythology is created—with improvisation, repetition (i.e. oral tradition) and maybe even a little "humbug". Though it is likely that the club's name came from Fess' early R&B hit with that title, recorded on Atlantic Records in 1953, the question remains—who or what is Tipitina? There are several suggestions: it was the name of a volcano that erupted around the time Prof. Longhair wrote the song; it was his affectionate nickname for an old two-toned car; it was a nickname of a girlfriend; it was street lingo for two joints (a.k.a. "jazz cigarettes") for two dollars.

In the early days, says New Orleans music writer and Louisiana Music Factory storeowner Jerry Brock, Tipitina's "functioned as a community center and you could go in any afternoon and there would be a lot of people there because they had good food and great juices and good music." All kinds of musicians, many the progenitors of 1950s R&B, played, and still play, Tipitina's, such as Huey "Piano" Smith & the Clowns, Lee Dorsey, Earl King, Jessie Hill, Chris Kenner, Benny Spellman, and Irma Thomas. All of Louisiana music is well represented with artists who are nationally known or little known.

Beat Street magazine's music editor points out that "Tip's" Homegrown Night every week turned the club into a "great incubator of local talent for 25 years". "The scene was loose: people would just show up and play, sit in with each other, take solos," says local photographer Pat Jolly, "and you might find anybody playing music in the afternoon, like Chief Jolly playing 'Monkey on My Back'."

For many, the spontaneity and intense energy of the music scene at Tipitina's resembled another Uptown nightclub that has since passed into mythology: the Dew Drop Inn, an unprepossessing hotel and adjoining nightclub that spawned a great number of New Orleans musicians, and, in the style of vaudeville, featured a bizarre array of shake dancers, drag queens, comics, and the like. Spencer Bohren, a Wyoming-born blues guitarist and lifelong student of New Orleans music, draws the parallels between the Dew Drop and "Tip's":

> *The society that happened in that room [Tipitina's] was totally avant-garde for the time. It was a community, and I think everybody know it was world-class and very deep. Bobby Mitchell used to stand around in his turban. Mr. Google Eyes would get up and rant and rave. My theory is that a lot of those guys had the Dew Drop mentality still fresh in their minds. They were used to shows with emcees and crossdressers and comedians.*

Creativity in the form of improvisation is key to the appeal of New Orleans and its music scene, whether underground, aboveground, or out on the streets. What people come to know, if visiting the city long enough, is that there are many talented musicians and a potent mix of ethnicities and races. At a club like Tipitina's, the music has a place to concentrate and become even more powerful, drawing people in, again and again. Says Scanlan: "It was scene that was so creative that it was almost out of hand. I wasn't around in the '50s, but I have to think that in the course of New Orleans music history, Tip's early days were one of the most creative and incestuous instances in New Orleans. I remember one night when the Rhapsodizers were playing, and Fess showed up and sat in. Then Bonnie Raitt's band showed up, and they sat in. Then Allen Toussaint showed up and sat in."

With all the great Louisiana musicians booked, such as zydeco "King" Clifton Chenier, the Neville Brothers, "Snooks" Eaglin, Dr. John and Deacon John, says Art Neville, "it's like Mardi Gras every day inside the building." Blues man John Mooney recalls, "I remember one night Fess was playing, it might have been around Mardi Gras time, and the joint was just jammed. There were probably 500 people outside on the neutral ground, and everyone was smoking reefer and dancing. That was intrinsic to the vibe whenever Fess or Clifton (Chenier) or the Nevilles played—everyone danced, inside, outside, all over the place."

End of the Line

"Sitting on the levee, up in Carrollton
I'm just waiting for my baby, her workshift's over at one.
She's slinging sushi to the clergy, from Notre Dame
and it's rumored that the Pope is incognito up in Carrollton.
A bend in the river, a turn of a phrase,
playing music all night, and sleeping all day,
we got poets, pirates, professors and thieves—
all night bartenders that you wouldn't believe.
I'm going to make a lot of money, playing at the Maple Leaf,
I'm going to buy a little shotgun cottage, up on Dublin Street.
If I find His Holiness, I'll ask him tonight
if he'll help me make that little waitress my wife,
and we'll be living slow and easy on the river up in Carrollton."
—Stephen "Spike" Perkins

When the St. Charles Avenue streetcar completes its arrow-straight course up its tree-canopied route, past Loyola and Tulane, past Audubon Park, it finally runs into the river bend, and then leans into Carrollton Avenue and the Carrollton neighborhood. Once a separate village, cut off from New Orleans by swamps and plantation lands, Carrollton was founded in the 1830s and named after General William Carroll, who had helped defend the city against the British. As the Port of New Orleans expanded, Algiers and Jefferson City became the 5th and 6th districts of New Orleans, and in the 1870s the town of Carrollton became its 7th. In the early years Carrollton was a summering spot for New Orleanians, and those lucky enough to have a summer home there traveled by a railroad whose cars were horse-drawn. Dilapidated Oak Street, which today wears the look of a Hollywood set for a 1940s "B" movie, was the main thoroughfare; now Maple Street supplants it with pleasant sidewalks that skirt restaurants, bistros, boutiques, bookstores and the like.

Maple on Oak

> *"The Maple Leaf Bar is quintessential New Orleans. The management, staff and clientele have always personified the unlikely mix of intellectualism, hedonism and eclecticism that defines the city."*

The Maple Leaf Bar, at the corner of Cambronne Street (General Cambronne was a Napoleonic War hero) and Oak may look shabby, with its old pressed-tin tiles on the inside, slowly turning ceiling fans, concrete floor with wooden benches lining the walls and a smoke-filled oblong called "the dancefloor". The stage is minuscule and barely manages to fit into a dark bay right at the club's front window, so anyone walking on the sidewalk up to the bar from the outside looks straight into the back of a drummer's head. The sounds inside slice into the night air, and as the bar's resident poet Everette Maddox once said, "ricochet over the heads of dancing, sweating revelers."

Like Tipitina's, the Maple Leaf has celebrated long-time service to its community: more than three decades, to be exact. It opened in mid-January 1974, adding to a neighborhood music scene that was in full swing—similar to present-day Frenchmen Street in the Faubourg Marigny. There was Jed's, which became Muddy Waters, Jimmy's Music Club, and Carrollton Station. "The Leaf" got its start when six investors went in on the opening (Carl Brown is the only original investor still involved with the bar today). Attorney, husband, father and jazz and ragtime enthusiast, Brown, like so many other serious jazzophiles who live in this city, could not get enough of the homegrown sound. He says:

> *At fifteen I'd go to Bourbon Street and hear bands like Paul Barbarin, Alphonse Picou at the Paddock Lounge, Sharkey Bonano at the Famous Door, Pete Fountain. I love music, the real stuff. I liked to watch Pork Chop and Kidney Stew [an old minstrel duo] dance... The place had been a laundromat on the side where the bar is. We couldn't decide on a name. I came up with the Maple Leaf. Jelly Roll Morton claimed that the "Maple Leaf Rag"—New Orleans style, the way he played it—was the first real jazz piece. He told that to Alan Lomax...*

John Parsons, the original talent buyer, was responsible for bringing the first Cajun and zydeco artists from rural Louisiana into the city, and for moving jazz Uptown. The Leaf became known as a showcase for the likes of James Booker, an eccentric music genius on piano, who could, recalls longtime friend Jerry Brock, "start [a] piece with a rollicking 'You Ain't Nothing But a Hound Dog'. After 30 bars or so [sneak] in Beethoven's 'Moonlight Sonata' with his left hand and to top that off adds a Sinatra favorite, 'Strangers in the Night', to the mix. He was simultaneously playing three distinct melodies creating a new composition. Beyond his extraordinary technique was this uncanny ability to interpolate material together that no one else ever thought of or tried."

Booker's performances at Maple Leaf are legendary and are now documented on two CDs produced by Rounder Records, culled from Parson's tapes: *Bayou Maharajah: Live at the Maple Leaf Bar* and *Spiders on the Keys: Live at the Maple Leaf Bar*. Another performer associated with the Maple Leaf is deluxe soul-singer and guitar maestro Walter "Wolfman" Washington. "Trained up" by New Orleans vocalist Johnny "the Tan Canary" Adams, Washington has so much energy that he and his band The Roadmasters (when in town) regularly whip dancers at the Maple Leaf into a frenzy, and keep them there until 3 or 4 in the morning. Add to these many others: blues man Roosevelt Sykes, Cajun balladeer Michael Doucet and Beausoleil, hip ReBirth Brass Band, the Tex-Mex Iguanas. And there are the visits by rocker Bruce Springsteen, the Grateful Dead's Robbie Robertson, Stones' Keith Richards, actors Dennis Quaid, Robert Duvall, Samuel L. Jackson and Kathleen Turner.

"The Leaf" is a little place with a big reputation. Most importantly, it is a place in which you feel like you belong. That is probably the spirit that Prattville, Alabama-born poet Everette Maddox (*The Everette Maddox Song Book* [1982], *Bar Scotch* [1988] and *American Waste* [1993]) felt when he decided he would never leave the Leaf. Having become homeless, and in waning years very ill with cancer, Maddox, who had begun a successful reading series at the Leaf, took up residence there, sleeping in the courtyard at the far reaches of the bar. Knowing that he was losing his battle with the disease, Maddox is rumored to have said: "If anybody tries to bury me in Ala-goddamn-bama, there's going to be some serious haunting going on."

Some of the poet's ashes were spread around the Maple Leaf's patio, and some were sprinkled into the brown Mississippi River. Maddox now has a headstone in the patio garden, and his picture graces the wall behind the long front bar. Annually, organizers host the Everette Maddox Memorial Poetry and Prose Reading Series, and irregularly an edition of *The Maple Leaf Rag* appears. It is an anthology of works by people who have performed in the club, or in some way contributed to, the ongoing creative life of the Maple Leaf on Oak.

Chapter Six
Mid-City: The New Bohemia

During the Second World War migrants flooded into New Orleans, as shipyards and industrial plants down to Venice, Louisiana, on the Gulf of Mexico, employed thousands of workers. Research and development into offshore oil began in earnest; petroleum and metal industries would be productive throughout the twentieth century until the late 1980s, when the price of domestic oil went bust, dropping to $10 from $40 a barrel. The massive refineries built all long the banks of the Mississippi prompted locals to start calling the waterway "Cancer Alley". Refineries lit up at night looked like, and still do resemble, some sort of alien city rising against the sky.

Suburban development during the war years increased solely to house the incoming number of *new* New Orleanians, and middle-class neighborhoods such as Metairie, Gentilly, and the lakeside area continued to be built up. Deluxe hotels and motels with swimming pools were built along Airline and Gentilly highways to accommodate visiting business people. The Mississippi River Bridge (also called the "Crescent City Connection") was a modern new span to connect New Orleans with Algiers Point and the West Bank, where more suburbs were expanding, such as Gretna, Westwego and Harahan.

Despite the expansion—and even despite a marked rise in crime in the late 1950s with rumored "Mob" activity headed by Carlos "Little Man" Marcello, notorious for his alleged involvement in the assassination of President John F. Kennedy—New Orleans continued to go by, and live by, its sobriquet: it was the "Big Easy". Though musicologists acknowledge that there was a Big Easy Hall in the early jazz years, the popularization of the name is attributed by *Gambit*'s local history columnist "Blake Pontchartrain" (a pseudonym) to locally well-known society diva Betty Guillaud. For a column she wrote in the old *States-Item* Guillaud sometimes compared the laid-back style of New Orleans, "the Big Easy", to the tension and anxiety of living in New York City, the "Big Apple". The name stuck; and it even became the title for a big box-office draw, the detective film starring Dennis Quaid and Ellen Barkin. Locals recognized its many inaccuracies. One *faux pas*, depicting New Orleanians as inner-city Cajuns calling one another *Cha (chère)*, is snickered about even today.

Good Neighbors

> *What's the loneliest bayou?*
> *By-you self.*

Making up the "real New Orleans" is its very real jigsaw of neighborhoods, from which arises the close connections between people. Mid-City, like Uptown, is really made up of a number of sectors that can easily be explored on foot. There is Bayou St. John: its comfortable suburban homes are reflected in the placid canal (bordering the original waterway that led Bienville and his men from Lake Pontchartrain to the site of the present Vieux Carré); there is Gert Town, predominantly working-class African-American, following Carrollton Avenue to City Park; Esplanade Ridge, following along Esplanade Avenue to the bayou (Downtown's St. Charles Avenue).

The prettiest "neighborhood" in Mid-City is the park that anchors it, where Esplanade reaches the juncture of the Bayou St. John. City Park's 1,500 acres were dedicated to New Orleans by philanthropist John McDonogh. Amid the park's collection of live oaks (this green space actually contains four 18-hole golf courses and 36 illuminated tennis courts) the New Orleans Museum of Art sits quietly and coolly beneath masses of vegetation (1 Collins Diboll Circle). It houses a $200-million permanent collection spanning centuries of French, American, African and Asian treasures, such as masterpieces by one-time resident Edgar Degas. NOMA is considered the Gulf South's premier art museum. Its newest counterpart is the Sydney & Walda Besthoff Sculpture Garden, showcasing the largest collection of modern sculpture in the South. City Park's Botanical Gardens bursts with plantings, including some from Thomas Jefferson's Monticello home as well as from Napoleon Bonaparte and Josephine's estate.

Yet the favorite Mid-City neighborhood venue must be Mid-City Lanes Rock 'n' Bowl (4133 S. Carrollton Ave.), where locals go to drink, dance, bowl and have fun accompanied by live music seven nights a week. This is ground zero for zydeco music, and, when the time draws near, it is known as the palace where the reigning "King of Zydeco" is crowned (after the passing of legendary accordionist Clifton Chenier, Boozoo Chavis became contemporary monarch). There are even neighborhood spots that no longer exist, but live on in some people's memories. This could be said of a little juke in the "'hood", known as Dorothy's Medallion at 3232 Orleans Ave. just off Bayou St. John, a popular club during the 1970s and 1980s. It was just a "joint," one in a network of many frequented mostly by African-Americans. It was located on the ground floor of a raised cottage with a simple brick façade and iron gate. Club-goers could enter under the stairs, evoking the feeling of being in a Parisian *boîte*. Dorothy was the black lady with blonde wig and large sunglasses who ran the place—in what seemed like pitch-darkness. And Charlie, her son, dressed respectfully in three-piece suits with wide ties and trademark large gold medallion, helped out. Says music writer "Spike" Perkins, Charlie's build, plus his quiet demeanor, "brought to mind a cross between a mob torpedo and a preacher." The crowd was mostly middle-aged African-Americans and, as Perkins notes, "a few young local white hipsters and music junkies, and an occasional European tourist who had heard about the place from local musicians out on tour." By the 1970s and 1980s, the younger black audiences of New Orleans preferred disco music to this sort of quirky, bohemian music scene.

Music at the Medallion began at 1 a.m. Irma Thomas ("It's Rainin'") and Lee Dorsey ("Working in the Coal Mine"), were still singing their 1950s and 1960s hits. It was practically a permanent gig for vocalist Johnny Adams, as well as Adams' protégé Walter "Wolfman" Washington. The story goes that Walter Lastie, so fired by his performances at Dorothy's, sometimes even stayed out and would hit the street the following morning. And that is how he died one Sunday morning, playing "When the Saints Go Marching In" in front of St. Louis Cathedral.

Dorothy's Medallion also featured scantily clad dancers in cages as part of the entertainment. "Mona" performed with a live snake. "Big Linda", according to Perkins was one of the club's shake-dancers, who "took the idea of plus-size beauty, weighing approximately 350 pounds, wearing a string bikini, to the limit… But big as she was, Linda had beautiful skin, and one got the sense that she could fulfill some foreign prince's wildest fantasies, if only one should happen into Dorothy's."

The club closed permanently in 1987 when Dorothy's husband "Pops" died. Son Charlie tried to open a Dorothy's Medallion in the Tremé at Esplanade Avenue and North Robertson Street, but it failed, and now, unfortunately, Charlie is deceased.

Keepers of the Flame

Many people who move to this city are music lovers. But especially passionate are the "jazzophiles" who are keen to inhabit the setting that became, as ethnographer Alan Lomax once called it, "the cradle of jazz". New Orleans has been the home for the growth of many kinds of musical oeuvres—"trad" and contemporary jazz, R&B, blues, gospel, hip-hop, Cajun, country, zydeco and more. There were pioneers, and now there are preservers. They have become a part of what might best be called the local cult of jazz worship. It is legend, but legend that can be "authenticated" any morning listening to the Morning Jazz Show on WWOZ FM Radio, or checked out during October, which is Jazz Awareness Month in New Orleans, or "dug up" in the treasure troves of any number of research venues in town: libraries public and private, archives, personal collections, posters, photographs, fine art, and recordings.

However, it is the people themselves who are the greatest repositories of music memories, and some take it as a personal calling to contribute to the continuation, interpretation and constant reinvention of New Orleans jazz. An original force for preservation is in the French Quarter—Alan and Sandra Jaffe's Preservation Hall on St. Peter Street, which kept the seminal sound alive even when it was not fashionable to do so. Here, in a simple room without the trappings of a nightclub atmosphere, visitors come to sit jammed together for a low cover charge and hear some of the "great men" (for there are far fewer women) of jazz. Preservation Hall was a showcase for such talents as "Papa" Celestin, George Lewis, the Humphrey brothers, "Kid" Thomas Valentine, "Papa" French and many others.

In keeping its jazz history alive, New Orleans has become an acutely nostalgic place, looking back, and looking in upon itself. It seems as if by living with past, present and future generations of music families, one feels a part of this evolution. Drummer Johnny

Vidacovich, a native New Orleanian interviewed in *Offbeat's* Q&A "Backtalk" in March 2002, conjectures:

> *There's a morphic subconsiousness here about music. It's part of the genetic history. There's so many musicians around here. I don't mean popular, fancy, well-known, rich ones—I mean natural musicians. Children being born, children coming up—it's morphic resonance. It's in the air. There's nothing sterile about music here. We're isolated down here. Nothing gets out, too, because we're below sea-level and it's hard to get that shit through a bunch of thick-ass water...*

Luckily, the forces for music preservation in New Orleans are legion: there are the teachers (Ellis Marsalis at University of New Orleans, father of the internationally renowned set of sons including Wynton and Brandford), or a singer/songwriter/impresario such as Harold Batiste or Allen Toussaint; there are the photographers, archivists and documentary makers such as Jules Cahn, Michael P. Smith, Phillip Gould or Pat Jolly, providing a "window to a hidden city" in their works, says author Jason Berry. There are institutions at work for the conservation of Louisiana's indigenous sounds, stewarding musicians and their accomplishments, such as the Louisiana Jazz Federation, the Louisiana Music Commission, and WWOZ radio station, an "organ" of the New Orleans Jazz & Heritage Foundation which oversees Jazz Fest; the media, such as *Offbeat* magazine, *Beat Street* magazine, and *Gambit*; the annual Big Easy Entertainment Awards; stores such as Louisiana Music Factory; and even musicians' unions.

The New Orleans Jazz & Heritage Foundation, the agency overseeing the New Orleans Jazz & Heritage Festival, contributes in large degree to the wellbeing of roots music in New Orleans and Louisiana, with outreach in many forms: SEED, a micro-loan small business development program, the New Orleans Musicians' Clinic for free healthcare, its "Jazz Journey Series" and "Tom Dent Congo Square Series" of lectures, a Foundation Archive, the Heritage School of Music, community grants, neighborhood street festivals, and a community outreach ticket program enabling everyone to get into the Fest. When WWOZ does its annual fund-raiser it promotes the "Brass Pass", which is given to people who have made sizable donations. Being able to bypass the entrance line at Jazz Fest for the entire eight days, as well as spending time and eating with the WWOZ staffers, rewards that generosity.

Now people are realizing that New Orleans, which has always had a few small-scale recording companies, should develop its music industry and compete nationally, or even regionally (for instance, with neighboring country music capital Memphis, Tennessee) as a dependable and ongoing source of great music. At the same time, the industry is charged with the responsibility of protecting musicians from what they have suffered in the past: most importantly poverty, as well as such abuses as copyright infringement or out-and-out piracy of lesser-known artist by "big names" and more influential studios. Brandford Marsalis has launched a new label, Marsalis Music, to add to those such as Rounder, Orleans Records, and Allen Toussaint's Seasaint and NYNO (New York-New Orleans). According to Marsalis: "The consolidation of the record industry into major conglomerates has turned the business into a mega-hit pop music machine with a very short-term focus. Artists who want to be musicians, not marketing creations, have very few places to record anymore. We formed Marsalis Music to provide a real alternative."

In the early 1990s, Dr. John (born Mac Rebennack), who has been one of the outspoken ambassadors for New Orleans music, "came back" with his Grammy-winning tribute album (traditional blues album category), *Goin' Back to New Orleans*, featuring some of the city's best talent, with R&B superstars the Neville Brothers, now-departed jazz raconteur Danny Barker, trumpeter Al Hirt, Pete Fountain and Alvin "Red" Tyler. *Goin' Back to New Orleans* is packed with such diverse New Orleans anthems as Jelly Roll Morton's "Milneburg Joys", "Litanie des Saintes", blending *fin-de-siècle* classicism with Afro-Caribbean poly-rhythms, the Mardi Gras Indian anthem "Indian Red", and a title tune that is an affectionate hymn to the city, performed by 1950s R&B artist Joe Liggins and the Honeydrippers (first performed by the Creole Kings of New Orleans on Specialty Records).

Dr. John confesses that his love for the indigenous sound is not something cerebral, but physical instead. Those who have grown up with New Orleans music know that the deeply moving experience of attending a jazz funeral, for instance, is not likely to be re-created in any other city: "It's just about feelin'. It's just about spirit. I mean, some band is playin'—a brass band is playin' for a funeral. It's rainin'. The instruments is out of tune. Everythin' is raggedy. Sometimes it feels so good to me I don't know. It don't matter about all these musical 'isms' that we was so brainwashed to. It just *feels* right." Ask Dr. John what makes the New Orleans sound—and the city itself—so distinct, and he will gladly tell you in his own musician's lexicon that it is the people and the almost two centuries of ethnic interchange between Americans, Europeans, Latinos, West Indians and Africans: "They all add their own piece," he says, "it's like, if someone came here playin' polka music from Poland, I think if they got here they'd have a little second-line feelin' to their polka." Like many others who prize this musical inheritance, Dr. John strongly believes that there is no room for commercial compromise. The sound is unique, and can only be found in Louisiana. He says: "There's a lot of people that's interested in tryin' to 'make it' in a *different* way, but what we do don't have to turn into something that it ain't. This is south Louisiana, we got our own little mud and bayou water floatin' in our veins... and you got to appreciate that what we do is something that's homegrown to just right here."

"Fest" Fever

I was here and had my soul renewed."
—Marcia, Jazz Fest 1997 (graffito on a bathroom wall)

"I'm not sure, but I'm almost positive, that all music came from New Orleans."
—Ernie K-Doe, New Orleans eccentric, fondly remembered among many other hits for the R&B classic "Mother-in-Law"

Since "Jazz Fest," or simply "Fest" as natives and pilgrims call the New Orleans Jazz & Heritage Festival, is always on the last weekend of April and the first of May, there is little hesitation about when one should get in the Jazz Fest "spirit". When that time comes, people in neighborhoods all over New Orleans clip their Festival music lineup from the newspaper, consult the NOJHF official website, or buy the program—and then they start to puzzle over how to be in five different places at one time to catch all the music. There is even a Jazz Fest mindset and style: citizens hook Jazz Fest flags to fly from their eaves and flutter Jazz Fest banners from the front of houses, they have festival parties, and, since it is usually the start of the really hot weather, wear very little clothing. Specially crafted flag posts, which are customized and held aloft once at the Fair Grounds, act as markers so that friends can find friends. They have become a form of folk art.

Jazz Fest animates the musical life of the city that is written about, told, depicted, and played throughout the year. Now, it suddenly comes to life in the spring, and crowds of people join in. They come from around the world—as many as a half million visitors—to hear music presented on more than a dozen stages, which hold as many as 1,500 musicians, for audiences 90,000-strong every day, for ten days over two long weekends. The open-air Louisiana Heritage Fair, as it is called, is staged over the Fair Grounds Race Course Mid-City, where hundreds of Louisiana dishes are sampled from booths, and where music (traditional and contemporary jazz, blues, R&B, ragtime, gospel, Cajun, zydeco, Afro-Caribbean, folk, Latin, rock, rap, country, bluegrass "and everything in between") is staged either under the sky or beneath giant canvas tents. Folklife demonstrations (oral histories and demonstrations on subjects as diverse as "How to Skin an Alligator") are generally hosted indoors.

Performances are designed to "preserve and perpetuate the area's rich music and cultural heritage" by reflecting the cultures of Louisiana, particularly highlighting the African-American contribution to this massive "root system". In a history of the festival, produced for the NOJHF, Jason Berry claims:

> *No other ongoing enterprise (not even Mardi Gras, which stretches back well over a century) has done as much to extol the African identity that marks New Orleans more deeply than any other American city... the fair's focus on heritage—a gathering of Cajuns and Indians, white rockers and gospel shouters, plus all that food—has enlarged the definition of heritage, the idea of culture, in these environs. Even before the word multiculturalism gained its currency, the human topography here reflected an almost mythical diversity: for there are many meanings to the word Creole—the deep French and Italian imprint; the mingling of Caribbean and southern folkways; and then the Creoles of color; that distinctive caste that produced so many of the seminal jazz musicians.*

Local musicians can count on their annual appearance at Jazz Fest as a source not only of eager listeners, promotion (for their new recordings and projects) and pay, but also for the tradition that it has become. Old-timers receive affirmation and new musicians get a start. The Festival, says Berry, is "a catalyst—rejuvenating careers of older musicians, showcasing younger artists, pushing a [onetime] tiny club circuit to grow, driving the expansion of a local recording and entertainment industry and, for ten days each year, focusing international attention on the city and culture of New Orleans. Beyond that, the festival holds up a mirror to the spiritual essence of this beautiful and exotic state."

One year, for instance, *Newsweek* reporter Annalyn Swan chanced to hit upon a performance by one of those local hidden music treasures—a woman who probably would never "rise" to the attention of a national music industry. The reporter wrote:

This year, 84-year-old Grandma Dixie Davis was an unexpected delight. A seraphic-looking lady who learned ragtime as a teenager by listening to W.C. Handy perform on riverboats, she proved to be a stride piano player who could bang it out with the best of them.

Every Jazz Fest experience is different: it could be a musical high, an adventure on stage that lasts only for just the length of the performance, an exchange with the people around you in the crowd (individually or collectively), or it could be the setting for a real drama like the story told by Dr. Michael White, clarinetist, traditional New Orleans jazz scholar, and impresario:

I started going to the Jazzfest when I was in college at Xavier. The only day I missed at school for about three years in a row, was to attend the Jazzfest. It sparked my interest in New Orleans jazz and gave me a chance to hear many of the great, great musicians—some that I would eventually perform with. One of my great memories is the first time I played the Fest with Wynton Marsalis. Miles Davis was performing too. We had just recorded an album which had not been released called "Majesty of the Blues." It was a very risky and experimental thing for Wynton to perform traditional New Orleans jazz—and this was the first time we had done any of the songs before a live audience. It was the year the tent blew down on the river. The New Orleans style stuff was a big surprise and the audience went wild. Two of the musicians on the album and who performed with us, Teddy Riley and Danny Barker, are now deceased. We did two songs from the album "Death of Jazz" and "Happy Feet Blues"— songs that Wynton had written. The people screamed so much my ears hurt, my ears went numb. And you know there was always this competitive thing between Wynton and Miles and people were so uplifted by our performance that when Miles came to the stage, a lot of them started to leave. Miles was pretty mad about that. But people are still talking about it.

"Fest" Future
The New Orleans Jazz & Heritage Festival has grown from a quaint folk festival into a giant undertaking produced by hundreds of people. In the fall of 1969, George Wein, creator of the Newport Jazz Festival,

met with several civic leaders to establish a jazz festival in New Orleans. The organizers wanted to follow the example of Newport in showcasing music, crafts and folk art. The so-called "British Invasion" taking over the pop charts—the birth of rock 'n' roll—had for many supplanted interest in local music. As Jason Berry points out, "Economically it was a fallow time for rhythm and blues too. Although 'Tell It Like It Is' had done well, [for the tremendously successful Neville Brother] Aaron Neville ended up working as a longshoreman. In the 1950s, records by R&B artists poured out of the city's single, small studio. Through Cosimo Matassa's recording doors moved Fats Domino, Shirley and Lee, Roy Brown, Professor Longhair, Irma Thomas, Allen Toussaint, to name but a few…" By the 1970s, however, the local scene was considered pretty provincial.

Wein needed organizers, and he identified them with the help of Dick Allen, then-curator of the William Ransom Hogan Jazz Archive at Tulane University. Wein drew his charges from the school body; they were to become local heroes. Allison Miner (a onetime staffer at the archive) would give tirelessly to the Festival, and, sadly, she passed away at a very young age of cancer. Quint Davis, an ethnomusicology student who had a passion for the Mardi Gras Indians (at that time unknown to most white New Orleanians), was a Jazz Fest pioneer, and today is its major domo. Miner and Davis were a team—young, highly enthusiastic, full of energy, and full of love for the music and culture of Louisiana. They invested thousands of hours seeking out musicians in remote villages and country churches, lining them up for their appearances at Jazz Fest.

The eclectic programming would present everything from Dixieland to pop music, and music from around the world. The first Jazz Fest was held outside Municipal Auditorium on a piece of grass that flanked Rampart Street, an area that in another century was part of historic Congo Square. There was absolutely no press coverage, and fewer than 200 people attended. In fact, some people actually wandered over to a public school across the way in Tremé and tried to give the tickets away. Wein was interviewed early on in the *Vieux Carré Courier*, saying that there was not enough appeal to the young African-American audience, and this was something organizers intended to fix quickly. Each year, the lineup of acts grew more diverse, and artists from around the world were invited to participate. Bai Konte, a kora player from

Gambia, was the first African artist to play, and that very year Duke Ellington joined in a second line snaking through the Fair Grounds. Organizers did whatever it took to attract people to the Fest. Bo Dollis, Big Chief of the Wild Magnolias, remembers:

> You know in the early days, the Jazzfest was one full week and there weren't too many people coming during the week. So we used to get the Mardi Gras Indians together, at least 15 or 20 of us, and we'd start from around Canal and Rampart and parade through the Quarter. We'd be singing the Indian chants and we'd go down Bourbon Street to Buster Holmes' Red Bean place and people used to join in and second line. We'd have tambourines and bass drums and cowbells and we'd be in our costumes and we'd wind up back at the Auditorium, and people would follow us and just buy tickets. We used to do it once or twice a day—it was a bunch of fun.

Organizers began to draw some big-name artists, such as Stevie Wonder or Louis Jordan, for evening concerts, and this effort kept ticket prices down. But at the same time, the festival was exposing younger and bigger audiences to traditional jazz and other roots music. It would not be until 1972 that it would move to the Fair Grounds. By that year it was attended by nearly 50,000 people.

Just as important as the perpetuation of New Orleans' music, Jazz Fest takes very seriously its role as a presenter of folkways that vary regionally across the state. Of course, in *foodways*, the serving of Louisiana Creole, Cajun and soul cuisines it gives the local flavor in a cornucopia of vividly seasoned dishes: fried frogs legs, pecan catfish Meunière, crawfish étouffée (a tomato stew), barbecued turkey wings, seafood cornbread, alligator sauce *piquante,* shrimp *macque choux* (shrimp with corn and rice), pheasant-quail-and-*andouille* gumbo, crawfish cakes, oyster-artichoke soup, crawfish *boudin* (sausage), alligator pie, shrimp and turkey tasso pasta, catfish Mardi Gras, *cochon de lait* (shredded pork cooked until tender in milk), jambalaya, red beans 'n' rice, stuffed peppers, "hot and sloppy" roast beef po-boy sandwiches, sweets such as pralines, sweet potato pie, peach cobbler, strawberry shortcake, coconut pie, sweet potato bread, pecan-praline cookies, Louisiana blueberry sorbet, and bread pudding with praline sauce.

Folklife demonstrations draw on oral tradition and craft presentations in booths or at small stages in one area of the fairgrounds. There it may be possible to see an alligator skinned, or to hear an elderly New Orleans woman speak of the "old days", when, due to hard times, if a bit of salt meat could not be procured for the making of a traditional Monday-night red beans 'n' rice, a few banana leaves would be thrown into the pot. "That's the jazz," says the octogenarian, perhaps summing up best the Crescent City's spirit of improvisation that has helped its people make the best of life's difficulties.

Gospel Testifies

"Instead of preachin' The Message, you're singin' The Message."
—Joe "Cool" Davis, New Orleans gospel singer and promoter

The tradition of gospel music in the South has its roots in the "ring-shout," a form of inspirational expression (hands clapping with rhythms, cries in crescendo imploring the Lord) sung by enslaved Africans. Ring-shouts were also the progenitor of the beautiful but sorrowful songs that we call "spirituals". Spirituals, indeed the church itself, are the source of so many other genres of black music. They are the "place" where sorrow is expressed and solace received.

While is seems hard to imagine it today, there was a time when spiritual and other gospel music had to be slowly introduced to audiences. This barrier was broken, as Jason Berry points out, by such groups as the Nashville-based Fisk Jubilee Singers, who spread the idea that spirituals were really just conventional religious songs. But as Samuel A. Floyd Jr. notes in *The Power of Black Music*, the focus of the spiritual was always "slavery and the possibility of freedom".

In the home town of gospel great Mahalia Jackson, who began her career singing gospel with a hit ("Move on Up a Little Higher") that sold eight million copies on the old Apollo label, the heartfelt sound of gospel is still influenced by the communal origins of the ring-shout, and its harmonic beauty is very much owing to the influence of traditional spirituals. Large portions of the community that would otherwise not hear the devotional music of African-American churches hear it at Jazz Fest: "the Gospel Tent introduced thousands of white people to the driving rhythms and soaring vocals of black choirs," says Berry.

Then, of course, there are always church "plates". The four words, "make him a plate," are, for the spiritually hungry, the happiest words, as one visiting writer found out:

> *I paid my respects to the ladies of the Second Mount Triumph Missionary Baptist Church, whose potato salad turned out to be even better than their chicken, and not wanting to provoke any schism among the Baptists, I had also sampled the barbecued chicken being sold by the ladies of the Second True Love Baptist Church. I also felt I should try both versions of jambalaya being offered, and both versions of red beans and rice. Fair is fair. Three hours after we had arrived at the Fair Ground I was settled under a tree, almost too full to finish my second hot sausage po' boy.*

Once fed, spiritually and physically, it may confidently be said that, more than any other genre of music exuding from doorways of the Crescent City, gospel best characterizes its deep spiritual life and spirit. It is where most of the musicians receive their earliest training. It is possible to hear great music every week—every Sunday in church. And it is still possible, despite his international obligations and busy schedule, to walk up the steps of Our Lady of Guadalupe on Christmas Eve and chance to hear burly Aaron Neville singing "Ave Maria". His trademark *falsetto* makes trills and modulations in the dark, which makes the darkness light.

Indian Red

In addition to Jazz Fest, what many New Orleanians associate most with the Bayou St. John and Mid-City neighborhood are "the Indians". For here on Super Sunday, on the banks of the bayou, the Indians gather for sets of primal drumming before the big march—a "pow-wow" if you will. They march from the bayou in the colorful tribes, and the people in the neighborhood hear them coming. Playing congas, bongos, tambourines and cans, driving out the rhythm, clapping hands, the Indians come in bright splashes of color and swags of plumes sculling the air. They chant and sing out strange syllables from dawn to dusk on their biggest day—Carnival. There are the big chief and his queen; second, third and trail chiefs; flag boy and spy boy; and children, faces framed with braids. Though weighed down by heavy beaded suits

that take a year to fashion and that can weigh upward of 100 to 150 pounds, they walk tall through some of New Orleans' oldest and poorest neighborhoods, Crescent City citizens "masking Indian."

The Mardi Gras Indians, or "Black Indians", are a splendid sight on Mardi Gras, wielding flashlights on St. Joseph's Day Eve, marching through neighborhoods on "Super Sunday" following St. Joseph's Day, or practicing at Dryades Street outside the H&R Bar or another well-known Indian enclave, The Glass House. They are a performance highlight at Jazz Fest time, usually on the Congo Square stage, or maybe leading a parade through the Fair Grounds.

African-Americans' veneration of Native American culture is a spiritual tradition that dates as far back as the early eighteenth century. This cross-cultural legacy is found only in New Orleans and is the result of a compassionate bond between peoples, born of shared suffering and subjugation. The tradition can also be traced logically to the actual mingling of the two cultures through intermarriage. As many who study Mardi Gras Indians point out, the tradition represents an enduring link to the spirit worship of African slaves, who came to Louisiana via the Caribbean. And the practice represents a joyous, artistic response to the oppression African-Americans have endured. The Mardi Gras Indian cult in New Orleans employs every metaphor of Native American culture, whether authentic or ersatz—from tribes and tribal "titles" to chants, dances, braided hair and popular approximation of "Indian lingo", i.e. "Me big chief."

The first recorded instance of a black man masking Indian in New Orleans dates to the early 1880s in the city's Seventh Ward, when Becate Batiste founded the Creole Wild West "tribe". Today, there are as many as fifteen tribes (one-time rival gangs) whose turf roughly divides Uptown (the Wild Magnolias, Golden Eagles, Creole Wild West, Gold Star Hunters) and Downtown (Yellow Pocahontas, White Eagles, Seminoles, Guardians of the Flame).

The Mardi Gras Indians' complex music and chanting rituals have had a profound effect on New Orleans music, particularly with the pervasive call-and-response style of singing (whose origin is gospel music born of old-time spirituals) and primitive rhythms. The Indians have also served as inspiration for many songwriters and singers, as heard in early R&B hits such as Dave Bartholomew's hit "Carnival Day" (1949), Professor Longhair's "Mardi Gras in New Orleans"

(1949) and "Tipitina" (1953), "Sugar Boy" Crawford's "Jockamo" (1954), and Huey "Piano" Smith's "Don't You Know Yockamo" (1958).

The Wild Magnolias' hit 45-rpm recording of "Handa Wanda" produced by Willie T. (Wilson Turbinton) in 1971 began a number of collaborations that teamed Mardi Gras Indians with other New Orleans musicians, and ushered the Indians onto the concert stage. Such famous recordings as "Wild Tchoupitoulas", which featured the Indians, the Neville Brothers, the funky Meters, and Allen Toussaint, are close to New Orleanians' hearts. In 1998, the Wild Magnolias celebrated three decades together with a commemorative album release on Aim Records called *Thirty Years and Still Wild*. It was a musical event that featured Big Chief Emile "Bo" Dollis, one of the most visible and legendary Indians, Chief Monk Boudreaux of the White Eagles, some of the Magnolias' longtime fans in the music industry (Robbie Robertson, Bruce Hornsby), talented "homeboys" and "homegirls" (the Nevilles, Willie and Earl Turbinton, Davell Crawford, Marva Wright, Rockin' Dopsie Jr.), and special songs written and arranged especially for the occasion by such Crescent City collaborators as Toussaint, Dr. John and Wardell Querzergue. Other tribes that have recorded include the Golden Eagles, the Wild Tchoupitoulas, Bayou Renegades, the Flaming Arrows and Guardians of the Flame.

Listeners can buy recordings that feature the Indians, but there is nothing that approximates the experience of actually seeing this indigenous Louisiana folklife on the street, the ritual repeated generation upon generation. Musicologist-author John Sinclair believes that it is important to see them in their own milieu—down in the street:

> ...emerging in all their magnificent finery like eye-popping apparitions out of the doorways of dilapidated inner-city houses and project apartments to strut and swagger down the middle of the beat-up streets where they struggle just like everyone else to make a living and somehow survive the crime, the violence, joblessness and grinding poverty of their neighborhoods... That's the real-life context of the Wild Indians at Mardi Gras, and year after year they manage to rise above the morass of their daily lives to make themselves over as creatures of immense beauty.

Michael P. Smith, perhaps the best-known photojournalist of New Orleans music and culture (really an artist in his own right, and a friend to the subjects he has immortalized with his images), brought musicologist-ethnographer Alan Lomax (collaborator on the Jelly Roll Morton autobiography and author of a musical memoir called *The Land Where the Blues Began*) to some Mardi Gras Indian practices. Said Smith: "I showed him a little of the New Orleans underground." As Smith further explains, "Lomax was reaffirming things I already felt, respecting different ways to express one's intent, one's spirit. Mardi Gras Indians… have deep respect for Native American culture and express that in rites of the church and all kinds of ways." This deep New Orleans culture is soon to be treated in a new film entitled *Under the Surface.*

Under the Surface is a project that has been in pre-production for more than two years. The documentary will capture the multitude of musical genres that are naturally expressed in New Orleans, particularly during Carnival, through the chants and practices of the Mardi Gras Indians, in the undying brass band tradition, and in street music of all kinds. The title's watery, subliminal imagery reveals refers to the fact that the city is below the level of the Gulf of Mexico—below sea level—but also reaffirms that most tourists and non-residents must immerse themselves in New Orleans' cultural life if they want to return to the surface with something more than just the most superficial image of the city and its music.

Chapter Seven

CANAL STREET, CENTRAL BUSINESS DISTRICT, AND THE WAREHOUSE DISTRICT: BOOMS AND BUSTS IN THE "BIG UNEASY"

"New Orleans has always been, and still is, a city of canals, making it properly symbolic that the city's main street should be so named. Against Venice's 28 miles of canals, New Orleans in 1945 counted 108 miles! Neither does this include the city's Grand Canal—the Mississippi river."
—John Churchill Chase

On a weekday in New Orleans, white-collar workers are lined up in their cars in traffic-jammed parades as though it were Mardi Gras, coming in over the Highrise, stop-and-go, hoping to get to work on time. And on Canal Street blue-collar workers are making it their job to get wherever they need to go just a bit late. This is not really the frenetic movement of "New South" Atlanta—a capital city that is home to more than a score of Fortune 500 companies—and this is certainly not the melee of northern urban centers.

In Atlanta it is all luxury import cars, not a late-model car to be seen. In New Orleans, on the other hand, you can see the most fantastic jalopies barely held together with rubber bands and coat hangers. Often there is no license plate, just a cardboard sign dangling for the rear-approaching NOPD officer: "Tag applied for" in hand-scrawled lettering.

Canal Street, a thoroughfare devoid of any architectural charm, is New Orleans' central business artery, a transportation corridor, and it is an access route to the city's many small enclaves, neighborhoods and outlying districts. This is where working class meets leisure class, where

white collar mingles with blue, and where teenagers with dog collars and pierced tongues loll about. Back in "the old days" that people still frequently recall—during the 1940s and 1950s—Canal Street was the place to go for ladies of leisure. Mary Lou Widmer in her book *New Orleans in the Forties* remembers the boulevard this way:

> *The shops… were beautiful and their window displays breathtaking. When ladies met for a shopping expedition, they always met under the clock at Homezes', that is the way it was said. Canal Street theatres were like palaces. Trips to Canal Street still meant dressing up with hats and gloves… A good place to have lunch on a shopping day was at Homezes' restaurant, sitting at the lunch counter. They made wonderful seafood gumbo…*

Today, the bus named Desire lumbers along spewing exhaust, not nearly as romantic as Tennessee Williams' streetcar of the same name, which is now put, for historic not mechanical purposes, up on blocks. The lurching Freret bus (Freret Street, named after the nineteenth-century cotton industrialist/mayor William Freret) is taking on its load of passengers headed Uptown. The faithful cross themselves each time a shrine or church is passed. And the 150-year-old army-green streetcar, the oldest continuously operating trolley in the United States, is making its capacious swing from Canal onto St. Charles, clanging out the berth to pedestrians as it starts out on its oblong route loop Uptown.

A bit of progress is being made: a Canal Street line has recently been laid, a "retro" sort of conveyance, says *The Times-Picayune*, which can help people to "catch up on a little history and a lot of local color along the line." But bemoaning New Orleans' usual idiosyncratic way of doing things, the same reporter writes disapprovingly about the line's debut: "Well, you won't be overburdened with useful information in New Orleans. At this writing, there are no maps or schedules whatsoever… You'll know it's almost time for a car to arrive when you see the headlight coming down the track; it's that simple. They seem to arrive every 20 minutes or so." The air-conditioned ride, from the lower French Quarter near Esplanade Avenue to the "Cemeteries" end of the line at Canal Street and City Park Avenue, takes about an hour. Into the "CBD" (Central Business District) heads the trolley, windows opened wide to allow riders some fresh air.

Canal Street is the northernmost boundary of a roughly rectangular segment of the city bordered by the river and the World Trade Center/Ernest N. Morial Convention Center to the east, La Salle Street and Louisiana Superdome to the west, and the I-10 overpass as a southern demarcation. Canal is actually more than a street; it is a cultural division that has always cleaved Downtown from Uptown, which historically meant Creoles from Americans, and francophones from anglophones. From the riverfront to Rampart Street, not a single street name remains the same as it crosses Canal—and neither do address numbers cross it. Canal Street and the river are the "T" points for geographic orientation. Establishments going Uptown or Downtown all begin with number 100 at Canal. Ironically, there was never a canal put into Canal Street. An Act of Congress dated 3 March 1807 decreed that land should be used for the purpose, but in 1807 the Orleans Navigation Company went bankrupt and lost its charter to engineer the task. The street stayed its 171 feet wide—*sans* canal.

Dreams of "SoHo South"
Whether by trolley or on foot, the first impression is that New Orleans' inner city is not very large, nor very "inner" even. It is a lasting impression. The sidewalks are never crowded, even on a weekday at noon. The skyline does not bristle with skyscrapers. And once the 9 to 5 day is done, there are few souls walking these windy corridors, save perhaps the praline man selling his wares from the old-style box, leather strop around his neck, standing at his post outside the telephone company. Flanking Poydras Street are the main office megaplexes, including those of international oil and mineral exploration giant Freeport-MacMorRan, one of the bigger employers. In the CBD, one is compelled toward the river for cultural value—not the values of Mammon—and thus toward the most vitally growing region in the life of the arts in New Orleans.

There has been so much happening here in recent years that one can almost sense the new ideas brewing, growing more robust, like the coffee beans that used to be stored in the warehouses before roasting. A recent civic pride campaign for the City of New Orleans pre-Katrina showed the city's blue-and-white ceramic sidewalk tiles with the names of actual streets writ large: Liberty, Commerce, and Desire. Underneath the mayor exhorts in print: "Break Free From Apathy and Cynicism…

If You Want It Bad Enough It Will Happen… This City Has What It Takes To Be An Economic Power… Embrace Diversity And We'll All Be Rewarded." The biggest tiles spell out the words "I Care." Increasingly, as a result of interaction between people in the visual, culinary and performing arts—through the mouthpiece of cultural tourism—the city will continue to be reinvented. Culture, with a capital C is growing ever more accessible, popular, and multifaceted.

The waterfront sector, between the CBD and Uptown, has become known as "the Warehouse District", and it is where, prior to the 1984 Louisiana World Exposition (a financial flop), blighted brownstones, row houses and cavernous turn-of-the-century warehouses were sandblasted into shape for museums, art galleries, auction houses, bistros, law offices, design firms. Some were turned into condominiums for those who like "loft living". Not far from here, before the advent of the steamboat, flatboats unloaded at a harbor off Tchoupitoulas Street. It was an area of great disrepute called "The Swamp", lined with brothels and gambling dens. (It is the flatboat men who are credited with originating the term *dix* for the ten-dollar denomination used pre-Civil War, thus helping to coin the term "Dixie".) In passing centuries, The Swamp has dried up and disappeared, to be replaced by trendy Julia Street, a main thoroughfare for galleries and museums, including the trendsetting Contemporary Arts Center, which weathered the very first years of change.

Indeed, New Orleans had needed a change. Sleeping in Euro-Caribbean lassitude, during the 1960s and 1970s the city languished. Administrators, politicians and citizens themselves had become overly reliant on revenues from the offshore oil and gas industries and, of course, the New Orleans mainstay: tourism. Locals complained vehemently about corrupt politicians who were on the take in good times and even in bad, and the city was lampooned on late-night television: "Now for the news from New Orleans"—(the man on the street reporting digs in his trench coat pocket and takes out a big red plastic clown's nose, then attaches it to his). During the mid-1990s, the city was rocked (or regaled, as the case may be, since many New Orleanians tend to find political hi-jinks amusing) when a one-time Ku Klux Klan member (David Duke) ran a gubernatorial race with Edwin Edwards, who had been charged with racketeering. The former won 600,000 votes; the latter eventually won the office of governor. A bumper sticker slogan from this era read: "Vote for the crook. It's important." (David Duke was imprisoned at Big Springs, Texas, Federal Correctional Institute, and former governor Edwin Edwards did federal time, charged in 2001 with being involved in extorting payoffs from businessmen seeking riverboat casino licenses.)

Then came the bust. During the 1980s domestic oil crisis, the Big Easy struggled with an economic downturn that would ultimately have a worse impact on the standard of living than the Great Depression. In the period between 1981 and 1987 alone, employment fell by eight percent. This was devastating for everyone, but particularly for the 35 percent of half a million people in New Orleans who already lived in grinding poverty and squalid government housing projects named after their geographical location, such as "Desire" (ironically), "Calliope", and "the Magnolia".

On top of all that, despite the fact New Orleans was held up as the ultimate travel destination and convention meeting spot in the country, it seemed that the city's infrastructure, on which travel and tourism relied, was simply worn ragged. The roads were a mess. The Union Terminal, for instance—end of the line for The Crescent from the East Coast, The City of New Orleans from Chicago, and the Sunset Limited from Los Angeles—was in need of a facelift, being, as it was, outdated and dangerous. Louis Armstrong New Orleans International was also in need of a serious overhaul and expansion. Even City Hall would ultimately receive an inside-out makeover under the administration of young Mayor Marc Morial in the waning years of the 1990s. This included customer service training for the many civic employees who did not seem to have a clue how to deal with the public, and an overhaul of the police force by then-police chief Richard Pennington, currently the chief of police in Atlanta. New Orleans correctional facilities were notoriously inadequate and the police force viewed as brutal or, at best, incompetent. An overflow of inmates at the jail on Broad Avenue was handled with makeshift shelters, which became known as "Tent City". It did not help much; citizens feared they could be thrown in jail, and no one would know they were there for weeks at a time. What could prevent the Crescent City from becoming a Euro-Caribbean Third World city in the Computer-Age US—a good-time town with a banana-boat economy?

River Gamblers

Many New Orleanians put their money on big-time gaming as a chance to recoup economic losses. In 1995 a consortium of players—ten local investors known as the Jazzville group, Harrah's Casinos (with major operations in Atlantic City, New Jersey, and Nevada) and developer Christopher Hemmeter of Hawaii—hoped to draw a full house to what they would create as "the world's largest casino". *The Times-Picayune* started to call the seemingly inevitable event "Blackjack on the Bayou". Just a dice-toss down the Mississippi River from the French Quarter, the new casino cost as much as $260 million to build and it spread over five acres of prime downtown real estate (about the size of two football fields). The look of the complex borrowed heavily from Monte Carlo's 1861 casino, employing a dome, towers and finials in combination with classical elements such as an elegant column-flanked main portico. In addition, the architects wanted to echo the spirit of the New Orleans 1885 Cotton Exposition and Chicago's 1893 World's Columbia Exposition for the buildings' design.

Architectural authenticity aside, it was not hard to underestimate the importance of a new gambling house to the city of New Orleans. The Mississippi Gulf Coast had already realized a big profit ($30 million in the first nine months of operation) from its flotilla of gambling boats alone. The developers in New Orleans claimed that a single land-based casino could pull in as much as $780 million in annual revenues. Yet many also worried about a possible increase in crime and the effect that it might have on New Orleans' reputation as a first-rate conventioneers' city if it were to turn to gambling as a seedy source of revenue. Many noted, in turn, that the Big Easy could hardly stand on virtue when it came to gaming. In Storyville, at the turn of the century, there were more than 200 bordellos, barrelhouses and juke joints where games of poker, faro, three-card Monte, craps, escarte and brag were played. As the famous guitar standard every neophyte plays always warns: "There is a house in New Orleans/They call the Rising Sun/It's been the ruin of many a poor boy/And, Lord, I know I'm one." The Louisiana Lottery was urging locals to "Get Lucky Every Night." They needed little prompting—what with fast games of "skin" or blackjack from the tailgates of trucks one of the favorite sports in town.

Crime statistics and personal safety were of concern, but so, too, was the health of the historic districts. City conservationists had been particularly vigilant since the summer of 1992, when 44 interested developers responded to the call for bids from prospective casino builders. Their concerns centered on three historic neighborhoods—the Vieux Carré, the Warehouse District, and Algiers Point—which would suffer should the rush to develop ignore residential needs or alter the historic flavor of these areas. Already, five mid-nineteenth-century commercial buildings in the Warehouse District had been saved from the wrecker's ball; they sat on land that at one turn during negotiations was to be annexed for parking space. According to Lary Hesdorffer of the Historic District Landmarks Commission: "[Large-scale casino development] is different from the 1984 World's Fair, which we recognized as a temporary event. Any inconveniences resulting from not having our i's dotted and our t's crossed we would have survived. But history is vital to New Orleans' economic health. We depend on it."

After lengthy negotiations and a long stall, Harrah's paid the state $125 million for the right to build Louisiana's exclusive land-based casino on the site of an old exhibition hall at the foot of Canal Street where it meets the river. The goal: to bring in an estimated one million new tourists, thousands of jobs, and millions of tax dollars each year. Harrah's New Orleans Casino (512 South Peters St.) is now doing big business. Still, it does so with a nod to the arts community in sculptures by New Orleans masters George Dureau and Robert Warrens on the outside pediments. A recent "experiment" by a *Times-Picayune* reporter determined that it only takes a half-hour to lose $100 at the blackjack table, and that future winnings would require frequent trips to the ATM banking machine (an acronym, standing for "automatic trouble machine").

MetroVisionaries and New Orleans Ingenuities

> *"One morning a policeman found a dead horse lying in the street at the corner of Common and Tchoupitoulas streets. He took out his notebook to record the incident. After several futile efforts to spell Tchoupitoulas he grabbed the horse by the tail and pulled it a block down the street. 'Dead horse in the street at the corner of Common and Magazine,' he wrote."*
>
> —Old New Orleans anecdote

It is the steadfastness, the sheer imagination, of this enterprising policeman of lore and yore that is quintessentially New Orleanian: the will necessary to make a difficult job turn out alright, even if it means taking some effort and creative thinking. The world's largest convention center and the sprawling Riverwalk shopping and entertainment complex, in the CBD, at the riverfront, are legacies to New Orleans left behind following the re-creation of the city for the Louisiana World Exposition. They are now indispensable to the health of the local economy. Organizations such as the Historic District Landmarks Commission and the Preservation Resource Center continue to do their duty in maintaining the integrity of the past. And it has also been advantageous for the city to have a future facilitator, such as the Downtown Development District, or "DDD", to keep the Downtown attractive and drawing as many visitors and residents into the heart of the city as possible. Louisiana SuperDome, completed in 1975, also helps keep New Orleans afloat financially with some cultural events, such as the Essence Festival, which attracts thousands of African-Americans into town for big-name entertainers and partying. There are sporting events, too, such as the "Final Four" college basketball tournament, and of course that annual spectacle of American excess—National Football League's Superbowl.

One creative economic initiative was MetroVision, effectively the development arm of the New Orleans Regional Chamber. Its goal was to provide a sort of stewardship of local economic fate and it called for the diversification of New Orleans' industries, compensating for the fact that the city has a very small manufacturing base. The idea was to put the emphasis on fields already doing well, such as the healthcare-related business of medical supplies, as well as to give attention to industries that could complement and support resources-based industry (i.e. shrimp processing and packing).

MetroVision proposed that New Orleans was, and continues to be, a good place to do business due to its strategic geographical position between the three Americas—South, Central and North. It encouraged such efforts as Inter-Cambio 2000, a trade conference aimed at identifying buyers for New Orleans goods in places such as Mexico. The Port weighed in, spending $250 million on construction to accommodate containerization. New Orleans business also took advantage of lower tariffs on the heels of the North American Free

Trade Agreement (NAFTA) and shifted emphasis away from Pacific Rim markets to emerging ones in Latin America, the Caribbean and South Africa.

Arts District

In the sphere of the arts, many organizations and countless individuals can be credited with rallying to help keep New Orleans a place where people would want to reside, despite what happens economically or politically: the New Orleans Ballet Association, the New Orleans Symphony Orchestra, the New Orleans Opera among them. There is a vital cultural arts scene, and through cultural tourism New Orleans has positioned itself to show people that it is about far more than cliché riverboats, plantations, magnolias, and mint juleps.

The New Orleans Arts Council has been one such organization instrumental in bringing the creative works of regional artists to a wider public. Its various programs geared to keeping the visual arts alive and well are locally well known. The Arts Council has, in fact, an innovative project which is soon to further transform a major sector of the Warehouse District at Lee Circle, where Carondelet Street and Howard Avenue intersect. Formerly a dingy traffic loop—and still the place where the streetcar ends its Uptown route moving Downtown along Carondelet—the circle in times past supported a decrepit location of the local YMCA as well as a number of flophouses, barrooms, and greasy spoons that were the hangouts of transients and itinerant laborers.

(In a way it is a tragedy for the Downtown to lose its seedy little "joints"; they are the last vestige of a bygone era: the twentieth century. Tennessee Williams actually spent his first night in the city in a rooming house on St. Charles Avenue near the Lee Circle "Y". The disappearance of "Mom & Pop shops" and other sole proprietorships is the down side of mainstream North America's fascination with franchises and multi-location "theme" establishments. It is a trend that has taken over even in New Orleans, a city that values continuity of the past, and it seems there is little that can be done about it. Modestly cloaked Confederate General Robert E. Lee stands stock-still in the very center of Lee Circle, watching over these generations of changes, always vigilant and keeping his eye on the North. Perched atop his periscopic ionic column, surrounded by a bull's eye of flowers and grass, he looks to see if New Orleans is re-inventing itself but keeping faithful to its roots and identity. It seems he is happy with what he sees.)

The Art Council's new facility is called "Louisiana ArtWorks." It is a 90,000-square-foot cultural creation space/exhibition place that comprises four large shared-studio workshops. Each has state-of-the-art equipment, dedicated, respectively, to the genres of ceramics, metal, glass, and printmaking. Artists may rent time in these studios or one of the fifty other individual studios. The more than 250,000 annual visitors expected at ArtWorks will be able to take an interactive stroll or even mount a catwalk strung over the workspaces in order to observe artists. An exhibit gallery, where people can "make and take" pieces they create, is part of the overall creative experience.

ArtWorks joins the much-celebrated, recent debut of the Ogden Museum of Southern Art, University of New Orleans, which is situated close to another new venue, the National D-Day Museum around the corner on Magazine Street. It will definitely contribute to this vibrant new growth of cultural facilities in the Warehouse District. The Ogden, an affiliate of the Smithsonian Institution, contains works of artists working in all media from 15 southern states and from the District of Columbia, thus making it the largest assemblage of southern art in the world. Its raison d'être, as expressed by novelist-historian Shelby Foote, is to present "the inner heritage of the South through the media of artists from the eighteenth century to the present"—what another writer described as the South's "regional hagiography". The South has produced such great artists as Jasper Johns and Robert Rauschenberg, but has not really been put on the national map of American art; the Ogden may change things. The prime mover of this collection is Roger H. Ogden, a lawyer and developer, who with the State of Louisiana provided $7 million toward the museum's $11-million cost, and who donated his own 1,200-piece collection. The new Stephen Goldring Hall houses the museum's twentieth- and twenty-first-century works. It traces the history of the South from its agrarian roots through the First World War, the Depression, and the Second World War, and from the Civil Rights movement to the present day, depicting the evolution of Old South through to New.

This is a wonderful counterpart to what the Contemporary Art Center (CAC) at 900 Camp St. is doing as a showcase of contemporary works. Founded in the mid-1970s, it has been the Warehouse Arts

District's hub from the start. It is the place where leading-edge painting, photography, sculpture, theater, dance and music was given a dynamic forum in one of the first warehouses (at the cost of $5 million for restoration), rescued from total obscurity as it sat in the shadows of riverfront docks and storehouses. Creative programming by the CAC's curators has included a welcome balance to the more traditional venues—like the New Orleans Museum of Art in City Park—with such different happenings as a round-the-clock "Insomniac-athon", performances devoted to American "Beat" poets and their chief chronicler William Burroughs (Beat spirit still infuses much of New Orleans' art scene and bohemian ethos), as well as a Drum Summit that celebrated the city's reputation as a cradle for rhythm-makers, with seasoned artist Earl Palmer, young lions such as Shannon Powell, and the ghost of at least one who has "passed" on—James Black, whose work was recently nationally celebrated at Lincoln Center for the Arts in New York City during its year of "The Drum".

In years past, it was to Robert Tannen, a founder of the CAC, that many looked for intellectual and artistic leadership. This quirky "visual-poet" arrived on the New Orleans art scene from his native New York in the late 1960s. For more than thirty years he has brought his intense vision to bear on such urban issues as housing, transportation, land use, waste management, water conservation, agriculture and the city's economic and cultural development. As an architect/artist-cum-urban planner, Tannen has expanded the "outsider" role of an artist and, according to former *Times-Picayune* art critic Roger Green, "bade New Orleanians to consider aspects of their environment, and to become more alive by responding to them intellectually and/or emotionally."

Tannen has called his pieces "models" for their impromptu combination, in sculptural assemblage, of what most people would think unrelated or unlikely materials: inner tubes, bricks, plastic bags, timbers, taxidermied fish... Surprised viewers have been asked to invoke both imagination and thought as a way to comprehend Tannen's conceptual one-liners, which to date have included installations (a village of tiny shotgun-house structures nestled by the heft of the Louisiana Superdome); shows (such as the 1978 "Sportsman's Paradise" in a New Orleans antique shop ritualizing sports fishing images); and timely sculptures ("Redfish Cadillac", created for the 1984 Louisiana World Exposition, which consisted of a pink 1955 Cadillac convertible suspended from a structural column in the Louisiana pavilion). Though Tannen is not currently represented by any one gallery, passers-by can see a good selection of his work in the sculpture garden surrounding his home in the Marigny, at 2326 Esplanade Ave.

The CAC has also championed the works of a school of artists that has been associated with New Orleans and south Louisiana. These artists are known as "visionary imagists". In brightly colored, finely crafted, patterned creations, the works of Andrew Bascle, Jacqueline Bishop, Charles Blank, Douglas Bourgeois, George Febres, Ann Hornback and Dona Lief transcend the conventional boundaries of regionalism to raise issues of national and universal concern. Though their paintings, constructions and sculpture are endowed with a dream-world symbolism that emanates the region's peculiar psychology and semi-tropical environment, the artists' work also resonates with additional levels of meaning. Both consciously and subconsciously, such timely issues as environmental pollution, sexual domination and the decay of civilization's myths are incorporated into these multimedia meditations.

Every year, the CAC is home to the largest art happenings in the city: White Linen Night (in the blinding heat of August) and Art for Art's Sake in October. These events begin with gallery hopping and street parties, and wind down with an after-party in the CAC's sleek glass-wood-and-steel-beam open atrium. As many as 4,000 people turn out during these festivities, walking the streets to see and be seen. Either one of these nights is an opportunity to visit some of the galleries in the area, each with its own specialty, such as the Arthur Roger Gallery, showing contemporary paintings, sculpture, photography by national and international artists, d.o.c.s., a studio/gallery of contemporary art with works by emerging artists from throughout the US, LeMieux Galleries, exhibiting Louisiana and "Third Coast" contemporary artists, and Stella Jones Gallery, featuring African-American, Caribbean and contemporary African fine art and photography.

The CAC does not charge admission on Thursdays. A recent *New York Times* article sums up the prevailing ethos of "art for everyone": "Like the food revolution, the design revolution is built on the lovely paradox that what is special should be available for everyone's enjoyment and that good taste can at last shed its residue of invidious social differences." The CAC, along with all the other galleries, centers and museums that have lined the streets of the Warehouse District undoubtedly comprise the starkest example of urban transition and the largest concentration of art houses in the South.

Chef Super Stars

> *"I first came down here believing that eating in New Orleans meant dinner at Antoine's. What I discovered dining at Bayona, Stella!, Restaurant August, Peristyle and the Bistro at the Maison de Ville will surprise no one who has been keeping up with the local restaurant scene: this remains a fabulous eating town, right up there with New York and San Francisco and maybe superior to either because of the distinctive nature of the indigenous cuisine."*
> —Frederick Turner, *The New York Times*

New Orleans' entrepreneurial spirit is alive in the kitchen and in the Downtown corridor of new restaurants in the CBD and Warehouse District. That is because Creole cuisine is conducive to reinvention, a stalwart blend of ethnic influences upon which to improvise, swinging with the spice of cayenne seasoning (every chef with his own "special" blend), and favoring flavorful one-pot dishes coaxed from the best of local ingredients, which are handy and cost-saving at the same time. New Orleans' cuisine is hailed around the world, but that can be attributed to the charisma of the chef super-stars who promote it, not only in their signature restaurants, cookbooks, spin-off products, and cooking schools, but by the very force of their personalities. This may all perhaps be traced back to Paul Prudhomme's popularization of Cajun cuisine.

One such culinary superstar who has transformed the landscape of the CBD and beyond is Emeril Lagasse. His empire spans the television networks, from the prime-time cable show "Emeril Live", broadcast to an audience of more than 25 million, to his hosting of "Good Morning America" on ABC. His aphorisms have become legendary, for when he cooks, he peppers his methodology with shouts of "Kick it up a notch!" (as he adds an ingredient) or "Bam!" (when he adds even more). With attitude akin to that of a rock star, Lagasse looks like a movie star with dark hair and winning smile. He has a faithful following of besotted females, children (who go for his high-energy cooking) and men, who prove to be the largest demographic category in his ratings. Although he is actually a native of Fall River, Massachusetts, he is often called "Mr. New Orleans" or even "The Ragin' Cajun" when he travels, probably because he got his start at Commander's Palace on the heels of Paul Prudhomme, who himself went on to achieve chef superstardom. The name, which he unashamedly pronounces "La-GASS-ee," is actually of French-Canadian origin.

Lagasse's namesake restaurant is located in the Warehouse District at 800 Tchoupitoulas St., where the menu of "*nouvelle* Creole" cuisine is ever in a state of reinvention. He has purchased and reopened the old-line Delmonico's, at 1300 St. Charles Ave., with a massive $4-million renovation and a twenty-first-century update to the Creole classic menu. In the past few years, other locations have been added to his *bouquet garni* of dining rooms, including NOLA in the French Quarter, Emeril's New Orleans Fish House in the MGM Grand Hotel in Las Vegas, and Emeril's of Orlando at Universal Studios (where Steven Spielberg is creative director), as well as locations in Miami Beach and Atlanta.

A Louisiana-inspired cookbook Lagasse has written, co-authored by Marcelle Bienvenue (of St. Martinville, Louisiana), is called *Louisiana: Every Day Is a Party*. The book covers festivals around the state and enumerates all indigenous foods, beverages and comestibles. Lagasse writes: "I go into the country, to the various state fairs, and show how we celebrate them with food. We'll do St. Patty's Day, a great tailgate party, the Christmas festival in Nachitoches; it will be a blast." Asked what perfection in an indigenous Louisiana meal would be, Lagasse dreams up not only his, but any diner's meal to relish:

> *I would have a lot of good friends over at Emeril's, and fix Louisiana chanterelles with pasta and truffles as the first course, then a Creole tomato salad with maytag blue cheese and, next, a double-cut pork chop with a tamarind glaze on mashed potatoes, with fresh beans and crispy bacon. And then I would definitely consume as much banana cream pie [Emeril's signature dessert: 1,548 calories in one piece] as I could get in my mouth. I would also enjoy several great bottles of wine from Burgundy. To end it all, a great cigar and a glass of brandy… I'd munch on that cigar until God came down and took me off the planet.*

Adding spice to the New Orleans "foodie" scene is Susan Spicer, a doyenne of Crescent City cuisine. In the past few years this young woman has been a culinary force whose exceptionally popular restaurant Bayona, at 430 Dauphine St. in the French Quarter (voted Number One in *Gourmet* magazine's "Readers' Choice Poll of America's Top Tables"), has led to openings of still more upscale venues in the Downtown sector, including Cobalt (333 St. Charles) and Herbsaint (701 St. Charles Ave.). She began her career as apprentice to Chef Daniel Bonnot in the deluxe Louis XVI Restaurant in 1979 and went on to a four-month training with Chef Roland Durand at the Hotel Sofitel in Paris. In the late 1980s she opened the Bistro at Maison de Ville and finally in 1990 Bayona with Regina Keever. She has blazed a gastronomic trail with her creations such as cream of roasted garlic soup, eggplant caviar and tapenade, grilled shrimp with black bean cake and coriander sauce, and grilled venison.

Spicer could never be faulted for not using her imagination. During the Tennessee Williams Festival recently, Cobalt (along with scores of other restaurants, bistros and diners around town) served up a special, fashionable Creole-meets-the-new millennium dish to celebrate one of the playwright's best-known works: "*Camino Real* lobster enchiladas with red chile rice and aged jack-charred scallion crema". This joined other such imaginative "New World" pairings as "Crawfish and fontina 'jammed' pork tenderloin with dirty rice pilaf and an apple-bourbon reduction". During the festivities for the bicentennial of the Louisiana Purchase, the Louisiana Office of Tourism, in conjunction with a cruise company, hired Spicer for a seven-night sailing to the Caribbean. She adapted several Louisiana Purchase Bicentennial dishes from her restaurant menus and served them on board: pecan-crusted fish with orange-thyme meunière, chicken and andouille gumbo, fried oyster and spinach salad, Herbsaint crème brûlée, shrimp and green chile grits (the cornmeal baby food only a Southerner could love) with tasso cream sauce, a tuna *muffuletta* sandwich, goat cheese crouton with mushrooms in Madeira cream... It was a wonder the boat remained afloat.

Southern Repertory and a Cat That's Black
The Downtown and CBD is a district of theatres: two of the lovely grand concert halls are located downtown, the Saenger Performing Arts

Center on Canal Street, as well as The Orpheum, just a few blocks into the CBD at 129 University Place. Southern Repertory (365 Canal Place), located in the Canal Place center, across from Harrah's Casino, has offered creative programming since the mid-1980s. And at 715 St. Charles Ave., not far from where the homeless used to gather at Lee Circle Y, Le Chat Noir is staging a comeback of the cabaret milieu, hosting drama, jazz, readings, performance art and other live entertainment. Le Chat Noir's prime mover, Barbara Motley, says that she took her inspiration from the 1881 Paris progenitor by the same name, a place "reserved solely for artists... a trendy salon of sorts, a place where the creative minds of Paris would gather to critique social issues of the day, while drinking away the night." The intimate rooms of Le Chat Noir also include the Bar Noir (staffed by hip bartenders) where actors, writers, directors and musicians are, indeed, often in the audience. In keeping with the retro Paris ambience there is tango on Tuesdays.

The cabaret lives up to its promise of delivering thought-provoking theatrical fare with productions that take aim at local manners, such as a musical revue called *The Black and White Blues*, which looks at New Orleans' obsession with food, restaurants and celebrity chefs from a waiter's perspective. "Politics with a Punch" is a round-table discussion of Louisiana politics led by local pundits, media commentators, and comedians, while a local production called *Galatoire's Monologues* uncovered the story surrounding the firing of one of that fine-dining institution's favorite long-time servers.

Nouvelle New Orleans

In his famous essay called "New Orleans *Mon Amour*", Walker Percy considered the fate of the city to which he, as many others, felt drawn. There is something that New Orleans is doing right, according to Percy, which has helped the city and its people endure poverty, contagion, war, racial strife, and climatic extremes. It would, indeed, be ironic if this battered old place were to somehow, finally, rise above the others:

> *If the American city does not go to hell in the next few years, it will not be Berkeley or New Haven, or Santa Fe or La Jolla. But New Orleans might. Just as New Orleans hit upon jazz, the only unique American contribution to art, and hit upon it almost by accident and*

despite of itself, it could also hit upon a way out of the hell which has overtaken the American city...

Lewis Lawson in *Literary New Orleans and the Modern World* characterizes New Orleans' ethos as a "mutually moderating effect of two major behavioral patterns, an Anglo-Saxon seriousness of purpose and a Mediterranean mellowness". Perhaps this is what explains the fact that, though the CBD is being gentrified, it is still on a scale that is human and inviting. The old buildings are still there, and they have put on a change of clothes. New Orleanians are coming out to their evening performances, to dinner dates, concerts and gallery openings— albeit arriving just a little late.

Chapter Eight
THE LAKEFRONT: CROSSING THE CAUSEWAY

From New Orleans' earliest colonial history to the present century, travelers and residents have escaped the pull of the city's inward spiral by passage outward to lakeshore towns settled along the north and south shores of Pontchartrain's flat, sparkling expanse. New Orleans planters had good reason to seek the open air and water. In order to survive, they had to escape the outbreaks of mosquito-borne yellow fever that historians acknowledge were the nemesis of New Orleanians in the eighteenth and nineteenth centuries.

The lake, approximately 40 miles long and 24 miles wide, is unusually shallow (only 16 feet at its deepest) and appears unimpeded by any islands or inlets as far as the eye can see. Interestingly, Pontchartrain is a mixture of fresh and salt water, by virtue of the fact that it is attached to Lake Borgne, to the east, by a strait called the Rigolets (Borgne is actually a bay leading inland from the Gulf of Mexico). In 1956, when the single-span, 24-mile Lake Pontchartrain Causeway was built to cross the lake's surface and join the north and south shores, development of St. Tammany Parish, hitherto resort country, could begin in earnest. The second span, opened to the public 13 years later, on 10 May 1969, made the Causeway the longest concrete bridge in the world. Commuting to New Orleans proper from the leafy subdivisions of "the North Shore"—for it is was now an identifiable region—became *de rigueur*. Today, more than 30,000 cars cross the causeway daily, and then head back to suburbia at 5 pm.

Milneburg Joy
Work aside, it was here, on Pontchartrain, the body of water Iberville named for France's colonial naval minister, that generations of New Orleanians found refreshing breezes to blow away the work day and humidity; recreation in the form of boating, swimming, fishing,

crabbing—every other sort of summertime fun—was *lagniappe*, something extra. When a New Orleanian hears the jazz standard "Milneburg Joys" (written by "Jelly Roll" Morton and still played today by young lions of jazz), he or she is likely to conjure a grainy black-and-white photograph of the docks at Milneburg. It was a resort town at the northernmost terminus of the Pontchartrain Railway (no longer extant), on the lake end of Elysian Fields leading out of Faubourg Marigny. New Orleanians boarded a train they called "Smokin' Mary" to reach the destination. We can imagine, perhaps, the venerable Washington or Arch hotels of long ago, where jazz musicians from New Orleans gigged, playing syncopated melodies that drifted out over the water, to which well-dressed couples danced through the night.

In 1839 the town of Milneburg consisted of just a few houses, the Washington and Arch hotels, a grocery, two barrooms, and a bakery. The Milneberg pier was constructed a little later with the "camps" (cabin-like structures built along the docks) that were rented for parties, and they were where jazz flourished.

Another historic subdivision resulting from the railroad was a place called Darcantel. It was located halfway between the river and the lake at the intersection of Elysian Fields and Gentilly Road. As historian John Churchill Chase points out, all that remains of this suburb, now totally enveloped by the city on all sides, are a few street names: "a real Creole jambalaya is this list: Carnot was a French general, Stephen Girard, a French-American financier, Pelopidas a general of ancient Thebes, Caton a Roman book of ethics, and Foy a neighbor…"

Well acquainted with the citizens' need to escape the tribulations of the city for the summer pastimes the lake afforded, William Faulkner set his second novel, an arch novel of manners called *Mosquitoes* (published in New York in 1927 upon recommendation by Lillian Hellman), on the expansive waters of Pontchartrain in the doldrums. Once Faulkner has his affected *nouveaux riches* characters aboard the yacht, while cruising between New Orleans and Mandeville, they are unable to debark—and he unmercifully skewers their pretensions. The characters he sets up for scrutiny are the very same "types" National Book Award-winning author Walker Percy indicates he sought to avoid by moving to the suburbs of Covington, on the north shore of the lake:

The occupational hazard of the writer in New Orleans is a variety of the French flu, which might also be called the Vieux Carré syndrome. One is apt to turn fey, potter about a patio, and write feuilletons and vignettes or catty romans à clef, a pleasant enough life but for me too seductive.

Milneburg, too, was the destination, some decades earlier, of William Makepeace Thackeray, who traveled across Louisiana overland in the 1850s, via Pontchartrain Railway, to arrive at the Washington Hotel's dining room in time for supper. In a published advertisement, the hotel had boasted of its venison dinners served "on arrival of the quarter past 3 o'clock car", as well as its bouillabaisse. Thackeray ordered the latter and praised it exuberantly in his journal, saying, "At that comfortable tavern on Pontchartrain we had a bouillabaisse than which a better was never eaten at Marseilles, and not the least headache in the morning, I give you my word; on the contrary, you only wake with a sweet refreshing thirst for claret and water." Milneburg's joys as a resort town were ended, unfortunately, when squat wartime housing was developed there.

The lake's heyday includes summertime memories of Pontchartrain Beach and Lincoln Beach. Many Crescent City citizens have childhood memories of the former resort areas. Pontchartrain Park had an enormous midway with rides and concessions, a public beach with pristine white sand much like a seashore, honky-tonk vaudeville shows, and beauty pageants for men and women alike ("Mr. New Orleans" elected annually). Pontchartrain Park closed in 1983 when it not only faced competition from such big-name entertainment venues such as nearby Walt Disney World, but also the local Louisiana World Exposition threatened its existence.

Lincoln Beach, which lay several miles to the west of Pontchartrain Beach "[was] for Negroes," states Oliver Evans perfunctorily in his 1950s-era history *New Orleans*. He goes on to describe the subtleties of race relations at the time: "Integration has recently been extended to the public transportation system but not to the swimming pools or to the beaches." (In other words, next-to-naked white people did not want to swim with next-to-naked black people.)

Integration, which effectively closed the beach in 1963-4, may have been granted, but perhaps not entirely desired by the recipients.

This is what one contemporary New Orleans poet, Arthur Pfister, implies in his hometown homage called "My Name Is New Orleans," a sort of dramatic monologue with the city itself as speaker:

I am memory
I am legacy
I am history
I am the Deep South (the Dee-ee-ee-eep South)
I am "2-4-6-8 We don't wanta in-te-grate"
I am Pontchartrain Beach and Lincoln Beach

Now, in an age of mega-stores, chain-operated restaurants, and franchised amusement, New Orleanians seek out a new lakefront super-theme park, Six Flags New Orleans, on Lake Forest Boulevard, for summertime thrills and spills. The rides may still be good fun, but what else is there to recommend it?

Saving the Lake

"An Amazing Number of Shrimp
1 Louisiana's ranking as US shrimp producer
10 Number of feet on a shrimp
40 Percentage of US shrimp produced by Louisiana
80 Calories in one serving of shrimp
120 Galatoire's daily shrimp serving in pounds
9,722 Number of Louisianians working in the shrimp industry
70,058 Amazon.com sales rank of The Bubba Gump Shrimp Co. Cookbook
500,000 Eggs produced by a single shrimp each spawning
121,000,000 Louisiana's annual shrimp harvest in pounds"

Just beyond the Orleans Parish line along Lake Pontchartrain is the community of Metairie. It is the part of suburban Jefferson Parish that closely flanks New Orleans and contains many affluent neighborhoods, shops, restaurants and boutiques. Metairie was once the site of a Colapissa Indian village built on the banks of the bayou that formed a trail to New Orleans. This ridge was a prosperous farming region, thus named *metairie* by settlers, a French term for a "farm worked on shares".

Today tradition-bound Old Metairie runs along the original trail, which is now called Metairie Road. It is a short trip to the lakefront from here.

The small fishing community of Bucktown is below Lake Pontchartrain's levee and adjacent to the Orleans Parish lakefront. Places like Fitzgerald's Seafood Restaurant, Deanie's Seafood, and SidMar's of Bucktown have long catered to New Orleanians who, of course, have come to take for granted the abundance of such catches as soft-shelled crab, shrimp, and oysters brought in daily from the Gulf via Lake Pontchartrain.

Shrimp, as well as oysters, are harvested, then sold and cooked in abundance in this city, and they may be sampled in true New Orleans style as the main ingredient of a "po' boy" sandwich. Although every coastal region of the world boasts shrimp, Louisiana is the largest shrimp-producing state in the US, fishing out as many as 121 million pounds from Gulf estuaries annually. Oysters see a bountiful harvest, too. Louisiana is America's largest oyster producer, supplying approximately 70 percent of the nation's bivalves (1.6 million sacks, or 10.22 million pounds of oyster meat).

In recent years, there has been much concern over the state of Lake Pontchartrain, which had grown to be very polluted. Work in reclamation has had to be done by such groups as the membership-based Lake Pontchartrain Basin Foundation to clean and conserve the large body of water and bring it back to its former glory. Back to the Beach is an annual festival in August dedicated to this cause, a lakefront party re-creating past summers' diversions and raising the funds necessary to carry out the foundation's valuable work. This has included the Pontchartrain Artificial Reef Working Group's bid to create barriers offsetting the loss of Louisiana wetlands, the so-called Comprehensive Management Plan, dealing with pollution caused by sewage and urban or agricultural runoffs, the Big Branch Marsh Refuge for protection of St. Tammany Parish's wildlife, and modifications to the Mississippi River Gulf Outlet, preventing erosion caused by ocean-going vessels.

Now the lake and parishes surrounding Orleans Parish have become far more than resort destinations. Increasing numbers of people choose to live outside Greater New Orleans, with the lake and its communities in St. Tammany Parish such as Covington (population 8,500), across the causeway and directly north, Abita Springs (population 2,000), to the east of Covington, and Mandeville (population 11,000), also directly north of the causeway, supporting more than weekend diversion. The North Shore has become a desirable place for New Orleanians to raise their families, and many people who were formerly sworn to enjoying the cultural life of the city have chosen to leave New Orleans' inner-city headaches (i.e., crime, poverty, poor schools, traffic, pollution, tourist crowds) in favor of supplying themselves and their children with the benefits of the suburbs.

In the past two decades, the population of St. Tammany has increased tremendously, to nearly 200,000 in 2002 from just over 50,000 in 1970, with a 74 percent growth spurt in 1980 alone. The median family income has also increased, to a high of $56,000 in 2000 from around $20,000 in 1980. Clearly, mostly those who can afford it are choosing the suburban experience over the urban. According to the national census, inner-city New Orleans' Caucasian population in 2000 was just 28 percent.

Across the Causeway

But are there intelligent signs of cultural life in the suburban universe? Walker Percy, a one-time resident of Covington, thought so. He once said that,

> *It's very easy to sneer at mass society or the American suburb, but there are many beauties there. So, this business of alienation can certainly be overdone. But, of course, alienation, after all, is nothing more or less than a very ancient, orthodox Christian doctrine. Man is alienated by the nature of his being here. He is here as a stranger and as a pilgrim, which is the way alienation is conceived in my books.*

Percy arrived in New Orleans in his twenties circa 1946, to woo Mary Bernice Townsend. When she accepted, they were married in a local Baptist church, spent their honeymoon at an uncle's summer home in Sewanee, Tennessee, and returned to New Orleans in 1947 to stay at the Pontchartrain Hotel on St. Charles Avenue. They then moved to a house on Calhoun Street in Gentilly, a community in New Orleans East bordering the lake. There, Percy worked on first draft of his first novel *The Moviegoer* (1961), which placed the existential struggles of his hero, Binx Bolling, in the contemporary wasteland— Gentilly, characterized by one critic as a "pleasant nonplace". Ultimately, Percy and his family would settle in Covington, which had, as the writer called it, a "certain persisting non-malevolence".

The tone of this remark calls to mind the same timbre of John Kennedy Toole's sardonic character Ignatius Reilly when he comments that New Orleans has a "certain apathy and stagnation" that he admits finding "inoffensive". It is, in fact, Percy whom we have to thank for rescuing Toole's manuscript of *A Confederacy of Dunces* from possible anonymity. One day, the older author received Toole's mother in his office at Loyola University while he was teaching a creative writing workshop there. Her son had shortly before committed suicide, and, after his death, his mother, Thelma, dedicated herself to finding a house that would publish the languishing manuscript posthumously. It was this book-in-progress that had made Percy "gape, grin, laugh out loud, shaking [his] head in wonderment" when he read it. Though Toole had had his story rejected again and again, then sent though the editorial wringer with one large publishing house (in large part the reason for his depression), the novel was eventually published by Louisiana State University Press in 1980. It is the rollicking story well loved by New Orleanians for its hilarious descriptions of life in the Crescent City.

So, perhaps when considering the suburban experience, we should take seriously the opinion of Toole's protagonist, Reilly, whose characteristic invective affirms that of many an avowed city slicker: "Outside of the city limits, the heart of darkness, the true wasteland begins." There are, it is true, some cultural diversions across the lake, notably the season at Columbia Theatre for the Performing Arts at Southeastern Louisiana University in Hammond, the Abita Springs re-creation of the old-time Piney Woods Opry (popular Town Hall presentation of country, bluegrass, and traditional southern gospel), and such events as the Three Rivers Art Festival in Covington. Otherwise, for unrepentant urbanites there still exists only the improbable prospect of contagion as a reasonable cause to cross the Causeway.

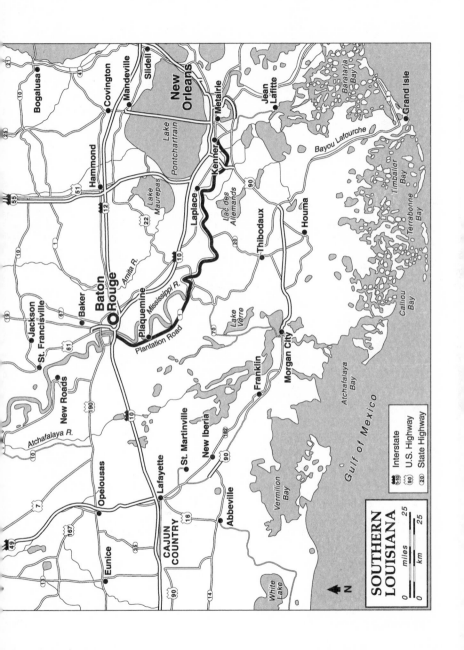

SOUTHERN
LOUISIANA

| Interstate |
| U.S. Highway |
| State Highway |

0 miles 25
0 km 25

Chapter Nine
CAJUN COUNTRY: LAFAYETTE AND BEYOND

"It had been a wonderful ride up from New Orleans, past towns and villages with strange French names, such as Paradis and Des Allemandes, at first following the dangerous winding road that runs beside the levee, then later the meandering Bayou Black and finally the Bayou Teche. It was early January and hot as blazes though a few days previously, coming into New Orleans, the cold was so mean and penetrating that our teeth were chattering. New Iberia is in the very heart of the Acadian country, just a few miles from St. Martinsville [sic] where the memories of Evangeline color the atmosphere."

—Henry Miller

It may come as a surprise to many people, including the modern American rambler-writer Henry Miller, that Henry Wadsworth Longfellow, author of the epic poem *Evangeline* (1847), never visited Louisiana, not even for a brief sojourn. While Longfellow's masterpiece is certainly a moving portrait of star-crossed Acadian lovers, it is entirely a work of the imagination. Written in traditional hexameter verse, the poem is based on the eighteenth-century expulsion of Acadians from Canada and tells the tale of two lovers separated by this event. Still, it is unlikely that the very real suffering of families and loved ones separated through this exile can ever really be fully documented or expressed.

Miller cannot be blamed for strongly associating Acadiana, and in particular St. Martinville, with Evangeline and Gabriel, the lovers whose historical counterparts planned to meet at the "Evangeline Oak" in the center of town. Longfellow's poetic rendering of Acadiana and the mythology he created were wildly popular in his day. For decades afterwards, schoolchildren were made to declaim the lines from

Longfellow's verse, thus duly honoring the great poet's work. It is safe to say that for a long time this mournful poem was most outsiders' one cultural touchstone for an exotic Southern people—Louisiana's Cajuns—about whom very little was known.

Moving to the twentieth century, when Opelousas, Louisiana-born Chef Paul Prudhomme and his popularization of cayenne-powered "blackened" cuisine provoked a fad-like interest in all things Cajun in the US (actually, Cajun cuisine is not customarily highly seasoned), people all over the world wanted to know who the Cajuns were. And just what was their relationship to the Acadians? they wondered. Interest came on the heels of a 1970s cultural awakening regarding ethnicities nationwide (i.e., the books, recordings, journals and documentaries of Alan Lomax, who in the 1930s crisscrossed the southern states, exploring roots music and other cultural expressions). Tabasco sauce, manufactured by McIlhenny Co. on Avery Island since shortly after the Civil War, was one thing everyone could associate with south Louisiana. But people wanted to know more, and they wanted to know about the folk still speaking French "down on the bayous".

Up until the 1920s and 1930s, not many visitors had traveled to Acadiana. That is probably because many had conceived of Cajuns as clannish and reclusive, or, worse, had been deterred by unflattering stereotypes the media had often heaped upon the people who inhabited the 22 parishes traditionally called "Cajun Country". The apotheosis of this treatment is the 1948 documentary produced by Robert J. Flaherty entitled *Louisiana Story*, which depicted a boy and his dog traveling about the swamps in a *pirogue* (a hand-hewn boat of cypress wood) and suggested that Cajuns were hardly better than barefoot, swamp-dwelling hillbillies. The debut of this film, which caused quite a stir in Acadiana, was treated in a satirical play entitled *The Picture Show on Magdalene Square*, directed by Wade Russo and presented at the Abbey Players Theatre in Abbeville.

Such misconceptions are alive even today. The caricature of "Cajun Man" for prime-time television's *Saturday Night Live*, for instance, is of a "coonass" (an unflattering epithet, referring to an uneducated beer-swilling rube who talks pidgin French, eats strange creatures out of a swamp, and wrestles alligators between hunting trips for nutria rat—a rather large rodent that looks like a beaver minus the flat tail). Many Cajuns are obviously at pains to dispel these ideas, and one book recently published, entitled simply *The Cajuns*, by Shane Bernard, may go a long way to ending the derision. Indeed, it fully chronicles and laments these misconceptions, ruing the process of Americanization that has meant a loss of culture for generations of Cajuns following the First World War, particularly in 1921 with the adoption of compulsory education,  which meant that French-speaking on school grounds was prohibited. Bernard's book makes interesting reading for those acquainted only with the prevalent, quaint notions about Cajun culture.

A key organization devoted to defending and retaining francophone culture in New Orleans and Louisiana is the Conseil pour le Développement du Français en Louisiane, the Council for the Development of French Language in Louisiana, better known as CODOFIL. The inspiration for the founding of this cultural force in 1968 was reaction to a 1969 *Life Magazine* article, "A Waning Echo From Cajun Country", in which the demise of French culture ("there will be no French found in Louisiana by 2000") was predicted. In his governor-appointed role as president of this force for cultural outreach and change, Warren Perrin, a lawyer from Lafayette, is extremely visible in carrying out the CODOFIL mission to "do any and all things necessary to accomplish the development, utilization, and preservation of the French language as found in Louisiana for the cultural, economic and touristic benefit of the state." He routinely hosts foreign dignitaries, curious visitors and media types from around the world to southwestern Louisiana, presenting Cajun culture to outsiders.

Perrin's Petition

Perrin's task of acquainting more people with the hardships foisted upon Louisiana's early Acadians sometimes means educating his own people, even closer to home. On a special weekend, more than a hundred Broussard relatives are expected at Perrin's family reunion, which takes place at his *Nonc* (Uncle) Edier's fishing camp perched on the edge of the wetlands bordering Vermilion and Lafayette parishes, a region that is home to some 400,000 descendants of the eighteenth-century French colonists who once settled Canada's Bay of Fundy region.

One only needs look to history to see that close-knit families meant—and still mean—survival to later generations born of the original displaced Acadians. These refugees were "scattered to the wind" when British colonial landlords expelled them from what are now the Canadian provinces of Nova Scotia and New Brunswick. As many as six thousand Acadians were exiled in the first of a series of deportations beginning with *le Grand Dérangement* (The Great Disruption) of 1755.

In "New Acadia" (Louisiana), where twenty-five hundred exiles from the Canadian colony found refuge, the Acadians huddled together, facing challenges of rigorous colonial life and, despite rural isolation, the ever-present threat of cultural assimilation. As their communities grew, spreading across the state's bayous and prairies, neighboring people shortened Acadien to 'Cadien, then arrived at "Cajun". Today, Cajuns inhabit a roughly triangular area that stretches from the outskirts of New Orleans to overlap, for a few miles, the Texas border. It is Deep South countryside, with gleaming fields of sugarcane and rice paddies.

At the site of the reunion are the one thousand acres of natural-gas-producing land that have yielded Edier Bares and the Broussard family a modern fortune. A ghost story is told, then the tale of Acadian folk hero and insurgent "Beausoleil" Broussard, a direct relation to the family. Perrin's book about his fourteenth-generation relative, entitled *Acadian Redemption: From Beausoleil Broussard to the Queen's Royal Proclamation*, traces the life of the insurgent Broussard who conducted forays against the British in Acadie and who led a group of 193 Acadians from St. Domingue (Haiti) to Louisiana and up the Mississippi River Valley after their exile.

The story begins with the Acadian exodus, mythologized by Longfellow in *Evangeline*. Perrin relates how more than 6,000 Acadians were torn from verdant lands, which they had farmed peaceably for more than a century and a half. France and Britain vied for those fertile pastures, and Britain won sovereignty in 1713. Four decades later, at the beginning of the French and Indian War, the security-conscious British decided to deport the "French neutral" tenants when they refused to take an iron-clad oath of allegiance to the Crown.

That action resulted in their forebears' dispersal aboard overcrowded ships and under miserable conditions. The Acadians fled to British seaboard colonies (Massachusetts, New York, Pennsylvania, Virginia, and the Carolinas, among others) and places much farther away: France, England, Haiti, and the Falkland Islands. Many never completed their journey. Some succumbed to malnutrition, typhus, or smallpox. Others were turned away as "Papists", as was the case with the Virginia-bound Acadians, or were forced to eke out what they could through scrounging or the dole. In 1785, 1,600 of these refugees left France to make the difficult passage to New Acadia, Louisiana, thus beginning a new chapter in a new land, in new millennia, for the wandering Acadians.

In preparation of a landmark legal action, lawyer Perrin has added thousands of hours' work and travel to his already busy schedule as president of CODOFIL. His unwieldy adversary: the Crown of England, or, more precisely, Her Royal Highness Queen Elizabeth II, former British Prime Minister Margaret Thatcher, the British high commissioner in Canada, and the Canadian commissioner in Great Britain.

It all began with the creation of what Perrin has styled an "amending petition", initially hand-delivered to Queen Elizabeth and Thatcher and later faxed to the other parties. Perrin's petition augments an historic letter originally sent to King George III in 1763 by Acadians languishing in exile in the British colony of Pennsylvania and restates their plea for clemency. The carefully researched 25-page document traces the history of the Acadians and their expulsion by the British from Nova Scotia and New Brunswick, seeking, in essence, an official end to *le Grand Dérangement.*

Following the delivery of his document to the Queen and Thatcher, Perrin began polite "quiet negotiations" with a Texas law firm. The law firm was the representative chosen by the Crown to smooth over what it viewed as a public relations matter.

Technically speaking, the Queen of England is immune from legal action. However, on 9 December 2003, as recognition of the Acadian cause, a Royal Proclamation was signed acknowledging the wrongs that occurred during the deportation. Recently, it has been established that Queen Elizabeth II is constitutionally bound to consult further with Canada's Parliament on the matter. In other words, Britain's official position is that, by protocol, the "successor government" (the Canadian authorities), must deal with this complaint. Though some say Perrin's litigation is destined to be unfruitful, Cajun cognoscenti are motivated to persist in the matter, motivated by what they perceive as a human rights violation that stunted the growth of their family tree.

In sum, the petition seeks no redress in the form of a monetary reward, unlike many other reparations proceedings around the world. The document puts forward five requests: restoration of the status of the Acadians as French neutrals; inquiry into the tragedy by a fair panel; declaration that the tragedy did occur; acknowledgement that the action occurred contrary to existing international and/or British law; and a symbolic gesture of goodwill by the erection of a small, simple monument with appropriate inscriptions to memorialize the end of the exile.

The Acadian Museum (203 S. Broadway) in Erath, just outside Lafayette, is an interpretive center that tells the continuing Cajun saga. For close to a decade the museum has been sponsoring a program it calls "Living Legends" to honor citizens who do outstanding work on behalf of the state's Acadian population. These efforts will endure. Similarly, more and more travelers will be extended a welcome in Acadiana and become acquainted with the real denizens of French Louisiana who have maintained their culture since 1764, when they first arrived in Louisiana.

Cross-Country Roadtrip

In order to seek out Cajun culture in the places it springs up, it is necessary to leave the city of New Orleans—for Acadiana is primarily a small-town, or rural, experience. Spring, early or late, when the swamps and bayous are new again with flower, is particularly beautiful. It is the very fecundity of the wetlands, in contrast with the dry piedmont-like prairies, that is remarkable. It was what Miller responded to, as he traveled bayou back roads and wild swamplands, piling up the names of the flora and fauna to convey the overwhelming abundance of life:

> *January in Louisiana! Already the first signs of Spring were manifesting themselves in the cabin door-yards: the paper-white narcissus and the German iris whose pale gray-green spikes are topped by a sort of disdainful white plume. In the transparent black waters*

*of the bayous the indestructible cypress, symbol of silence and death,
stands knee-deep. The sky is everywhere, dominating everything.
How different the sky as one travels from region to region! What
tremendous changes between Charleston, Asheville, Biloxi,
Pensacola, Aiken, Vicksburg, St. Martinsville [sic]! Always the live
oak, the cypress, the chinaball tree; always the swamp, the clearing,
the jungle, cotton, rice, sugar cane, thickets of bamboo, banana
trees, gum trees, magnolias, cucumber trees, swamp myrtle,
sassafrass [sic]. A wild profusion of flowers: camellias, azaleas, roses
of all kinds, salvias, the giant spider lily, the aspidistra, jasmine,
Michaelmas daisies; snakes, screech-owls, raccoons; moons of fright-
ening dimensions, lurid, pregnant, heavy as mercury. And like a
leitmotif to the immensity of sky are the tangled masses of Spanish
moss…*

Travelers and locals alike do their best to avoid the summer's zenith.
According to naturalist John James Audubon (1785-1851), who loved
the area for its uncultivated beauty, the wetlands during a certain time of
year were unendurable, particularly during a certain time of day: "Late
in the afternoon of one of those sultry days which render the atmosphere
of the Louisiana swamps pregnant with baneful effluvia. . ."

Heading west out of the Crescent City on US 90, soon the
highway turns to sleepy back roads through cypress-haunted swamps
bearded with swags of Spanish moss. The yards and fields of
southwestern Louisiana exhibit their rural eccentricities—and in
between the odd suburban strip mall each hamlet seems caught in a
time warp somehow stuck in the 1940s or 1950s, with homemade
signage, whirligigs, and other quirky décor.

There are hundreds of cultural touchstones that will convey the
lifestyle of contemporary Cajuns, but of international note is the annual
Lafayette, LA, Festival International de Louisiane which brings together
actors, intellectuals, writers, artists, dancers, musicians and chefs from
all around the francophone world to express the individuality of this
unique culture. Each year, the celebration is organized with a specific
theme, and events take place through town. Some of these are in the
authentically interpreted Acadian Village (200 Green Leaf Dr.), which
approximates life in colonial Acadiana with a restored Cajun settlement
and buildings dating to the 1800s. The Evangeline myth, as it rises

from the pages of Longfellow's poem, can be explored at the Longfellow-Evangeline Historic Site (215 Evangeline Blvd.). Established in 1930, the Evangeline-Longfellow State Commemorative Area comprises four museums: Acadian Memorial, Duchamp Opera House, La Maison Duchamp, and the African-American Museum.

Heading toward the little town of Eunice, sojourners and Louisiana natives alike seek out the live broadcast of the weekly *Rendezvous des Cajun* radio show, a tradition akin to the Grand Ole Opry, at which one can sit in as audience while performances are put on air. There is also the "Eunice Cajun Music Show" at Liberty Theatre (200 W. Park Ave.) every Saturday night, with live music and dancing. In a town called Opelousas is the now-famous roadhouse Slim's Y-KiKi (9389 Hwy. 182), which, truth be told, looks like someone's tool shed, situated across from the local "Piggly Wiggly" grocery store. North from Eunice is Mamou, where Fred's Lounge (420 Sixth St.) picks up a broadcast of the best bands in Cajun Country.

Mamou is best known at Carnival time in Louisiana as host of one of the quaintest and least commercial celebrations of Mardi Gras: the Cajun *Courir de Mardi Gras.* Towns such as Mamou, Eunice, and Church Point—and even quasi-metropolitan Lafayette—celebrate the spectacle of Cajun Mardi Gras with gusto and with more than a *soupçon* of difference from New Orleans' festivities. It is a day trip, a short drive out of New Orleans (an hour or two perhaps), to take part in one of these smaller, rural celebrations. The *lagniappe* is that visitors see authentic Cajun folk expression, and also savor the results of a whole day's worth of gumbo cooking.

This slow-simmered stew, stirred in gigantic cauldrons in the center of town, is the focal point of a folk observance that is the semi-spiritual, semi-secular Cajun Mardi Gras. Much like traditional celebrations, *la course de Mardi Gras* (Mardi Gras run), enacted in country byways and public spaces of Acadiana, involves a procession—but with an unusual twist. What townsfolk and out-of-towners witness are the hi-jinks of a ragtag band of dusty, often inebriated, masked horsemen (sometimes women) garbed in bizarre home-made costumes reminiscent of the Middle Ages. The revelers are seen at stages along their route to beg, cajole, entertain and otherwise mildly terrorize local homeowners out of gumbo provisions. Flour, rice, onions, oil, even money, are acceptable gifts to the horsemen who *faites des macaques* (make monkeyshine). But the most valued prize is a live chicken corralled by the celebrants, whose chase after the squawking prey is comically hampered by costumes and too much beer.

It may all seem rather strange. But this unique, frontier-spirited tradition, the vestige of a medieval European begging ritual called the *fête de la quémande*, continues to draw and ever-increasing number of visitors, cultural historians and ethnographers. Planning for the Mardi Gras run takes place weeks in advance; in fact, *le Capitaine,* who leads the charge in a flamboyant cape of Mardi Gras gold, green and purple, is chosen *for life.*

The ride starts early on Mardi Gras morning, when riders trot down country roads to assemble at a pre-chosen spot, usually near the center of town. Homespun whimsical costumes cloak clowns, monsters, movie heroes and villains, but there are also comical hats (a parody of medieval noblewomen and long associated with fools), mitres (a poke at the Roman Catholic clergy) and, less frequently, mortarboards (spoofing scholars and clerics) and false female bosoms and bottoms—all in the spirit of Mardi Gras' mystical pre-Lenten power to transform.

Le Capitaine, who keeps mayhem at an acceptable pitch, rides ahead of the band and approaches a farmhouse alone. Blowing his primitive *corne de vache* (cow's horn), he announces his band's presence and inquires whether the group might be allowed to entertain in return for a small gift for the gumbo that night. If the answer is yes, the *Capitaine* drops his flag and riders thunder into the farmyard as if to take it. The scenes that ensue kick up a lot of dust: singing, dancing, impromptu skits, displays of machismo and horsemanship, maybe even a mock abduction of pretty wife or daughter. Finally, dust settled, the man of the house brings out that day's offering. If it is a chicken, the bird is thrown high into the air for the rabble to run after. *Le Capitaine* then blows his horn to call the raiders back to order, and on to another house. This frivolity is repeated as many times as is necessary to win the makings for the collective gumbo-making. For as the words to the old folk song go:

Allons se mettre dessus le chemin,	Let's get on the road,
Les Mardi Gras se rassemblent	The Mardi Gras riders get together
une fois par an demander la charité	once a year to ask for charity
—poule grasse. Capitaine,	—fat chicken. Captain, Captain, wave
Capitaine, boyage ton drapeau!	your flag!

At dusk, everyone tastes from the communal pot; in it is the complex local flavor that has been centuries in the making.

Chank-a-Chank

"Well I'm standing on the corner in Lafayette/Across from the Public/Heading down to the Lone Star Café/Maybe get a little conversation/Drink a little red wine/Standing in the shadow of Clifton Chenier/Dancing the night away."
—Paul Simon, "That Was Your Mother", *Graceland*, 1986

Those fascinated with Southern "roots" culture know that, besides the food it is the music in the form of heartfelt Cajuns ballads and rollicking, syncopated zydeco that sticks in the memory. At any feast day, or at an event such as September's Festivals Acadiens in Lafayette, whenever the music is "cranked", the dancers seem to appear out of nowhere, taking the dance floor (whether dirt, grass, concrete or wood) by storm with their bandanas and T-shirts, old-timers and first-timers. It is music that conjures the resilient spirit and the very essence of Cajuns and Creoles, people who, despite the vagaries of climate and topography, made their lives on the bayous and prairies of this state. It may give Hollywood film aficionados used to John Wayne a shock to see a black cowboy—but chambray shirts, bolos, denim jeans, cowboy hats and boots are the apparel that is *de rigueur* in town, on the farm, and even in the sweltering dance clubs all across all of Acadiana.

Cajun music is vigorous, and for the most part upbeat music, despite the struggle that lies at the heart of the Acadians' exodus to the South following the deportation from their homeland. The adaptability of Cajun people is also reflected in the complex blending of French heritage with Creole, Native American, Spanish, Afro-Caribbean and Anglo-American folk traditions. Such youthful performers as Kristi Guillory and Wayne Toups, as well as seasoned artists such as Allen Fontenot or Zachary Richard are preserving the language and culture of their Cajun forebears while entertaining audiences with their danceable music.

And whether it is the traditional two-step and shuffles of earlier zydeco, or the new R&B- and rap-influenced sounds, a dancer can feel the energy of this homegrown Creole country music when the accordion and the *frottoir* (rub board) start up. Zydeco, like Cajun music, is a folk expression, a living artifact of cultural survival. It is the country music of Louisiana's black Creoles (see Chapter One, Neutral Ground) and has evolved in fascinating ways over the past 150 years. Zydeco is fast, syncopated, and shows influences from Cajun, African-American and Afro-Caribbean cultures. It is said that zydeco was given its strange-sounding name when it was dubbed with a "Creolized" pronunciation of the French *les haricots* ("snap beans"). Zydeco musicians are taking their music from such popular country festivals as the Zydeco Extravaganza in Lafayette and the Zydeco & Blues

Festival in Mamou out into the international arena. Spirited R&B-infused zydeco anthems have become as popular as Louisiana cuisine and hot sauce around the world.

The new "princes" of zydeco—even a five-year-old fiddle player Guyland Leday and three-year-old Kevin Ballou on rub board—are always ready to make the "chank-a-chank" sound. Musicians such as C. J. Chenier & the Red Hot Louisiana Band ("King of Zydeco" Clifton Chenier's son and "heir"), Terrance Simien & the Mallet Playboys, Buckwheat Zydeco, Geno Delafose & French Rockin' Boogie, Chris Ardoin & Double Clutchin', as well as Rosie Ledet, whom they call the "Sweetheart of Zydeco", are heard playing gigs around the state as well as around the world. The New Orleans Jazz & Heritage Festival showcases scores of Cajun and zydeco artists every year at "Jazz Fest" time—in fact there are special tents set aside for these genres—but it is also possible to hear the music out of town at celebrations in smaller venues across the state of Louisiana. There is, for instance, the Festival International in Lafayette, the always-dependable Zydeco Festival in Plaisance (going on now for more than twenty years), the Zydeco Breakfast in Opelousas, and the Giant Omelette Festival in Abbeville, when chefs come out to break 5,000 eggs to create the world's largest omelette in the largest skillet (12-feet) for a "street" breakfast.

"Ragin' Cajuns"

Although events such as these are celebrated with four-color zeal in the pages of tourism brochures dedicated to promoting the unique cultural makeup of Louisiana, there is an even deeper movement afoot that seeks to claim redress for the Americanization of francophone people—both white and black—throughout the twentieth century. Even though it is rare to hear French spoken today (but not so rare to hear it sung in such ballads as *Tan Patate—La Tchuite* [When Your Potato's Done It's Time to Eat]), as mentioned previously, Cajuns of the "baby boom" generation and their parents still remember a time when receiving an education meant that no French could be spoken in state schools or even on school grounds. Cajuns of multiple generations recall this fracturing experience.

For this reason, and to preserve Cajun French as a viable dialect, CODOFIL fills its role as a conservationist body, because with cultural awareness comes political awareness. In 1960s it was legally established that Louisiana's children should have the right to a bilingual education—that is, standard and Cajun French would be studied. At the state level, in the capitol buildings of Baton Rouge, the Commission on French was formed to assure that curricula across the state would begin to incorporate both idioms. In contrast to visits from dignitaries hailing from France, Belgium and Canada, it may seem oddly "small town" to have children singing French songs in the Louisiana Senate, but if that is what it takes to promote pride in Louisiana's francophone cultural legacy, then so be it.

Meanwhile, the work and word of Cajun pride go out abroad. Pejorative uses of the term "coonass" in the media, and even the inappropriate coining of the term "Cajun", such as in a remark on ABC News Radio referring to the "Cajun Taliban", are addressed by letters sent out by CODOFIL. Individuals doing noteworthy things at home and abroad are acknowledged, such as one Louisiana businessman covered in a *Le Monde* article entitled "Lafayette Lifestyles". Within the US, students at Stanford University in California are putting together a dictionary of Louisiana Creole through intensive archival study and interviews. In international forums, where cultural allegiances are established or dismantled, Cajuns are taking sides. For instance, with the recent nationwide "French bashing" in conflicts among nations reacting to the conflict in Iraq, articles are appearing with such headlines as "Anger Should Focus on French Leaders, Not French People". Even the *L.A. Times* conjectured about the adverse effects on Louisiana from the rash of anti-French sentiment.

Today, being Cajun in Louisiana is actually a cross-cultural matter and, in fact, many people "claim" to be Cajun even though their ancestry does not strictly support it (i.e. Cajun bloodlines are identified by a small number of family names, such as Richard, Broussard, LeBlanc, etc.). Even non-Cajuns feel they must get in on the cultural bandwagon; a young Anglo businessman from New Orleans has created, and is now marketing, his electronic "Cajun In Your Pocket®" key ring, which shouts out such expressions as the Cajun call to dance, "Aiieeeeeeee-e-e-e!" And, recently, in a bold move, McDonald's announced its first all-Cajun restaurant, to be piloted in New Orleans.

In keeping with the wave of the future, there are whole websites devoted to Cajun culture. With a look at these resources, such as Action Cadienne (www.actioncadienne.org), L'Alliance Française de la

Nouvelle-Orléans (www.af-neworleans.org) and Le Consulat Genéral de France à la Nouvelle-Orléans (www.consulfrance-nouvelleorleans.org), we can look to the future and see that it looks bright for Louisiana's Cajuns, as well as Acadians everywhere.

Congrès Mondial Acadien

Indeed, Acadians are pro-actively seeking unification for Cajuns and Acadians all over the world. And the unifying force is the Congrès Mondial Acadien. This organization has provided the way for Acadian family trees to remain intact and flourish over the years, and it allows growth to continue by holding a giant family reunion every five years to which Acadians flock, no matter how far they must travel. The first Congrès took place in New Brunswick, Canada, in 1994, and the second one in conjunction with FrancoFête '99, the anniversary celebration of the founding of the French colony of Louisiana. The third, attracting 100,000 people, took place recently in Nova Scotia, commemorating the 400th anniversary of the founding of Acadia. The CMA website, www.cma2005.com, has page after cyber-page devoted to Acadian traditions and "photo albums" of families whose members range globally.

Between these larger events, family reunions take place where the concentration of Acadian families is great, i.e., in Louisiana. These are enormous *fais do-do* (see Glossary), requiring months of advance planning and pulling thousands of family members into the state. The Guidry family holds its reunions in Vermilionville. In the small town of Rayne (Frog Capital of Louisiana), as a prelude to the bigger Congrès Mondial Acadien family reunion, 10,000 Acadian descendants of another Cajun family converge. Concurrently, Nova Scotia senators have sponsored a bill in the Canadian federal government to recognize National Acadian Day, while back in Louisiana dedication ceremonies are held in St. Martinville to memorialize the replica of Grand Pré (Nova Scotia's) cross, marking the first Acadian settlement. A grant from the Acadiana Arts Council has been put to work to fund the creation of a mosaic design incorporating Acadian family crests to encircle an eternal flame. This montage will symbolize the Cajuns' ever-present longing to keep the Acadian spirit burning for its Southern tribe.

Chapter Ten

CULTURE OF CELEBRATION: MARDI GRAS AND OTHER SPECTACLES

"More than the inhabitants of most cities, New Orleanians live by the pleasure principle: the right to enjoy oneself by means of the senses is commonly conceded to be inalienable, and the greatest sin that one can possibly commit is to be unhappy. Mardi Gras in New Orleans is not a holiday; it is every day—or rather, it is one day which distills the essence of all the other days, recapitulating and symbolizing a whole way of life and a very definite attitude toward it."
  —Oliver Evans

"In New Orleans, culture doesn't come down from on high, it bubbles up from the street."
  —Jazz patriarch Ellis Marsalis

Tennessee Williams called New Orleans "one of the last frontiers of Bohemia". Throughout the 1940s and into the 1970s "The Bird" would swoop down, survey the shabby streets of the French Quarter, and choose his favorite bars, bistros or restaurants in which to meet other writers. Among them was the Court of Two Sisters (where he worked briefly as a server in the early 1940s), or The Alpine (not the present-day bar and grill) which served as setting for a scene in *The Mutilated*, a dramatic work that, like *Small Craft Warnings*, drew on the playwright's intimate knowledge of barroom riffraff and "characters" of every type.

After his daily writing regimen—sustained by several cups of robust New Orleans coffee—Williams could retire to a place like the Bourbon House at the corner of St. Peter and Bourbon streets, an establishment described by mystery writer Erle Stanley Gardner as "something of a Bohemian place... Quite a few of the prominent authors, playwrights, and actors ate there when in New Orleans."

Williams and his literary companions relished the *laissez-faire* attitude that prevailed in the Crescent City of the 1940s (today it presents an even rarer anomaly among the capitals of American materialism). New Orleans was a place that flouted the bourgeois work ethic and was perceived to favor play over serious endeavor. The city had (deservedly) gained a reputation as "Sin Central of the South", and the darker side of French Quarter milieu also proved a potent lure for young Williams, drawing him into recesses of the night. Kenneth Holditch in *Tennessee Williams and the South* names some of them:

> There were other bars, of course, those that catered to the kind of lifestyle that Tom had found decadent on his first exposure to it in 1938 but had subsequently embraced. On Exchange Alley were several gay bars: Ivan's, an all-night establishment with a shady reputation, and between Iberville and Canal, the even more notorious Society Page. Where Royal Street meets Canal there was Monkey Wrench Corner, a generic name in all port cities, according to Lyle Saxon, for favorite meeting places for sailors and merchant seamen. Traditionally they referred to each other as monkeys and would sometimes put a "wrench" on one another for a loan.

In New Orleans Williams shed inhibition to explore his desires. Today people still think of the city not only as a place where can you do what you want to do (the chorus of a popular contemporary brass band anthem enjoins, "Do What Ya Wanna"), but also by extension where you can be who you want to be. This credo gives libertines license, and it is the backdrop against which feast days and festivals unfold, even those of those of a spiritual nature.

Sometimes it is hard to discern who is bohemian and who is just in costume for a feast day, as in the run-up to Mardi Gras, Southern Decadence (the annual gay fête on Labor Day Weekend) or Halloween. No matter, for New Orleans proudly celebrates a cult of the individual—and, even though it sounds like an oxymoron, individuals just have to blend in. A number of eccentric individuals are seen elevated in a rogues' gallery of ethereal black-and-white portraits posted on a website called eccentricneworleans.com. It seems that residents have not only come to tolerate these bizarre personae who wander around town, but have even come to love them: the crooked

Lucky Bean (or Bead) Lady, dressed in black distributing fava beans or strands of Mardi Gras beads to passersby; Ruthie, the Duck Lady, now relegated to a nursing home with her quacking entourage; Chicken Man, the voodoo practitioner; Banjo Annie... In a humorous book with the title *Ballooning Alligators* (1990), a tale is told of an 1858 item included in the *New Orleans Bee* that covered the antics of two thrill seekers. They are reported to have soared over the French Quarter astride two eleven-foot alligators suspended from balloons—just for fun.

In an interview with local author Jason Berry, jazz raconteur Danny Barker observed: "New Orleans people are unique... somebody goin' to jail? Give him a party. Somebody died? Give him a party. They'd throw a party for a dog's birthday." The Big Easy's reputation as an unconventional safe harbor from everything "straight" is by now something that has to be upheld at all costs, and is especially propagated by tourism. Much is made of New Orleans as a party destination, and even among New Orleanians themselves partying is considered a fine art that requires long apprenticeship. It has become customary to compare tales of outrageous excess. A monthly digest, *Scat magazine*, regales its readers with what the editors call "Talk of the Town" yarns of intrepid adventures interwoven with scraps of material from the bottomless rummage bin that contains "New Orleans Stories". Their dénouement usually reads like a jaded just-so fable: ". . .and that is why too much was not enough."

Capitalizing on Excess

In his article "Marketing Mardi Gras" published in the scholarly journal *Urban Studies*, author Kevin Fox Gotham suggests that superficial "place marketing" (i.e., pitching iconic images of places such as Disneyland, Las Vegas and Times Square) actually overshadows true appreciation of New Orleans' complex cultural history. It is the result of a phenomenon he calls "commodification". Place marketing is business, and it is conducted by an organized, specialized network of professionals, says Gotham. Dedicated to growing tourism in cities, place marketing seizes on one or more regional "attractions" as a way to revitalize an urban center.

This is especially true of New Orleans. As far as its economy goes, marketing Mardi Gras is essential to bolstering municipal budgets.

Carnival signals an annual incoming high tide of drunken humanity, "the bibulous throngs" one writer calls them, as well as the wave of profit that comes in its wake. As the hordes arrive, the dollar bill—and plenty of garbage—flies. There are probably few places on earth that gauge the success of an event by calculating how many tons of garbage is produced, but in New Orleans trash is considered cash. Though few people know it, the very last event of Carnival takes place when "the Clean-Up Squad", mounted New Orleans Police Department officers, form a cordon across Bourbon Street with steeds posted four or five abreast. This cortège moves tightly toward Canal Street on Bourbon, turning out droves of partiers from the French Quarter. And that is when Carnival closes officially. Then, behind the horses come the final parade vehicles: garbage trucks that suck up the litter and spray disinfectant as though actually capable of scrubbing away the night's debauchery.

A good Mardi Gras means that at least 1,000 tons of garbage is generated. That refuse translates, according to a University of New Orleans study, into as much as $860 million for City Hall's coffers. Despite its reputation as a city of lassitude, during special events the city's infrastructures must mesh and run together like a well-oiled machine. Indeed, NOPD officers, with their law enforcement expertise and miles of metal interlocking traffic barriers, are routinely "rented out" to other American cities for special occasions or municipal needs relating to crowd control.

When it comes to the marketing of "place" in current times, the role of tourism as purveyor of culture cannot be underestimated, says Gotham, and the process can be quite complex: "One can find conceptualizations of tourism as a sacred crusade, pilgrimage or search for authenticity... a form of colonialism, conquest and imperialism... a type of ethnic relation... a force for historical and cultural commodification... a form of migration..." In a curious marriage of form and content, the culture and cultures of New Orleans—particularly Mardi Gras—are promoted as "spectacle". The positive effect of this process is that more people are dazzled into choosing New Orleans to visit. But according to Gotham, marketing spectacle results in a domination of media images and consumer society over the individual. It "'distracts' and 'seduces' people into using the mechanisms of leisure, consumption and entertainment as ruled by the dictates of advertising," he laments, perpetrating "a form of mass seduction that leads to more harm than good," and ultimately leading to a distortion of history.

Lately, the most obvious successfully generated statewide cultural celebration was the bicentennial of the 1803 Louisiana Purchase. This historical event, travestied in tourism circles and brochures as "the real estate deal of the eighteenth century", was eagerly promoted by the Louisiana Convention & Visitors Bureau. A wide variety of cultural programming prevailed throughout the year: there were special TV broadcasts, art gallery openings (New Orleans Museum of Art's "Jefferson's America and Napoleon's France"), lectures (Louisiana State Museum's "One Nation Under God: The Church, the State, and the Louisiana Purchase"), and visits from French, Spanish and US heads of state. A new nickel was struck to commemorate the historic event; a stamp was minted in its honor. Even the Coca-Cola Company "participated" by imprinting a "special Louisiana Purchase logo" on its bottles of Coca-Cola. The point is that efforts toward selling New Orleans' international image as "the Big Easy" will not only endure but be redoubled, with city and state tourism, as well as local business, ready to promote the stereotype.

Regarding Mardi Gras, a day devoted mostly to having fun, it may seem mean-spirited to point out that such major corporations as Bacardi, Southern Comfort, Coors beer, Kool cigarettes and others make their respective pitches to a "sinful" captive market niche they conveniently find in town during Carnival. Nationally and regionally, companies relish the opportunity to bolster their good-time image to participants in the event. One advertising executive conveyed prevailing and superficial ideas people have of a unique cultural expression that has always been called "The Greatest *Free* Show on Earth": "People have a clear sense of what Mardi Gras is about. It's about fun, losing your inhibitions, and celebrating life… These companies are interested in appending those characteristics through their association of products to Mardi Gras."

Gotham notes that in the past, "Mardi Gras developed as a relatively indigenous celebration for local residents that existed outside the logic of market exchange and capital circulation." Now it is a mostly divorced from deeper religious meaning and covered as a newsworthy spectacle by media from around the world, and featured in documentaries made by the Travel, Discovery, Learning, and Playboy TV channels.

Imperative to Party

The bittersweet truth about New Orleans is that the city's poverty may have actually intensified the need to celebrate. "New Orleans: Third World and Proud of It", reads a local bumper sticker. Tourism has provided the city with hope for better times. Beginning with the period following Reconstruction, civic leaders undertook to promote as much commercial investment and population growth for the city as possible. By the early 1900s, commerce on the Mississippi also meant a growing market for leisure and entertainment alternatives. With its Storyville legacy and worldwide fame as the birthplace of jazz as the draw, city fathers realized that there might be marketing potential in glorifying the city's "sin industries" while recalling hedonistic glory days of yore.

The 1930s oil boom propelled chemical and petroleum research and development. By the Second World War New Orleans had also developed into a national hub for military shipbuilding and shipping. However, after the oil bust, tourism had to step in to fill the gap, and in the past three decades it has replaced the other sectors as the major source of jobs for people in the metro area. City leaders equated this move with "progress", yet the shift towards tourism has been paralleled by an erosion of the tax base. Between 1960 and 2000 the central city of New Orleans lost nearly 143,000 inhabitants (or 22 percent of its citizenry). The racial composition of the city changed radically: in 1960 whites made up 62.6 percent of the metropolitan area and blacks 37.2 percent. But according to the 2000 census, population reversed itself, with blacks comprising 67.3 percent of the city's population and whites 28.1 percent. Today, the poverty rate for the City of New Orleans is approximately double that of the surrounding suburban communities. Sadly, as recently as 1995 more than half the children living in New Orleans were living below the federal poverty level—existing, effectively, in a state of socio-economic and racial segregation.

Despite these depressing statistics, New Orleanians always rally and are exceptionally proud of their city and its role as a meeting and convention mecca. Celebration is considered an utterly egalitarian activity: every soul should "pass a good time." And the colloquialism gives a subtle hint as to just how long having a good time has been held important, since "to pass" must derive from the French infinitive *passer*, or "to have". In the same way, the local expression "makin' groceries," ("I've just been to Winn Dixie, makin' groceries") derives from the French construction using the helping verb *faire*, to make. *Laissez les bontemps rouler* (Let the good times roll) is the customary call to party.

Even in these ascetic, health-conscious times, alcohol is consumed at business meetings, conferences, and awards banquets in New Orleans. For the well heeled, cocktails are served at the venerable Boston Club (an exclusive, traditional men's venue on Canal Street), or after work perhaps the Bombay Club for martinis of prodigious proportions. On a late Friday afternoon on Bourbon Street, it is in the bald glare of Galatoire's signature lighting that one finds many Crescent City movers and shakers, media types, and upstart entrepreneurs who meet for power lunches that go on forever. The best of the old-line restaurants, such as Antoine's, Brennan's, The Bistro at Maison de Ville, and Windsor Court's Grill Room, have extensive wine cellars (Brennan's is routinely rated best in the country) with thousands of bottles—some costing in the thousands of dollars—to encourage conviviality. For plebeians, there is also no shortage of places, albeit more unprepossessing, to drink. In New Orleans proper there are, according to the local restaurant association, at least 3,000 places licensed to sell alcohol.

Saints Alive!

Ironically, a good number of feast days and festivals in Louisiana and New Orleans are tied to the Christian calendar of worship (though most are by now much secularized). As author and *Times-Picayune* columnist James Gill notes in his excellent study of Mardi Gras, *Lords of Misrule*, sacred occasions must not preclude a drink or two:

> *The religious pretext for the celebrations* [in this case Carnival] *had always been more or less a fraud in New Orleans, and even in the early days the arrival of Lent was not accompanied by widespread abstemiousness. Until the turn of the century, for instance, a live bull, or Boeuf Gras, appeared in Rex parades, supposedly to provide the last feast before the coming rigors* [of Lent], *but it was, in fact, regularly butchered to be eaten on Ash Wednesday. Drunkenness was always common in New Orleans at the best of times; at Carnival late-night promenaders were not infrequently obliged to pick their way through young men passed out in pools of vomit.*

Whether before Carnival or after, most citizens keep a keen eye on the calendar for the next feast day, the next festival, and they begin receiving guests who come with partying on the agenda. New Orleans and the rest of the state are only too glad to oblige: immediately, restaurant and bar fare, taxi and hotel rates become unfixed and begin their steady ascent. When it comes to major events such as Mardi Gras (always 47 days before Easter, usually falling in the last two weeks of February or the first week of March), and the New Orleans Jazz & Heritage Festival (always the last weekend in April and the first weekend of May), people citywide start thinking well ahead about their parties, putting together guest lists and planning the menus. Visitors must make their arrangements well in advance: if a hotel is not booked at least a year ahead for either of these two main events, in particular, there is certain to be slim pickings in the way of accommodation—from top-name hotels down to the smallest of guest houses.

In addition to the main attractions, namely Mardi Gras and Jazz Fest, there are several other festivals in Louisiana, many within a few hours' drive of the city. These local and regional fêtes exist often just to celebrate one food item: there are the beef, barbecue, alligator, shrimp, catfish, oyster and chicken festivals; there are abundant celebrations highlighting farmers' produce—Louisiana rice, the yam (or sweet potato), the pecan, the mirliton (a small yellow squash), the tomato, the watermelon and strawberry; and there are fairs devoted to cultural creations eaten with gusto by everyone, such as Bridge City's Gumbo Festival, a festival for the spicy Cajun sausage *andouille*, chili cook-offs, and a tamale festival.

The annual round of feast days begins in spring with the saints busily bestowing grace, New Orleans-style. "Wearing of the Green" is as enthusiastically embraced in New Orleans as in New York City (though only 4.5 percent of residents actually say they are of Irish descent). On 17 March, St. Patrick's Day, all stops are pulled for an intense party. On St. Patrick's Day Eve, the Downtown Irish Club marches from the Ninth Ward through French Quarter streets, stopping at various bars along the way. But on St. Paddy's Day proper, the celebration finds as its focus the aptly named Irish Channel (Uptown in and around the original Irish neighborhood, marshaling near the benevolent Kingsley House). This is where Irish immigrants settled in the mid-nineteenth century, in the area surrounding Adele Street running vertical to the river from Tchoupitoulas to St. Thomas (and which later grew to include the rectangular sector bounded by Tchoupitoulas and Magazine, Felicity and Jackson).

The Irish Channel Parade wends it way Uptown up narrow Magazine Street, with its seedy 1940s storefronts, many of which are being gentrified with trendy boutiques, bookstores, cafés and curio shops. Some of the floats in this Uptown parade are even more kitsch-looking than those of Mardi Gras, and loads of children, or else jazz pick-up bands, are loaded into rigs that look like nothing more than large vegetable carts. The crowds are forming under the merchants' awnings as people gather to catch the day's favored "throws". They are makings for Irish stew: potatoes, cabbages, onions, and carrots...

Separated by just one day on the calendar from St. Patrick's, St. Joseph's Day, on 19 March, is a feast day of deeper religious symbolism and veneration. It occurs halfway through Lent and during the season called "Micareme". The centuries-old holy day honoring Sicily's patron saint calls St. Joseph's family, friends and soon-to-be-friends together to break bread. The day's centerpiece is a symbolic banquet set out to draw passersby, a *tavola di San Giuseppe*, whose superabundant spread of pasta dishes, fried and fresh seafood, fruits and vegetables, and exquisite breads and *dolci* are designed to inspire and impress. The entire city turns out for an annual Mardi Gras-style St. Joseph's Day Parade, complete with gondola-shaped floats, and altars around town in private homes, businesses and churches (a spectacular display is at St. Joseph's Church in Gretna), are well documented in days leading up to St. Joseph's Day in *The Times-Picayune*.

This is a special feast day, imported by Sicilian immigrants. The first émigrés—merchants and many purveyors or brokers of tropical fruits—established themselves in the Port of New Orleans during the 1880s to drum up business. These first Italo-Americans settled their families in Creole-dominated Vieux Carré. They were much admired for their frugality and industry and shared with the Creoles who lived there as their next-door neighbors strong affinities for the Church, large families, and such popular diversions as opera and horseracing.

St. Joseph's Day altars spread for the spring's key feast day provide a stunning visual feast. They are featured in filmmaker-photographer Neil Alexander's documentary *Island of Saints and Souls*. "Whatever saints do for people spiritually crosses the division of religious background," says Alexander, noting that celebration of St. Joseph's Day is a pan-cultural celebration and a shared ritual:

> ... *to a Baptist person in New Orleans' Ninth Ward, say, the powers of St. Joseph may have just as much control over his life as anything else. People in New Orleans have always grown up together. It wouldn't be uncommon for a Sicilian family to be living on the same block with a black family and an Irish family. "Uncle Salvatore was sick and prayed to St. Joseph, and he's okay now, so we're putting on an altar!" St. Joseph's Day is about celebration, mystery, and miracles, and in New Orleans the miracles get passed around.*

Other churches and denominations, such as the African-American Spiritual Church, which on St. Joseph's Eve sets its meatless altar with votives and tropical fruit, celebrate St. Joseph's Day services.

Many may think it, indeed, a modern-day miracle that any group of families, or one family, Sicilian or otherwise, could produce such a copious amount of food for a single event. But St. Joseph's Day honors the unity of the Holy Family—Jesus, Mary and Joseph—and therefore it extends to all parents and children. By dint of familial cooperation, the work does get done, sometimes weeks or months in advance. Tables erected by the men are often arranged in three tiers to represent the Trinity. Spread upon the impromptu "altar" is an embarrassment of dishes, most inspired by the regional cuisine of Sicily and Italy, many symbolic in nature, and all employing to advantage local Louisiana produce. From the recipe cards of generations of Sicilian women come thick lentil soup, minestrone, pasta Siciliana with its tomato sauce and fish base of anchovy or fresh sardines, wild anise greens, *pignoli* (pine nuts), currants, and topping of seasoned bread crumbs known as "sawdust of St. Joseph the Carpenter". There are fried sardines, baked Louisiana redfish, twelve fried trout to recall Jesus feeding the multitudes, Gulf-fresh oysters, shrimp and soft-shelled crab.

On candlelit tables set with floral arrangements, icons, and gaily waving Italian and American flags are additional *piatti* (courses) of vegetable and egg: chunks of chilled fennel, glossy black olives, stuffed escarole rolls, fried cauliflower rosettes, spinach and asparagus omelettes. The breads and sweets are, in themselves, amazing to behold both for their beauty and complexity of design. *Cuchdati* (large, golden-brown breads with sesame seeds) are shaped as wreaths to represent a crown of thorns, hearts for the sacred hearts of Jesus and Mary, crosses to evoke the Crucifixion, or chalice and monstrance symbolizing Mass. *Pupacoulova* (baskets of colorfully dyed eggs) foretell the coming of Easter with seasonally tinted icings—pink, white, purple, yellow—which top *biscotti* (cookies) flavored with almond, vanilla, lemon, anise and chocolate.

As people pour in to sample the fare that has been placed on the groaning St. Joseph's Day tables, donations pour in, too. Baskets are placed discreetly for any proffering. Jugs of wine and oversized bottles of soft drinks are put down where people are eating. Young and old are involved in this labor of love, wishing all visitants a *Buona fiesta di San Giuseppe* as they leave with bags containing some blessed St. Joseph's Day bread, a fava bean (which if placed in a wallet means "You will never go broke," or, if on a pantry shelf "You will never go hungry"), fig or anise cookies, *pignolatti*, and a holy picture or medal.

Prayers to St. Joseph, or a petition left for him on the altar, request protection against illness, accident, poverty, or privation. New Orleanians ask of this patron saint of workers, and of carpenters in particular:

Primu di l'arma e pi du la corpu
Datinini aiuta, ripara e conforta.
Scura ai e agghiorna dumani
La pruvidenza na anti a mannari.

(First for the soul, and then the body
Give aid, strength, and counsel.
Whether it's today or early tomorrow
You will send your providence.)

Many families believe that having a St. Joseph's Day altar can bring good fortune. It is common to hear about favors received, which are attributed to the patron saint: it is a sort of spiritual contract. Unless the contract is fulfilled, the powers of St. Joseph may be turned against an individual. But it is St. Joseph's powers as patron saint of the Roman Catholic Church that are truly legendary. It is no wonder. In a largely working-class city such as New Orleans, St. Joseph's hagiography is something with which most people can identify. And in this fragile, subtropical region—like Sicily an "island" culture of sorts, but surrounded by canals, wetlands, and the Mississippi River instead of ocean—it is believed that a blessing can also fend off a Gulf hurricane. First, some St. Joseph Day bread must be saved. Blessed crumbs thrown to the wind fly into the eye of a blast as a supplicant prays, "St. Joseph, make the storm go away!"

In New Orleans, as doors are opened for anyone to enter and taste from a carefully prepared St. Joseph's Day feast, it seems that, for one day at least, differences of race, religion, and ethnic background disappear. This is what Barbara Jean Lichtfuss points out in *Island of Saints and Souls*, as she is putting the last edible flourishes on a feast-day altar. A city worker, Lichtfuss is not of Sicilian, or even Italian, extraction. "It's incredible to see people from all levels of society," she says, "the way we work together. It doesn't matter where you come from, or who you are. St. Joseph's Day brings people together, not just in the making, but also in the visitation of the altar. So, it's a gift that we can say has come from the Sicilians, and has just been embraced by all."

Pagan Party

"This was New Orleans, a magical and magnificent place to live. In which a vampire, richly dressed and gracefully walking through the pools of light of one gas lamp after another might attract no more notice in the evening than hundreds of other exotic creatures..."
—Anne Rice, *Interview with the Vampire*

In the fall, on the last night of October, the ancient ritual known as Hallowmas is on the streets of New Orleans—and it arrives with a vengeance. In contrast to the Christian spiritual expression St. Joseph's Day represents, this is a widely celebrated, and very secular, pagan Celtic festival designed to mark the new year by welcoming spirits of the dead and assuaging supernatural powers. "All Hallow's Eve" is second only to Mardi Gras' power to draw masked revelers from their homes, galvanizing costume-makers into creative frenzy and whipping celebrants into bizarre behavior with the mask of anonymity for protection.

Walking the entire length of Bourbon Street, from Canal Street all the way to Esplanade, thousands of ghouls parade not only their elaborate costumes, but also the monstrous (whimsical, outrageous, legendary, etc.) personae they have become. R&B music emits from clubs with doors thrown wide-open as the "hanks" (ghosts) descend on the French Quarter's countless hidden places, making everyone "hankity" or scared.

An interesting aside: a real reflection of New Orleans' true nature is its citizens' love of becoming "other" through costuming and donning masks—a habit perhaps retained from the city's colonial French origins. There have actually been periods throughout New Orleans' history when masking was banned due to political and/or racial unrest. During the Civil War, when Federal troops occupied New Orleans, one Union official turned up dead on a doorstep on Mardi Gras morning, wearing a scarlet clown's costume stained with blood. Quickly, masking that year became illegal.

Costuming for Mardi Gras, in particular, has been part of the spiritual roots of this feast day. Altering one's identity is traditionally an integral element of the religious rituals preceding Lent, which call for the attenuation of self in order to achieve spiritual enlightenment ("farewell to the flesh" or *carnem levare*, means to put aside flesh). This implies that the exterior world of appearance and ego must be traded in for Lent, all the better to access the spirit. Mardi Gras, like Halloween, has at its origin a pagan ritual—called Lupercalia—once celebrated by imperial Rome with mass orgies, wretched excess, and mayhem. Part of the proceedings, historians tell us, was for these first maskers to dress in drag. So it is perhaps not surprising to see the custom re-enacted today (for instance, ample plastic bosoms and round rubber buttocks become popular pieces for many a male Carnival costume).

With the secularization of Carnival not only in New Orleans but, indeed, in other Mediterranean and South American cities, costuming may represent simply a personal freedom. It is the chance to mask and become anonymous for a day or two, to let off a little postmodern stress. Costuming finds its best expression at Carnival time, but it is evident at many other times of year, such as Southern Decadence, the annual French Quarter gay festival. In John Kennedy Toole's *Confederacy of Dunces* we read that in New Orleans "you can masquerade and Mardi Gras all year round if you want to… really sometimes the Quarter is like one big costume ball."

On Halloween night, as the crowd mills up Bourbon and down, everyone looks at one another's costume. But no one looks for too long at a couple of foot soldiers from the army of holy rollers bussed in from far-flung southern towns. Every year this Christian Army is on hand to save lost souls on All Hallow's Eve and Mardi Gras, too. They carry huge wooden crosses made of four-by-five-inch timbers which, once held aloft, form crucifixes as high as five or six feet. LED displays recessed into these huge crucifixes flash the converters' clarion call: "Sinners repent!"

Throughout the French Quarter, voodoo shops' votive candles flicker from storefronts with *gris-gris* (amulets and charms) strung up to put a spell on passers-by (or to help them empty their wallets on souvenirs). Not far from here, in aboveground cemetery St. Louis No. 1, candlelight vigils usher in All Saints' Day, 1 November, the occasion for many New Orleanians to venerate their ancestors. There, they tend to the gravesites, whitewashing tombstones and decking them with fresh flowers. Every year extra traffic police must be laid on outside the Cities of the Dead as Baptists, Episcopalians, and Catholics, black and white alike, converge at their family plots to carry out this annual homage to ancestors.

In Armstrong Park, not far from St. Louis No. 1, a ceremony in honor of the acknowledged "queen" of voodoo takes place. But if Marie Laveau were looking on, she might well wonder at this ersatz ritual enacted in her name beneath the park's dark canopy of live oaks. A clutch of people, mostly tourists, sways to the flurry of primal drumming, and their shadows stretch out in lurid shapes, twisting into shadows of the trees. But in close proximity to this commercial ceremony, a bona fide wedding is underway at the voodoo Spiritual Temple on North Rampart Street. Priestess Miriam Chamani presides over the wedding of a couple from Dallas, Texas. The contemporary hybrid of centuries-old voodoo, incorporating diverse elements of belief (Afro-Caribbean, Roman Catholic, Native American, and others) draws many celebrants seeking meaning in their lives. Priestess Miriam observes of the All Hallow's Eve nuptials: "Halloween is a celebration of new beginnings... the end of the old and bringing in the new... new thoughts and new energy."

To close the haunted night of celebration is a host of other strange events, some well publicized, some hosted by private societies, and many others secret. The annual "MOM's Ball" (Mystic Order of Orphans and Misfits), is a loose affiliation of artists, aging baby boomers, bohemians, and assorted partiers. Anne Rice's Vampire Lestat Fan Club Coven Party draws faithful readers—attendees must be club members—costumed through the streets. Under the ghostly Spanish-moss-swathed live oaks of City Park, the Orleans Parish Sheriff has his charges build a haunted house as a make-work project for parish prison inmates. It is a maze through which people walk in the dark, and is rigged with *trompe l'oeil* tricks and gothic sound effects. Meanwhile, people in neighborhoods build their own haunted houses, and no expense is spared in decking front yards with orange and black bunting, Halloween décor and miniature Cities of the Dead.

Pointe du Mardi Gras

So, with its more than 400 annual feast days and festivals, New Orleans has become known as a place that perpetuates year-round excess—even when the Mississippi River's waters threaten to inundate the city (i.e.

the vaunted hurricane parties). But, of course, it is Mardi Gras that most people think of when they think "New Orleans", and it is the quintessential feast day that reflects the character of the city. In *Lords of Misrule*, subtitled "Mardi Gras and the Politics of Race in New Orleans", James Gill notes:

> ...[it] *is a year-round obsession for many people and inspires the fervor of a pagan religion. Much of the city's social intercourse centers on krewe get-togethers and the endless planning for the next parade. Mardi Gras is a major industry, and helps define the subtle gradations of the city's social and racial caste system...*

Today, perhaps because of tourism's mass marketing of Mardi Gras, fewer and fewer people know of, or perhaps even care about, the social complexity at the heart of the Carnival's history and its present-day makeup.

The "krewes" to which Gill refers—formerly secret Carnival societies that consisted of maskers, who as early as the 1850s chose mythological names and began what we know as the themed parades of floats and tableau balls concluding their parades—have always been the elite of New Orleans. Only recently have Carnival organizations opened their doors to include a wider cross-section of the populace and even nonresidents. The traditional founders of Mardi Gras, according to Gill (British and a columnist for *The Times-Picayune*) "made old-world society look like a hotbed of social mobility... Mardi Gras may be best known to the outside world as a public festival, but upper-class New Orleans knew that its real significance lay in the annual reaffirmation of social eminence over merit."

The celebration of Mardi Gras finds its roots in France, having first arrived in the US with settlers during the 1700s. In fact, New Orleans' founding father, Pierre le Moyne, Sieur de Iberille, and his men remembered their homeland custom with a simple ceremony at a spot along the Mississippi River some sixty miles south of the nascent city. And they dubbed their camp "Pointe du Mardi Gras". It was 3 March 1699. No doubt, these first émigrés to the New World comforted themselves with re-enacting the kinds of rituals they would have practiced back home. In the latter part of the eighteenth century, residents of the new colony began holding pre-Lenten balls, but later

Spanish governors banned them in an attempt to curb the French influence in the city.

There is much disagreement as to whether the first official parade on Mardi Gras was in 1835 or 1838, but newspaper accounts document the fact that six New Orleanians, who had taken part as "Cowbellions" during New Year's Eve celebrations in Mobile, Alabama, paraded as early as 1835 in New Orleans. Although interrupted during the Civil War as well during the First and Second World Wars, by the end of the century the first old-line krewes (membership groups) were well established. The famous four old-line Carnival organizations are the Mystick Krewe of Comus, founded in 1856; Momus, founded in 1872; Rex, also originating in 1872; and the Krewe of Proteus, founded in 1882.

The early Carnival parades reflected the taste of the day. Though the floats were crude conveyances, built on wheeled carts and drawn by horses, their themes were often sophisticated, employing subtle classical references. An organization would choose a subject that had the best visual possibilities. In the early years, works of literature made favorite subjects, something such as Dante's *Inferno*, for instance, or Homer's *Iliad* and *Odyssey*. As Oliver Evans notes, adding his own reminiscences, the possibilities were endless:

> ... *Theseus threading his way through marvelous labyrinths to slay the Minotaur; the Morte d'Arthur, with its dragons and Launcelot holding high the golden Grail; and Alice in Wonderland, with the magic mirror, the Queen of Hearts, the March Hare, and Alice herself, wearing a wig of long blonde hair and a mask that gives her a curiously sexless look...I still remember with a thrill of horror a float which I saw as a child, depicting the execution of Mary, Queen of Scots (I think the subject of the parade was "The History of England"): the axe was gigantic, ten times as awful as the real weapon could possibly have been, and blood, of course, was every-where—the whole float was daubed with it.*

Political satire was an especially favored subject for Mardi Gras floats—and to this day it still is. One historical example of note is the year 1873, when, during the unpopular Reconstruction administration of Henry Clay Warmoth, the subject of the Comus parade was "The Missing Links to Darwin's 'Origin of the Species'". The parade did not get too far before parade-goers realized the significance: it was an elaborate satire of the occupying government—and each "missing link" was an important Union official—a hyena wearing a mask resembled General Butler, a tobacco grub was made up to look like President Grant, and so on. The parade wound up in chaos and disbanded before it reached the final destination.

By fin de siècle, Mardi Gras was celebrated with wildly extravagant balls and parades, still seen as the preserve of the white male establishment; however, into the first half of the twentieth century Carnival would see the birth of the first all-women's and African-American parading krewes, as well as a marked increase in the number of city and suburban parades. The first black Mardi Gras organization, the Original Illinois Club, was launched in 1894. Two years later, Les Mystérieuses, Carnival's first female group, was founded and presented an elaborate Leap Year ball. Membership in the old-line krewes, however, was strictly by invitation only. The members themselves were known as "the Cast", comprising businessmen and their families whose identities were traditionally kept secret, except for the queens and debutantes of Rex, Comus, Momus and Proteus. Their shining debuts were featured during Carnival season in society pages of *The Times-Picayune*, "along with the rest of the gilded youth in their make-believe courts," quips James Gill, adding, "Blacks, women, Jews and anyone of Italian heritage were personae non gratae, although Rex, the largest of the elite organizations, had fallen victim to a creeping liberalism, allowing nouveaux riches and even a few whose Gentile credentials were questionable to infiltrate its ranks."

Following a historic and hotly debated anti-discrimination ordinance that took place in 1992 and was finally passed the same year by New Orleans City Council (see below), Momus, Comus and Proteus reverted to ball-only organizations staunchly to retain their all-white-male traditions, Rex was left as the last of the old-line krewes, and it did finally allow African-American members. Meeting the ever-increasing size of parades, and in some sense combating the demand for bigger, flashier, some say crasser floats, Rex took over Comus' role as maintaining more high-brow standards. But its first post-ordinance parade was still a "little gauche", maintains Gill, noting of the 1993 parade entitled "Royal British Scribes":

... "scribe" was hardly an adequate term for any of the honorees, none of them was royal, and one, Jonathan Swift, was Irish, while another, "Beowolf," was an Anglo-Saxon epic poem. Edward Hancock [an early Comus krewe member attributed with helping to found Rex] *would never have been so sloppy. The other "scribes" honored with a float in the Rex parade of 1993 were Wells, Shakespeare, Milton, Lewis Carroll, Coleridge, Spenser, Blake, Stevenson, Chaucer, Sir Thomas More, Wordsworth, Beatrix Potter, Walter Scott, Kipling, Conan Doyle, Dickens, Tennyson and the Bronte sisters.*

The celebration of Carnival has grown, and its spectacle has developed exponentially to include as many as 135,000 participants, attracting hundreds of thousands of people to the city each year. The Bacchus Krewe set a precedent during the 1960s with the largest floats in Carnival history, and there would be no turning back. Parade captains seek to outdo each other with increasingly stunning costumes—thousands of rhinestones are sewn onto the already elaborate silken suits, bedecked with ostrich plumes—loose capes, collars, hoods, masks and veils to conceal identities.

The Krewe of Bacchus is known for doing everything on a grand scale: even its membership (upwards of 6,000) draws participants who cross the country to be in the Bacchus parade. Formed in 1968 by culinary patriarch Owen "Pip" Brennan Jr., of Brennan's restaurants fame, and a group of his friends, it is Bacchus that is credited with resuscitating the energy of the event when it was failing in the 1960s and 1970s. The Greek god of wine is always played by a celebrity: over the years by actors such as Kirk Douglas, Raymond Burr, and Charlton Heston, comedians such as Bob Hope and Dom DeLuise, or American culture icons like pop music arbiter and *American Bandstand* host Dick Clark. The parade's more than 25 signature floats include several so-called truck-mounted or truck-pulled "super floats," such as the "Bacchagator", the "Bacchasaurus", and the "Baccha-Whoppa". Bacchus holds its parade on the Sunday before Mardi Gras Day, drawing crowds of several hundred thousand every year for the black-tie Rendezvous Party that winds up inside the Morial Convention Center, a venue that can accommodate the throngs of intensely partying celebrants.

While between 1857 and the 1930s only four to six parades rolled on Mardi Gras Day, today there are more than fifty. The number of organizations marching has expanded geographically, too—to the West Bank (across the river), in Jefferson and St. Bernard parishes, and in smaller outlying towns. The names of the krewes, often making classical or mythical allusion, sound strange to the newcomer's ear—Endymion, Orpheus, Atlas, Oshun, Ashanti, Sparta, Caesar, Shangri-La, Alla, Centurion, Iris, Tucks, Ulysses, Thoth, Okeanos, Mercury, Napoleon.

Now the emphasis is on creativity and social synthesis; with each passing year, organizations seem increasingly outrageous as new krewes form, competing to attract more and more people—even animals—into their ranks. Bacchus is spoofed by the popular "Krewe of Barkus" parade. The members of this comic krewe are dog lovers and their faithful canines. Barkus "takes a walk" through the French Quarter a week or two before Mardi Gras. The dogs and their charges perambulate, dressed to be admired in outlandish, often-matching costumes. Then there is the Krewe de Vieux (pronounced "kroo de voo"), which parries city leaders and local politics and traditions using a keen satiric thrust, i.e. with the political hi-jinks of David Duke (former grand wizard of the Ku Klux Klan) running for US Senate and then the governorship. Social commentary is local and often understood by "insiders"—or locals—only. For instance, when favorite local pharmacy K&B closed its doors forever (bought out by a larger, national chain) the Krewe de Vieux marked the death of the Crescent City's favorite drug store with sentimental parade souvenirs: they were the trademark "K&B purple" matchbooks that only locals would cherish.

Carnival Time

"... if you visit New Orleans at Mardi Gras you will be seeing its most characteristic aspect: in the language of algebra, you will be seeing the spirit of the city raised at its highest power, for Mardi Gras is an accurate symbol of both the place and the people who value nothing quite so much as a good time."
—Oliver Evans

In days and weeks leading up to the big event on "Fat Tuesday" (Shrove Tuesday), worker productivity drops. This is especially true when king cakes start making their appearance at the workplace any time from Twelfth Night (or Epiphany) on to Mardi Gras. Such venerable bakeries as Haydel's and Gambino's can deliver them. Or perhaps the workers pick them up themselves on the way to work. Either way, king cakes interrupt the flow of the day. Everything stops as a cup of coffee is acquired, and the king cake is sliced as employees look on. Whosoever finds the one-inch plastic boy-child (a symbol of Christ and the start of Carnival season) secreted somewhere inside the dense, chewy round of pastry iced white, stippled with green, purple and gold—official Mardi Gras colors—must buy the next pastry ring. King cake babies find their way into many office morning confabs.

As Carnival approaches, workers—in fact anyone found Downtown late afternoon during the week preceding Mardi Gras—must be careful not to be left in the city as a night parade is readied. For instance, if one works in the French Quarter but is headed home Uptown or Mid-City, that person should leave work well before the scheduled parades start rolling. If not, there is a good likelihood that the barriers erected to contain the well-established routes will block the way until long after dark. Public transportation ceases. Stragglers may be forced to attend the parade until after 10 p.m. It is either that, or walk home, parting the wild, partying crowds. Preventing this scenario means taking careful note of parade schedules published in *The Times-Picayune*, or consulting the popular Arthur Hardy guide to Carnival, among many other parade sources for complete schedules of parades, detailed maps, full biographies of special guests and grand marshals, themes for the floats, and a list of the year's all-important parade souvenirs.

The main event will blast full-pitch starting on Lundi Gras, or "Fat Monday", especially during the Zulu's (see below) celebration at the riverfront's Golden Nugget Stage, which goes well past midnight on Mardi Gras. Mardi Gras is actually the culmination of Carnival season, a series of balls which begins on 6 January with Twelfth Night, or the Feast of the Epiphany. Local custom dictates that Carnival has its official beginning when a debutante at her "coming out" ball finds a golden bean in her slice of king cake at the Twelfth Night Revelers' Ball. She reigns as queen of the evening, served by maids who find their own silver beads.

Rex (whose mythical father is Old King Cole, and whose mother is Terpsichore, the Greek muse of dancing and singing) makes his ritual, regal appearance on Lundi Gras at around 6 p.m., when the king and his entourage of captains arrives on a Coast Guard cutter to be greeted by the mayor of New Orleans. During a brief ceremony, the mayor symbolically turns over control of the city to Rex for one day, reading the rules of conduct for the city celebration. Fireworks then light up the night sky in the colors of Carnival—purple, green and gold.

Mardi Gras Mambo

Then comes Mardi Gras morning! Excitement is in the air: the sky is full of outlandish possibilities. There are people in town from all over the world—and anything goes. The hawkers of cotton candy, programs and souvenirs are buzzing up and down the streets in pre-parade anticipation. Noisemakers erupt. Someone on a side street Uptown has plucked a cast-off mirror from a trash can and written on its cloudy surface: "See yourself drunk, 50 cents." Families up and down St. Charles Avenue are making their way to favored spots to catch the "throws". Many have even bought or fashioned wooden boxes atop ladders, seats in which to seat the children so they get an elevated look, above adult heads, at passing parades.

Early in the morning, first libations are poured. You can smell Mardi Gras in the air: sweet olive and smoke; the musty Mississippi. Whatever it is comes through louvered French doors and mixes, sensual as perfume, with the music. All the songs of Carnival, inseparable from the event as carols are from Christmas, pulse and blast and shout and chant from the radio, set on local station WWOZ, blasting from speakers placed on the tailgates of trucks and atop the balconies of houses lining the streets. Henry Roland Byrde—Professor Longhair—in perhaps the best-known Carnival standard, "Mardi Gras in New Orleans", sings: "When you go to Mardi Gras, somebody's going to tell you what's Carnival for." Listening to the songs of Carnival helps to enliven—and deepen—the mystery. They are unforgettable, omnipresent, and once heard, become embedded in the memory.

People are everywhere, and music is everywhere: first Art Neville and the Hawketts' 1954 R&B classic with a Brazilian beat, "Mardi Gras Mambo", or the late-great piano Professor Longhair's "Tipitina" and his 1964 hit "Big Chief"—the Professor on piano, Dr. John on guitar, and Earl King swinging his own composition: "I'm going to do everything I could, me big chief I'm feeling good." A group of about a half-dozen burly males wearing construction hard hats and little else have set up a stage from the flatbed of a truck and are dancing energetically to music blasting from enormous speakers they have brought with them. A multi-member family has chosen a "theme" costume involving dressing up in large boxes decorated to look like breakfast cereals (i.e. Special K, Corn Flakes, Fruit Loops). They wield large knives and carry hand-lettered signs reading "Cereal Killers". A very, very old man in front of a tavern on St. Charles Avenue is dressed all in white, and his scrawny form is practically obscured by a long, wavy, Godiva-like blonde wig. Over his groin area is placed a wooden box with a small-hinged door. "What's in there?" some naïve soul may ask. "Open the door!" is his command in response. The septuagenarian shows his treasure. It's a loose collection of peach-colored, flaccid rubber crabs he keeps hidden inside the box.

The parades march all day long in every quarter of the city. The hordes of people swell and surge. "Jockomo", another Mardi Gras Indian-inspired tune written and recorded first by "Sugar Boy" Crawford and the Canecutters, later by the Dixie Cups as "Iko-Iko", then by the Neville Brothers as "Iko-Iko/Brother John". For nostalgia lovers there is Johnny Wiggs & His New Orleans Kings on cornet with the almost-official Mardi Gras tune, "If Ever I Cease to Love". Whether or not, as local myth suggests, Russian Grand Duke Alexis really demanded to hear this song in 1872 as he tried to woo concert hall singer Lydia Thompson does not really matter, as long as it moves the feet. During Mardi Gras' earliest days the feet were waltzing, and doing quadrilles on boards they placed over theater seats at the New Orleans Opera House—to such songs as the "Kickapoo" and "Carnival" waltzes or the "Momus Polka".

Down in the Tremé, not far from the Quarter, crowds are forming. New Orleans R&B artist Walter "Wolfman" Washington & the Roadmasters are improvising in an empty lot between two shotgun cottages. It is only noon, but already the humidity settling into the little neighborhood has become oppressive. Then, a second-line parade happens down the street with the contemporary Rebirth Brass Band keeping time, and, then whooping around the corner in a wild yellow-ostrich-plume flurry come the White Eagles Mardi Gras Indians, chanting and singing African call-and-response, cowbells, hair combs on bottles, tambourines and whistles pumping up the "humbug": "Now the prettiest thing I ever seen/Mardi Gras Indians down in New Orleans…"

In the French Quarter, on Bourbon Street (where floats were at one time allowed to roll), jazz clarinetist Pete Fountain and his Half-Fast Marching Club join in with the joyous syncopation of traditional New Orleans jazz. While on Canal Street, as the Rex and Zulu parades pass, there comes the swell and pomp of high school marching bands—"St. Aug's Marching 100" in purple and gold. People throng Canal Street. Some businesses have opened their upper-story balconies for employees, friends and families to observe the proceedings in comfort.

The impossibly perfect might happen at the corner of, say, Canal and Rampart. Shoved atop a set of willing shoulders, a person caught up in the spirit of Mardi Gras catches a Zulu coconut, arguably the most prized possession of Carnival. (It is the hard fruit, denuded of hair, and spray-painted gold by Zulu krewe member-artisans, who also incorporate bands of black and white as well as sparkly mock-primitive designs.) Throughout Carnival season, the currency is the "throws" of each krewe (plastic cups, cheaply minted "doubloons") but especially beads, to be worn thick around the neck all day on Mardi Gras. Some people on the streets make elaborate or humorous signs to flash at the passing floats-riders in hopes of attracting their attention. "Hey, Dr. Bob—it's me, your patient Dave!" reads one, attesting to the local's knowledge of the krewe's upwardly mobile membership.

On select Central Business District streets bleachers are erected and may be rented for a fee. At Lee Circle, the celebrants go round and round all day—tirelessly—as the general continues to keep watch, decade after decade. He never gets dizzy watching the spectacle that even Lafcadio Hearn ("certainly the most effective promoter of [New Orleans'] exotic and romantic image," says Gill) found fascinating for its "artificial picturesqueness." Hearn wrote the following for a 2 February 1880 editorial in the *Item*:

> *The Night cometh in which we take no note of time, and forget that we are living in a practical age which mostly relegates romance to printed pages and merriment to the stage. Yet what is more romantic than the Night of the Masked Ball—the too brief hours of light, music and fantastic merriment which seem to belong to no century and yet to all?*

Mardi Gras Mocked

When in December 1991 the forces for and against the established conventions of Mardi Gras assembled in the basement of New Orleans City Hall, "the economic and social power of old New Orleans was about to collide with contemporary political reality," says James Gill. The ordinance to desegregate Mardi Gras parades and gentlemen's luncheon clubs would effectively change the course of Carnival history:

> *The old-line krewes regarded themselves as guardians of the true spirit and traditions of New Orleans Carnival, which, to them, meant demonstrating both their civic generosity and their social superiority. To older connoisseurs of Carnival, none of the season's public spectacles compared to the Comus parade, which was always built around some mythological or otherwise learned theme, and which, in the tasteful designs and rich colors of its floats and the striking costumes of its riders, proclaimed itself a gift of the rich and educated classes to the common folk on the street.*

Questioning the municipal cost of staging Mardi Gras, a public celebration that, *de facto*, supported organizations practicing discrimination, Councilwoman Dorothy Mae Taylor queried the council's legal adviser Bruce Naccari as to how much it cost the city's taxpayers to provide police, sanitation and other civic services: "The city provides a subsidization of about three and a half million," came the answer. Shot back Taylor, the reformers' champion: "Subsidization, eh? In other areas it's called welfare."

The fact that the old-line krewes and the establishment who composed them would finally come under fire may well have been foreshadowed—at least preceded by—satirical treatment of them. One of the strangest sights to see on Mardi Gras is the Zulu parade, with all of its stock characters: King Zulu, the Witch Doctor, the Big Shot, the Province Prince, the Governor, and so on. It is certainly peculiar to see African-American men decked out in black face paint and grass skirts throwing coconuts—and it occasions the question, "Why?"

The Krewe of Zulu has its roots in a Carnival marching club called the Tramps, which paraded at the turn of the twentieth century wearing white shirts, raggedy trousers and straw hats. The club's king, Willie Stark, mocking his white alter ego King Rex, wore a lard can for a crown and carried a banana-stalk scepter. In 1909, the Tramps attended a stage show at the Elysian Theater that featured an African skit entitled "There Has Never Been and Will Never Be Another King Like Me". This inspired the group to rename their organization after the Zulus. A man by the name of Paul Johnson invented a character called "The Big Shot from Africa". Poking fun at the white royal entourage, the Big Shot carried a big glass doorknob instead of a multi-point diamond. In 1912, King Peter Williams wore a white starched suit and a tie fashioned from a loaf of Italian bread. As a trenchant comment on the white krewe's racial stereotypes, riders in Zulu tinted their faces with black dye, which, ironically says James Gill, "became a continuing source of offense to many of the city's blacks, who thought it too close to Uncle Tom for comfort."

Reid Mitchell, in *All on a Mardi Gras Day*, comments that the "meta-fiction" of this play within a play, complete with racial double entendres, is deeply fascinating and just one example of the many strata of meanings that can be mined from Mardi Gras as a unique social expression:

In his way, Zulu did everything that Rex did. If Rex traveled by water, coming up the Mississippi with an escort from the U.S. Navy, Zulu came down the New Basin Canal on a tugboat. If Rex held a scepter, Zulu held a ham bone. If Rex had the city police marching before him, Zulu had the Zulu police—wearing police uniforms until the municipal authorities objected. All that Zulu did caricatured Rex; a black lord of misrule upsetting the reign of the white lord, a mocker of a mocker. Zulu was perhaps the best example of what Henry Louis Gates, Jr., has called the "double play" of black "vernacular structures"—a black Carnival parade that commented on white Carnival parades.

Zulu's most famous ruler was native son Louis Armstrong, who answered the call in 1949 to "ride Zulu" and had the opportunity to live out what was his boyhood dream, despite, as Mitchell points out, the fact that Armstrong felt a certain "bitterness" toward his home town:

… Growing up poor, the son of a prostitute, incarcerated in an orphans' home because of an exuberant and dangerous prank involving his mother's boyfriend's pistol… he never lived in New Orleans again. But he would return when he was asked to be king of Zulu, the city's oldest black krewe. Mardi Gras was part of his identity.

That day, Armstrong sat on the throne of the Zulu float saying, "Man, this is rich." And later, when a fight broke out between a bystander and the mayor of Zululand, Armstrong was heard to say, "My, my, just like old times." His portrait as Zulu king that year graced the cover of *Time* magazine.

Mardi Gras Rebirth

Mardi Gras passes and in but a few days no one knows what to do with the "priceless" plastic gems they have caught; in fact, these strands of beads, costing an average of four cents each, are soon stashed away in attics, hung on car rear-view mirrors, given away, recycled for the next year, or thrown away entirely.

But some people just cannot let go of Mardi Gras. An occasional partier is spotted, now reduced to working at having a good time, becoming drunk and disorderly, holding onto poles at street corners, shouting obscenities. Under the feet of these errant revelers are trinkets in drains, and the odd piece of well-trodden offal in the gutter. For a few weeks after the big day, uncaught beads still hang suspended from phone lines and drip in multicolored ropes from trees just an arm's-length from a St. Charles streetcar window. The magic is gone.

Yet the next Carnival is not far away on New Orleans' inexorable feast day calendar. How fitting in this economically challenged metropolis that 67 percent of the citizens respond in a poll that they are satisfied with the quality of their lives—even in a city where the 2000 national census found that 46 percent of inhabitants had an annual adjusted gross income under $20,000. Though it is true that almost a quarter of the population of New Orleans is without basic health care coverage, that does not seem to deter the average New Orleanian from feeling good.

The fun of Carnival is short-lived, but its old-time romance remains. As Lafcadio Hearn wrote over 100 years ago: "the glorious night is approaching—this quaint old-time night, star-jeweled, fantastically robed; and the blue river is bearing us fleets of white boats thronged with strangers who doubtless are dreaming of lights and music, the tepid, perfumed air of Rex's Palace... who will dance the dance of the Carnival until blue day puts out at once the trembling tapers of the stars and lights of the great ball." Well, the Mississippi may have been blue—but in all likelihood Hearn turned it that color for effect.

Despite mythic metaphors, romantic clichés—and any hardship—the deep-down spirit of New Orleans is a hard resilience that drives people's will to endure. As lyrics of the Wild Magnolia Mardi Gras Indian anthem promise, "Every year, for Carnival time, we make a new suit..." It is a custom that takes many shapes, a cultural metamorphosis. Mardi Gras Indian children are taught to sew new costumes using beads from the previous year's celebration. It is a special knack. New Orleans continues to fashion from something old, something new—and from a mosaic of cultures comes an indelible experience that is uniquely her own.

EPILOGUE

On 29 August 2005, Category 4 Hurricane Katrina battered New Orleans and the Gulf Coast. For many, it will take a long time before sickening views of New Orleans' rooftops, near submerged in dark channels of water, drain entirely from memory. We will not soon forget the scenes of mayhem in the Big Easy: citizens, many of them the poorest of the poor, the sick and elderly, some perched atop their roofs, wading in the channels or airlifted, then forcibly detained in the Superdome or Convention Center's squalid shelter, waiting for disaster relief that was a long time coming.

Nearly eighty percent of the city had to be drained of storm surge that breeched the levee system's floodwalls. In some parts of the Greater New Orleans region, a "toxic gumbo" of sewage- and chemical-laced water reached twenty feet (six meters) in depth. One million people were displaced by the storm along the US Gulf Coast. About half of those were from New Orleans.

In the weeks that followed the disaster, relief organizations such as the Red Cross and Salvation Army worked tirelessly to help displaced New Orleanians and Gulf Coast evacuees. Americans opened their homes to absorb thousands upon thousands of wanderers who relocated to points all over North America. And now, even as people are returning to the Crescent City, it is principally (affluent white) residents who lived in parts of the city left mostly unscathed by the storm's effects, i.e., where elevation was the highest, who are able to come back: the French Quarter, Central Business District, the Garden District, Uptown. Much of New Orleans' citizenry—and New Orleans' culture—is left adrift in cities such as Houston and Austin, TX, Memphis and Nashville, TN, Baton Rouge, LA, and Atlanta, GA.

As people repair or rebuild their homes, and as the city, its government, its necessary infrastructures and organizations pull together, New Orleans ex-pats endure until they begin their slow return home, as New Orleans great "Fats" Domino put it, before they start "Walkin' to New Orleans".

So it appears that New Orleans' soulful culture will be on parade in other people's streets. And it is happening that way all over the country—as when artistic director of "Jazz at Lincoln Center" Wynton Marsalis pulled together a five-hour "Higher Ground" relief concert at NYC's Rose Theater, interspersing performances by New Orleans musicians with songs and commentary and readings by other musicians, actors and authors. As when New Orleans' Cyril Neville celebrated his birthday at Threadgill's nightclub in Austin, TX, and a group of New Orleans musicians showed up to surprise him, including piano legend Henry Butler. As when, even halfway around the world, New Orleans-style celebrations sprang up to benefit the city. One triumphant supporter of Louisiana music wrote to radio station WWOZ, which in the days following Katrina began streaming its shows over the Internet from a makeshift studio in Baton Rouge:

> *John Verlenden in Cairo here. Our party on Oct 28 was a success, raised over $4K, and had a good time doing it. About 200 expats showed up, from a variety of nationalities. One barman was a Dinka Sudanese refugee who'd never served drinks in his life. The other barman was a Pakistani student whose family's house got destroyed in the quake there. He asked for a bottle of wine after the night was done—unusual for a Muslim. Special songs included "Iko-Iko". Quite a night. The money has already been sent to four relief agencies… Red Cross, Direct Relief International, Baton Rouge Area Foundation, Catholic Charities USA. 11/10/05.*

WWOZ continues to post information on its Web site designed to keep New Orleans musicians—and aficionados of New Orleans culture everywhere—informed and in touch. There is a list of musicians "Safe after the trials of Hurricane Katrina". There is a roster of "Benefits for 'NOLA' musicians." And there is a checklist of New Orleans music venues now "open for business".

As one "blogging" evacuee wrote: "New Orleans has brought two major things to the world—and that is, of course, its food and its music. The link, the common bond in these is soul—whatever nebulous definition you may use… as this new diaspora finds stability in relocation to other places, there will be seed after seed planted. If not of New Orleans music or food, then at least a bit of that NOLA voodoo, worldview, the remnants of Congo Square and Marie Laveau." As was true in the days when jazz was born, the spirit of New Orleans emanates from the mouth of the muddy Mississippi—and permeates everything it touches.

"The fire's gone out of the day but the light of it lingers."
—Tennessee Williams, *Camino Real*

GLOSSARY

New Orleans natives share many linguistic eccentricities. Surprising to some outsiders is the fact that you really don't hear the proverbial "southern drawl" in New Orleans but, rather, a Brooklyn-style "twang" emanating from many of the neighborhoods. It's suggested that this is because both the Big Easy and the Big Apple experienced waves of Irish and Italian immigrants at approximately the same time. As John Kennedy Toole notes in a passage on the flyleaf of his novel *A Confederacy of Dunces*:

> *There is a New Orleans city accent. . .associated with downtown New Orleans, particularly with the German and Irish Third Ward, that is hard to distinguish from the accent of Hoboken, Jersey City, and Astoria, Long Island, where the Al Smith inflection, extinct in Manhattan, has taken refuge. The reason, as you might expect, is that the same stocks that brought the accent to Manhattan imposed it on New Orleans.*

Many more additions from the African-American community contribute to the linguistic gumbo of New Orleans' vocabulary, supplemented further by Creole and Cajun French vernacular or colloquialisms.

banquette = sidewalk (in the French Quarter)

bayou = a natural canal created by the overflow of a lake or river or the draining of a marsh

crab boil/crawfish boil = the seasoning mix used to put in the water to boil seafood, also the event (having guests over to eat the aforesaid)

ersters = oysters

fais do do = party or country dance (a Cajun diminutive derived from baby talk used while putting children to bed, i.e., "go sleepy-by." When the children are finally asleep, the adults can party) *flambeaux* = the torches carried in Mardi Gras parades by the flambeau carriers, mostly African-American men who dance at intervals in the parade picking up coins tossed to them by the crowd

garçonnière = an outbuilding of a townhouse or plantation house used as a bedroom for guests or the older boys of a family

get down [from the car] = as opposed to "get out of the car"

gris gris = a charm, statuette or incantation given to recipient by voodoo practitioner to help solve a problem, or create a problem for an enemy

humbug = verbal parry between two Mardi Gras Indians, or argumentation of any kind

king cake = the special pastry rounds bought at Carnival time

krewe = an organization that masks and parades during Mardi Gras and attends the Carnival ball

lagniappe = a little something extra (i.e., the baker's dozen)

make groceries = go grocery shopping

Mom-an'-em = your folks (i.e., "Say hello to your Mom-an'-em for me")

neutral ground = the grassy strip between lanes of any street or thoroughfare, a throwback to the days when Canal Street was actually the cultural divide between Creoles and Americans

parish = Louisiana's counties, a legacy of the city's French and Spanish colonial rule, during which Roman Catholic parishes determined geographical divisions

picayune = a trivial matter, but also what the French called the smallest denomination of Spanish coins, worth 6 cents *rinch* = rinse

swimp = shrimp

y'at = term for a denizen of the working-class (perhaps from a locale such as St. Bernard or Plaquemines parish, derived from the local greeting vernacular: "Where you at?" meaning, "How are you?" [a side note: an answer to the question "Where y'at?" is a drawled "Awwri- ight."])

zink = sink in New Orleans (because they were made of zinc? or because it's the French word for bar and counter?)

FURTHER READING

Ancelet, Barry Jean, *Cajun Country*. Jackson: University Press of Mississippi, 1991.

Bernard, Shane K. *The Cajuns: Americanization of a People*. Jackson: University Press of Mississippi, 2003.

Brasseaux, Carl, *The Founding of New Acadia: The Beginnings of Acadian Life in Louisiana, 1765-1803*. Baton Rouge: Louisiana State University Press, 1987.

Churchill Chase, John, *Frenchmen, Desire, Good Children and Other Streets of New Orleans*. 3rd edition. New York: Collier Books, 1979.

De Caro, Frank, ed. and Jordan, Rosan Augusta, assoc. ed., *Louisiana Sojourns: Travelers' Tales and Literary Journeys*. Baton Rouge: Louisiana State University Press, 1998.

Evans, Oliver, *New Orleans*. New York: The Macmillan Company, 1959.

Gill, James, *Lords of Misrule: Mardi Gras and the Politics of Race in New Orleans*. Jackson: University Press of Mississippi, 1997.

Holditch, Kenneth and Richard Freeman Leavitt, *Tennessee Williams and the South*. Jackson: University Press of Mississippi, 2002.

Horton, James Oliver, *Free People of Color: Inside the African American Community*. Washington: Smithsonian Institution Press, 1993.

Kennedy, Richard S., ed., *Literary New Orleans in the Modern World*. Baton Rouge: Louisiana State University, 1998.

Kennedy, Richard S., ed., *Literary New Orleans: Essays and Mediations*. Baton Rouge: Louisiana State University Press, 1992.

Kennedy Toole, John, *A Confederacy of Dunces*. New York: Grove Press, 1980.

Larson, Susan, *A Booklover's Guide to New Orleans*. Baton Rouge: Louisiana State University Press, 1999.

Marquis, Don. *In Search of Buddy Bolden: First Man of Jazz*. Baton Rouge: Louisiana State University Press, 1978.

Mitchell, Reid, *All on a Mardi Gras Day: Episodes in the History of New Orleans Carnival*. Cambridge: Harvard University Press, 1995.

Smith, Michael P., *Spirit World: Pattern in the Expressive Folk Culture of African-American New Orleans*. Gretna, La.: Pelican Publishing Co., 1992.

Smith, Michael P., *A Joyful Noise*. Gretna, La.: Pelican Publishing Co., 1999.

Twain, Mark, *Life on the Mississippi*. Justin Kaplan ed. New York: Signet Classic, 2001.

Williams, Tennessee, *A Streetcar Named Desire*. New York: Signet, 1951.

Online Resources

General

www.neworleanscvb.com	New Orleans Convention & Visitors Bureau, Inc.
www.yatcom.com	Virtually New Orleans
www.where-international.com	WHERE Magazines International
www.neworleansonline.com	All About New Orleans: New Orleans Online
www.neworleans.net	NewOrleans.net: Destination New Orleans
www.louisianatravel.com	State of Louisiana Travel and Tourism site
www.new-orleans.la.us	City of New Orleans site (municipal government)
www.nola.com	New Orleans Regional Chamber of Commerce

Music

www.offbeat.com	Offbeat (monthly music magazine)
www.gnofn.org	Louisiana Jazz Federation/Louisiana Philharmonic Orchestra
www.louisianamusicfactory.com	Louisiana Music Factory (music store)
www.louisianamusic.org	Louisiana Music Commission
www.nojazzcommission.com	New Orleans Jazz Commission

www.satchmo.net	Louis Armstrong House & Archives
www.wwoz.org	WWOZ Radio 90.7 FM
www.nojf.org	New Orleans Jazz & Heritage Foundation
www.nojazzfest.com	New Orleans Jazz & Heritage Festival
www.jass.com	Early jazz resource site
www.nps.gov	New Orleans Jazz-National Historic Park
www.backstreetculturalmuseum.com	Backstreet Cultural Museum

Literary

www.tennesseewilliams.net	Tennessee Williams Festival/New Orleans Literary Festival
www.wordsandmusic.org	Faulkner House Books (book store and annual festival)
www.annerice.com	Official site of Anne Rice

Culinary

www.foodfestneworleans.com	Cuisine resource, reviews by noted critic Tom Fitzmorris

Research

www.nutrias.org	New Orleans Public Library
www.tulane.edu	The William Ransom Hogan Jazz Archive and the Amistad Research Center
www.specialcollections.tulane.edu	Tulane University Special Collections

Art

www.ogdenmuseum.org	The Odgen Museum of Southern Art
www.culturalicons.com	Jazz photographer Michael P. Smith web site
www.cacno.org	Contemporary Arts Center
www.noma.org	New Orleans Museum of Art

239

Other

www.degashouse.com	Degas House
www.mardigrasunmasked.com	Everything about Mardi Gras

INDEX OF LITERARY & HISTORICAL NAMES

INDEX OF PLACES AND LANDMARKS